Springer Series on Social Work

Albert R. Roberts, D.S.W., Series Editor

Anne E. Fortune, Ph.D., is an associate professor at Virginia Commonwealth University School of Social Work, where she teaches practice, human behavior, and research. She received her A.M. and Ph.D. in social work from the School of Social Service Administration, University of Chicago, and has taught at George Warren Brown School of Social Work, Washington University, St. Louis. Dr. Fortune has conducted research and published in the areas of runaway youth; work incentives; communication processes, outcome, and termination in social work practice; task-centered practice with the elderly; and social work education. Currently, she edits *tcNewsletter*, which disseminates new developments in task-centered practice.

Task-Centered Practice with Families and Groups

Anne E. Fortune, Ph.D.

With Contributors

Springer Publishing Company
New York

Springer Publishing Company, Inc.
200 Park Avenue South
New York, New York 10003

85 86 87 88 89 / 10 9 8 7 6 5 4 3 2 1

Library of Congress Cataloging in Publication Data

Main entry under title:

Task-centered practice with families and groups.
   (Springer series on social work ; v. 6)
   Bibliography: p. Includes index.
   1. Social group work—Addresses, essays, lectures. 2. Family social work—United States—Addresses, essays, lectures. I. Fortune, Anne E., II. Series.
HV45.T37 1985   362.8'253   84-14186
ISBN 0-8261-4460-8

Printed in the United States of America

Contents

Contributors

Mary Coppola earned her M.S.W. from State University of New York at Buffalo. She is currently enrolled in the D.S.W. program at Hunter College School of Social Work. Ms. Coppola is an Assistant Professor in Social Work at Siena College, teaching human behavior, communication skills, and field. Her research interests are in gerontology and social work education.

Charles Garvin is a Professor of Social Work at the University of Michigan. He has co-written or edited five books, including *Contemporary Group Work: Interpersonal Practice in Social Work, The Work Incentive Experience*, and *Gender Issues in Social Group Work*. He has written several articles on group work which have appeared in practice collections such as *Theories of Social Work with Groups*, the *Handbook of the Social Services*, and the *Handbook of Clinical Social Work*, as well as recent issues of the *Social Work Encyclopedia*.

Jane Macy-Lewis is currently employed by a human service agency in rural Wisconsin where she designed and now oversees a community support program for chronically mentally ill adults, in addition to serving as a case coordinator for developmentally disabled adults. Prior to this she worked as a Community Support Specialist for developmentally disabled adults, and has been a group facilitator for a wide variety of adults' groups, including Assertiveness Skills Training, Problem-Solving for Single Parents, and Divorce Adjustment. She earned her M.S.W. at the University of Wisconsin–Madison, where she assisted with graduate courses in task-centered treatment.

Paul R. Mills, Jr., Associate Professor, School of Social Work at the University of Alabama, earned his Master of Divinity from the Lutheran Theological Seminary in Philadelphia and an M.S.W. from Bryn Mawr College. Trained in psychiatric social work at the Menninger Clinic, he received a Ph.D. from Florida State University. His research and teaching interests are in the analysis and evaluation of clinical theory with particular emphasis on family treatment.

Kent Newcome is Program Coordinator of the Community Support Services, an integrated community mental health service delivery system for the chronically mentally ill, at the Madison County (Illinois) Mental Health Center. An M.S.W. graduate of the George Warren Brown School of Social Work, Washington University, Mr. Newcome maintains a private practice where he applies the task-centered approach and other forms of brief treatment with families, groups, and individuals.

Bageshwari Parihar, Assistant Professor at the School of Social Work, Louisiana State University, was formerly an administrator at Martha Washington Hospital's Alcoholic Treatment Center, Chicago. He holds an M.A.S. from the Institute of Social Sciences, Kashi Vidyapith, Varanasi, India; an M.A. from the School of Social Service Administration, University of Chicago; and a Ph.D. from Jane Addams College of Social Work, University of Illinois at Chicago. His latest work includes *Task-Centered Management in the Human Services*, and his professional interests include alcoholism, employee assistance programs, supervision, and management methods and systems in human service organizations. Dr. Parihar currently researches testing the application of the task-centered management model in different types of organizations.

Eloise Rathbone-McCuan, Ph.D., M.S.W., is Director of the Social Work Program at the University of Vermont, and was previously affiliated with the Schools of Social Work at Washington University and the University of Maryland. She is a gerontological social worker who has published numerous articles and books, including *Isolated Elders*. A Fellow in the Gerontological Society of America, she is Co-Chairperson of the Committee for Gerontology in Social Work Education.

William J. Reid is a Professor at the School of Social Welfare, the Nelson A. Rockefeller College of Public Affairs and Policy, State University of New York at Albany. In addition to teaching clinical practice and research methods, he is involved in research on task-centered family treatment. He co-authored *Task-Centered Casework* and *Research in Social Work*, and is the author of *The Task-Centered System*.

Ronald H. Rooney, Ph.D., is an Assistant Professor at the School of Social Work, University of Wisconsin, Madison. He has been a practitioner, supervisor, instructor, and researcher in the task-centered approach for ten years and has written material on task-centered practice with groups, in foster care, and in public social services.

Tina L. Rzepnicki is Assistant Professor at the Graduate School of Social Service, Fordham University at Lincoln Center, New York, where she teaches individual and family practice and child welfare. She was formerly at the Jane Addams College of Social Work, University of Illinois at Chicago, and received a Ph.D. from the School of Social Service Administration, University of Chicago. A project coordinator for the Parent Education Program and the Child Welfare Curriculum Development grant at the University of Chicago, she most recently directed the West Virginia field test of the Illinois/West Virginia Intake Decision Making Project in Child Welfare Services.

Eleanor Reardon Tolson is an Assistant Professor at the University of Washington, School of Social Work. She studied under and worked with William J. Reid and Laura Epstein at the University of Chicago, School of Social Service Administration. The author of several articles about task-centered practice, she also co-edited *Models of Family Treatment*.

Ronald W. Toseland is an Assistant Professor, School of Social Welfare, the Nelson A. Rockefeller College of Public Affairs and Policy, State University of New York at Albany. Dr. Toseland is also in private practice where he specializes in group work, gerontological social work, and other aspects of clinical social work practice. His publications include several articles on working with older persons in groups, and his most recent book is *The Group in Social Work Practice*.

Marsha Wanless, M.S.S.W., is Senior Social Worker, Adult Voluntary Services, Dane County Social Services, Madison, Wisconsin. She has worked with elderly and disabled clients for the past eight years.

The Task-Centered Model

Anne E. Fortune

Task-centered practice is a form of short-term, goal-oriented treatment appropriate for individuals, families, and groups. It focuses on alleviating client-identified problems in living through actions (tasks) carried out between sessions by client or practitioner. The task-centered model was developed initially for social work practice with individuals; recent work has reformulated and extended its principles to work with larger client units. Those modifications are the subject of this book. This introductory chapter provides an overview of the approach as background for in-depth discussion of its application to treatment of groups and families.

Characteristics of the Task-Centered Model

The task-centered model began in the early 1970s as a response to research evidence that short-term treatment was at least as effective as long-term treatment (Reid and Epstein, 1972). The initial formulation of the model incorporated elements of Hollis' (1964, 1967) psychosocial and Perlman's (1957, 1970) problem-solving approaches to casework, Studt's (1968) conception of client task, and experimentation with planned time-limited treatment (Reid and Shyne, 1969; Reid and Epstein, 1972). It continues to be both eclectic and empirical, with elements added as research evidence about effective practice accumulates. The task-centered model has evolved around a set of key characteristics which both define the model and provide its core. These characteristics include value premises (Reid and Epstein, 1972), planned brevity, specific treatment focus, contracting,

1

structure within treatment, action orientation, and empirical orientation (Reid, 1977b).[1]

Values

All treatment approaches—indeed all views of the world—include explicit and implicit assumptions about the nature of man, of behavior, and of behavior change (J. Fischer, 1971; Ford and Urban, 1963). Since these assumptions are often unverifiable, they are in effect value premises whose validity is confirmed by social consensus. In many respects, basic task-centered values reflect prevailing American attitudes.

The most important task-centered value is the emphasis on the client's expressed wishes, or the attitude that the client "knows best" what her problems are and what successful resolutions look like. This is not an absolute position, as the practitioner's expertise, the potential need to protect others, and legally defined behavior codes influence both definition of problems and expectations of outcome; indeed they may pose serious ethical dilemmas for a task-centered practitioner. Nevertheless, on a continuum from individual client "self-determination" to societal definition of problems and needs through the practitioner as society's representative, the task-centered model clearly requires favoring the client's expressed wishes. The emphasis is reflected throughout the model by the requirement that problems be acknowledged by the client, that tasks be formulated with and explicitly agreed to by the client, and that client–practitioner contacts not continue after the contract is completed unless the client requests. As corollaries to the emphasis on client's expressed wishes are implicit assumptions that the client wants to change and that problems are changeable.

Another major value premise in task-centered treatment is a present–future orientation. While the past is important in creating a problem—and may provide crucial clues for problem resolution—the primary concern is the client's situation now and what can be done in the near future to resolve the problematic situation. What has happened in the past cannot be changed (although perceptions of the past can be) and thus there is far less emphasis on analysis of the past than in some treatment modalities.

Planned Brevity

The task-centered model shares with some other treatment approaches an initial mutual agreement between practitioner and client to limit treatment

[1]The organization and content of this discussion is drawn from Reid (1977b).

to a relatively short period of time. Normally, task-centered contracts call for between 6 and 12 sessions over a two- to three-month period (after problems are determined). The rationales for planned brevity and the time parameters are several: (1) Research indicates fairly consistently that short-term treatment is at least as effective as open-ended treatment (D. Beck and Jones, 1973; Fisher, 1980; D. Johnson and Gelso, 1980; Reid and Shyne, 1969; Wattie, 1973). Thus, to extend treatment indefinitely or over a long period with little likelihood of increased benefit to clients appears inefficient and costly, even unethical. Further, long-term treatment may encourage client dependency and reduce capacity to function independently (Blenkner, Bloom, and Nielson, 1971; Fortune and Rathbone-McCuan, 1981), contrary to social work goals of increasing or maintaining client functioning. (2) Crisis theory suggests that the time period during which problems are experienced as crises and during which change is most likely is within six weeks (Ewing, 1978; Rapoport, 1970). While task-centered practice is not limited to crisis situations, it assumes that the desire to resolve problems also changes with time (Reid, 1978), that is, that client motivation and thus problem change is greatest during the time shortly after initial client–practitioner contact. (3) There is some evidence that when time limits are planned initially, a "goal gradient effect" takes place, that is, the individual works harder as the goal or time limit approaches (A. Goldstein, Heller, and Sechrest, 1966; Reid, 1981). In social treatment, a number of authors have noted increased activity by both client and practitioner in short-term treatment (Butcher and Koss, 1978; Reid and Shyne, 1969; Sucato, 1978) and qualitative changes in long-term treatment once a terminal date is set (Firestein, 1978; Lemon and Goldstein, 1978; H. Levinson, 1977). Thus, setting a termination date in the foreseeable future is likely to increase client and practitioner actions to resolve problems. (4) A pragmatic rationale relates to data on typical length of service. The average number of interviews received by clients is low [7.2 at Family Service Association of America agencies (D. Beck and Jones, 1973); 8 sessions in a private psychological clinic (Koss, 1979)]. A large percentage of clients drop out of open-ended or long-term treatment without mutual agreement (D. Beck and Jones, 1973; Ewalt, 1976; Garfield, 1978; Reder and Tyson, 1980), and clients generally expect treatment to be shorter than the practitioner anticipates (June and Smith, 1983; Rhodes, 1977a). Pragmatism suggests utilizing the short average time limits rather than attempting to keep reluctant clients in open-ended treatment with dubious benefits. Furthermore, several studies suggest that clients are less likely to drop out of treatment in planned short-term service than when they are not informed of time limits (D. Beck and Jones, 1973; Parad and Parad, 1968; Reid and Shyne, 1969).

Specificity of Treatment Focus

The breadth of change desired and consequently appropriate treatment goals distinguishes various approaches to social treatment. At one extreme are treatments which intend to change the individual's personality or reorganize the intrapsychic structure; at the other extreme are behavioral therapies which focus on specific, discrete behaviors. As Reid (1977b) notes, task-centered practice, with its emphasis on problems in living, falls somewhere between these extremes. For example, Reid found that three-fifths of target problems were specific or somewhat specific for two different groups of task-centered practitioners (Reid, 1977a). Several authors suggest that specificity of problems and goals is associated with better treatment outcome (Reid, 1969/70; Reid and Hanrahan, 1982; Rubenstein and Bloch, 1978; Wood, 1978), and VanDyck (1980) found specificity of goals related to outcome, but the direct evidence is as yet limited. However, practitioners in open-ended treatment often set more ambitious and broader goals than do clients and this sometimes leads to client dissatisfaction or dropping out (Maluccio, 1979; Silverman, 1970). Whether or not specificity is more effective or more satisfying to clients, it appears to be a necessary characteristic of short-term treatment, since it is difficult to attack global or amorphous problems in a brief time (Budman, 1981; Butcher and Koss, 1978; Reid, 1977b).

Contracting

A contract in task-centered practice involves a written or oral agreement between client and practitioner about the problems to be worked on (target problems), goals, and duration of service. The contract is formulated early in treatment, usually by the end of the second interview; it is renegotiable, but normally the contract guides the course of intervention and provides the parameters for structuring of interviews. There are drawbacks to contracts if they are too rigid or are used to exclude some client groups (Seabury, 1976), and there is difficulty in assuring practitioner accountability to the contract (Corden, 1980). However, their advantages are considerable. In task-centered practice, key elements of the contract include explicitness about target problems and goals and mutual agreement between client and practitioner (Epstein, 1980; Reid, 1977b). The explicitness reduces the well-documented client confusion about treatment purposes and consequent frequent dissatisfaction or poor outcome (Lishman, 1978; Rhodes, 1977a; Wattie, 1973). Further, there is evidence that when treatment goals are clear to the client, outcome is better than when no goals are set or goals are known only to the practitioner (Hart, 1978; LaFerriere and Calsyn, 1978; Willer and Miller, 1976).

Mutual agreement about what is to be worked on is of course a major value in task-centered practice; however, several studies also suggest that progress is more satisfactory when client and practitioner agree on problems or goals (Kanfer and Grimm, 1978; Rubenstein and Bloch, 1978; Sirles, 1982; Starfield et al., 1981; Wattie, 1973). Finally, many authors argue that as part of American and helping professions' values of client self-determination and practitioner accountability, the practitioner has an ethical responsibility through contracting to be clear and explicit about treatment (Corden, 1980; Hare-Mustin et al., 1979; Maluccio and Marlow, 1974).

Structure

Structure refers to the degree to which a treatment model provides procedures, steps, or rules to organize treatment process (Reid, 1977b). The task-centered model is relatively structured compared to many other treatment approaches in that it prescribes a series of problem-solving steps to guide intervention. This structure has become more clearly delineated as research on the task-centered model has progressed, but it is a framework, rather than an explicit prescription of each therapeutic move, and it is intended to be used flexibly (Reid, 1977b). When the basic structure is utilized, more task achievement and better problem alleviation are attained than when the structure is not used (Reid, 1975, 1978; Reid et al., 1980).

Reid and Epstein (1972) also conceptualize structure in terms of "systematic communication," or the extent to which the practitioner focuses on target problems and task-centered steps in an interview. The opposite is "responsive communication," in which the practitioner responds empathically and builds on the client's communications without regard to the "business" of problem-solving steps. As Reid and Epstein (1972) note, the effective practitioner must maintain a balance between systematic and responsive communication, although how much of each is necessary is unclear. Blizinsky and Reid (1980) found that outcome was better in cases where a greater proportion of time was spent on the target problems, but Fortune (1979a) found the proportion of time devoted to discussion of nontreatment matters related to outcome among children. Neither study directly investigated responsive and systematic communication, but they and other research on empathic and following communication indicate that some degree of responsiveness is important to effective practice (Duehn and Proctor, 1977). In short, while the task-centered model is relatively structured, it both permits and advocates flexibility and responsiveness within that structure.

Action

A major premise and strategy of task-centered treatment is that problems can be resolved through action and behavior (Reid, 1978). The action orientation is evident in the emphasis on changing problems in living (rather than personality), in tasks to resolve problems carried out in the natural environment, and in the greater practitioner activity and advice giving than in many treatment models. The model itself takes no position on whether internal or affective changes precede or follow changes in behavior, but the primary target for change is behavior or situation rather than internal processes. At the same time, however, the task-centered model involves the client and her cognitive capacities in the problem-solving process, as part of client self-determination (Epstein, 1980) and to enhance maintenance of changes (Fortune, 1981). Internal processes may also become the temporary focus of treatment when they constitute obstacles to task accomplishment (Reid, 1977a, 1978). Since the model assumes that the practitioner will use various theories to explain human behavior, the approach to internal obstacles may range from cognitive-behavioral to psychodynamic, depending on the practitioner's orientation.

The effectiveness of action by itself is unclear because action usually occurs with other treatment interventions. For example, tasks or home-work assignments lead to better and more durable treatment gain (Kanfer, 1979; Kazdin and Mascitelli, 1982; Pendleton, Shelton, and Wilson, 1976), but the effects of action to resolve a problem versus change being carried out in the natural environment cannot be separated. Such a distinction is not necessary for practice, however. What is important is that the typical client generally expects and prefers an action-oriented approach, whether defined as advice, problem solving, or concrete action (Balch et al., 1978; Frank, Eisenthal, and Lazare, 1978; Oxley, 1977; Silverman, 1970).

Empirical Orientation

The empirical orientation of the task-centered model has two aspects. The first relates to treatment model development itself: techniques and approaches which have demonstrated efficacy through research are more desirable than techniques which have not been tested. Thus, the model developers (Reid and Epstein) and numerous others have continued to test the model and its various components and to develop it based on evidence from their own and others' study. The second aspect of empiricism relates to the practitioner's orientation to practice:

(1) target problems, treatment goals, practitioner operations, and outcomes tend to be cast in forms that lend themselves to objective measurement;
(2) data obtained on these components are interpreted at a relatively low

level of inference: speculative theorizing is avoided; (3) reliance is placed on such data to guide treatment of individual cases and the development of the approach as a whole; (4) research methods and procedures are used to collect data on problems, interventions, and outcomes as a part of normal practice operations . . . (Reid, 1977b:14).

The task-centered model's emphasis on empiricism is value based. There is no evidence that empirically oriented practitioners are more effective than those who are not empirically oriented. In fact, the question is irrelevant unless the practitioner already has a scientific perspective.

Treatment Steps in the Task-Centered Model

This section describes the treatment process of the task-centered model as a framework for following chapters. Readers who wish a more detailed description of the model are referred to Epstein's *Helping People* (1980) or Reid's *The Task-Centered System* (1978).

Task-centered treatment can be divided into three phases depending on the predominant practitioner–client activity during that phase: Problem Specification, when the focus is on determining the problems the client wishes to work on (1–3 interviews); Task Planning and Implementation, when the focus is on formulating, planning, and evaluating task actions to resolve the selected target problems (usually 6 to 10 interviews); and Termination, when progress and treatment process are recapitulated and plans are made to increase durability of treatment results (1–2 interviews) (see Table A).

Problem Specification

Eliciting Target Problems. A problem is any difficulty in daily living. To be included as a target problem to be worked on in task-centered practice, a problem must meet three criteria: (1) the client must explicitly acknowledge the problem and be willing to work on it (although the practitioner may suggest problem areas); (2) the client and practitioner together must have the resources to resolve the problem; and (3) the problem must be reasonably specific (Reid and Epstein, 1972). If, as sometimes happens, there are multiple problems, no more than three may be worked on in a single task-centered contract; the three target problems selected should meet a fourth criterion of being client priorities for resolution. In groups, each individual normally has only one problem; in families, there may be both family and individual-member problems.

Table A. Activities in the Task-Centered Model

Interviews 1–2
   I. Problem Specification
      1. Establishing presence of acknowledged problem
      2. Specifying conditions to be changed
      3. Determining desired changes
      4. Developing working explanations
      5. Eliciting prior problem-solving efforts
      6. Obtaining contextual data
         a. History and development of problem
         b. Client's characteristics and functioning as person
         c. Client's social and other environments
  II. The Treatment Contract
      1. Establishing treatment goals and general tasks
      2. Agreeing on the amount and length of service

Interview 3
  III. Task planning and implementation
      1. Task planning
         a. Generating alternatives
         b. Task agreement
         c. Planning details of implementation
         d. Summarization
      2. Establishing incentives and rationale
      3. Simulation
      4. Guided practice
      5. Analysis of obstacles
      6. Work with others
         a. Enhancing incentives
         b. Facilitating task execution

All Middle Interviews
  IV. Task Review
    I. Problem Assessment
  III. Task planning and implementation

Final Interview
  IV. Task Review
   V. Termination
      1. Final problem assessment
      2. Planning direction for further progress and for maintaining gains
      3. Generalizing problem-solving ability through review of:
         a. General steps in problem-solving
         b. Examples from client's experience in task-centered treatment
         c. Applications to other areas of client's life

The requirements for target problems mean first of all that difficulties which are defined by others but which the client denies are not appropriate for task-centered intervention. For example, a schoolchild may deny that his behavior disrupts the class or an elderly woman that she is a burden to her adult children. Often, such difficulties can be reformulated in terms acceptable to the client; for example, the child may agree that his teacher gets angry at him and this is worth working on. At other times the practitioner may consider working with a different client unit, for example, with the children of the elderly woman around a target problem of their reactions to mother.

The exception to the criterion of client acknowledgment is when a problem is legally mandated, for example, school truancy, child abuse, theft, etc. (Epstein, 1980). If a problem is mandated, the practitioner must inform the client of this and negotiate target problems. If the client will not acknowledge the problem, there are two options: to include the mandated problems along with client-identified problems in a task-centered contract, or to separate the supervision, coercion function from the counseling function. There is no evidence regarding which option is more appropriate and both options have been used. Usually, however, careful problem exploration and negotiation can avoid the dilemma, and clients with mandated problems are often "motivated" to work when their own concerns as well as the court's or agency's are taken into account.

The process of problem specification initially involves eliciting the client's perceptions of any difficulties. Reid and Epstein (1972) discuss two levels of client expression of problems: at the first level, discussion may be free but is colored by client anxiety or expectations of treatment and by affect associated with the problems in themselves; at the second level, the client is able to describe her[2] most troublesome difficulties, which may be underlying the initial complaints. This distinction is important to prevent the practitioner from focusing prematurely on superficial or peripheral problems or problems the client has used as an "admission ticket" believing that is what the practitioner expects (A. Schwartz and Goldiamond, 1975).

In addition, the practitioner may explore a number of areas to place the problems in context or reveal factors affecting the problems: the client's work or school situation, family and peer relations, health status, housing and economic situation, cultural or ethnic beliefs, personality and intelligence, and general manner of relating to others. Each of these

---

[2]The female pronoun is used in the editor's chapters because most social work practitioners and clients are women. No discourtesy is intended. Unfortunately, the field has not yet invented a euphonic pronoun that includes both genders and would render explanations like this obsolete.

factors can profoundly influence both problems and strategies for re-solving problems. However, the exploration should be general unless an area presents a new target problem or is clearly related to acknowledged target problems; in-depth diagnostic evaluations are not normally part of task-centered practice.

When it is fairly clear what the target problems will be, the practitioner should elicit in considerably greater detail the specifics of the problem. The details included in problem specification include: what exactly is the problem, how often it occurs, when, with whom, where, with what consequences, with what antecedents, in what context, and with what meaning to the client (Epstein, 1980). This information provides data for later assessment of progress and for guiding interventions. Other infor-mation which is often useful in problem specification includes duration of the problem, how the client has attempted to resolve it, what courses of action are open to the client, and what the consequences of those actions might be. Again, the purpose of this exploration is to assist the practitioner to form a working hypothesis of causes of the problem that *can be changed* and to suggest resolutions. For example, repeating solutions the client has tried unsuccessfully in the past may be futile and frustrating, whereas the client may suggest other alternatives that have worked. Similarly, if a couple's marital quarrels began when the wife was promoted at work, the practitioner has a clue to possible causes and interventions around the husband's jealousy or wife's new stress and lack of confidence.

Some clients may not acknowledge problems or may find difficulty in specifying workable problems. The practitioner may then suggest a problem search—a contract for one or two interviews whose sole purpose is to explore potential areas to be worked on (Reid and Epstein, 1972). If a target problem cannot be found by the end of the problem search, contact should be terminated.

Forming the Contract. Once the practitioner and the client have a fairly clear idea of what problems will be worked on, they form an agreement about the goals and length of service. Normally that is accom-plished by the end of the second session. A task-centered contract includes the target problems, goals of treatment, and length of treatment, usually stated in number of sessions over a specific time (Reid, 1978). The contract may also include who is to be involved in treatment and general (organizing) tasks which outline the strategy to be used to achieve treat-ment goals (Epstein, 1980). If not already clear, the contract should also include an explicit understanding that the client and practitioner will work actively through tasks to resolve the problems.

The goals of treatment reflect the changes desired by the client and should be as realistic and specific as possible. As mentioned earlier, the practitioner should avoid the temptation to set too high or unrealistic goals; at the same time, the practitioner must avoid underestimating the client's capacity to change or to achieve personal goals.

Treatment length in a normal task-centered contract is between 6 and 12 sessions. The practitioner should be precise ("8 sessions," not "6 to 8 sessions") to enhance the goal gradient effect. Unfortunately, there are no clear guidelines about what length is ideal. However, contract length should relate to target problems, goals, and the feasibility of resolving problems within a particular period of time. For example, unemployment problems are more difficult to resolve in a depressed economy than in an expanding economy. If a client lacks employment skills, a longer period may be necessary or the goal may be to acquire job training rather than to become employed. Another factor to be considered is "natural" time limits, for example, impending marking periods for students with academic problems or discharge for a hospitalized patient. As a pragmatic matter, practitioner's and client's schedules should be considered in setting time limits. Practitioners sometimes forget that they will be unavailable during holidays or vacations; clients may be able to predict that a visit from relatives planned for the near future may slow down their progress. Finally, clients' own ideas of how long it will take to resolve a problem are often good indicators for setting time limits.

Who should be involved in treatment is not often discussed in task-centered literature. Ultimately, it is the client's decision, and her wishes should be the guiding factor in the decision of who to involve. However, the practitioner can make suggestions based on her assessment of the situation and knowledge of factors contributing to initiation and durability of change. Particularly with interactive problems, the client's immediate social system may be important to changing and is generally crucial to maintaining change in target problems. For example, weight losses are maintained longer when spouses are involved (Israel and Saccone, 1979; Wilson and Brownell, 1980), and children's new behavior is more durable if parents or peers are involved (Conway and Bucher, 1976; Patterson and Fleischman, 1979; Solomon and Wahler, 1973). In general, persons directly involved in a problem or those who are likely to be contributing to it should be considered for inclusion in treatment sessions (see also Chapters 6 and 7).

In many circumstances it may not be desirable or feasible to involve others in all treatment sessions but to include them occasionally as collaterals whose partial involvement and knowledge of the client's goals may contribute significantly to problem alleviation. Examples include peers or teachers in school (R. Rossi, 1977), adult children of the elderly (Fortune and Rathbone-McCuan, 1981), or key personnel in other agencies that serve the client (Epstein, 1980). The client must, of course, give permission to involve such collaterals.

General tasks, included in the contract, are used to organize treatment planning and give a direction for action without the explicit steps (Reid, 1978). General tasks always reflect the goals. In some cases they may simply restate the goal in action terms ("Jennifer is to become more independent of her family"); in others they also reflect a treatment strategy ("Jennifer is to become more independent of her family by finding a part-time job"). Treatment strategies, as used here, refer to various approaches to resolving a problem and will be discussed further in the next section.

The contract in task-centered treatment may be either written or oral. Written contracts have the advantages of clarity, reducing misunderstandings about responsibilities, and making it easier to maintain focus on the original target problems; in some agencies they may be useful in maintaining records and accountability. On the other hand, written social work contracts have doubtful legal status (Corden, 1980; Epstein, 1980), may be misused punitively (Seabury, 1976), and are aversive to some clients (Dierking, Brown, and Fortune, 1980). Oral contracts are also easier and quicker to formulate. Probably in most social work practice, oral contracts are sufficient; written contracts should be considered when accountability or clarity is essential and they may be particularly useful with young children, with adults who have memory difficulties, or with adults who prefer the implied seriousness and formality of a written document.

Target Problems and Treatment Strategies. The task-centered model suggests eight categories of target problems: interpersonal conflict, dissatisfaction in social relations, problems with formal organizations, difficulties in role performance, decision problems, reactive emotional distress, inadequate resources, and psychological or behavioral problems not elsewhere classified (Reid, 1978).

Placing a client's individual problem into one of these categories is useful only if knowledge of the category provides guidelines or suggested strategies for efficient resolution of the problem. This section describes the categories following Reid's (1978) definitions and suggests potential treatment strategies for each type of problem. The strategies are general approaches only; the specific tasks negotiated within a strategy depend on the particulars of the problem and the client's perceptions of what is relevant and feasible. Further, the strategies are not mutually exclusive; in most cases, the practitioner and client will pursue several approaches simultaneously.

Interpersonal conflict includes overt conflict where both parties agree that the problem exists, i.e., can be used as a category only when two or more clients are involved in treatment. One treatment strategy, frequently underlying behavioral approaches (e.g., Paquin, 1981; Rappaport and Harrell, 1972), is to have each individual define what he or she finds objectionable in the other and then plan tasks to reduce the objectionable behavior of each. A similar strategy is to have each individual define desired *positive* changes or traits in the other, and to work toward increasing occurrence of that behavior (Reid and Epstein, 1972). The positive approach may be difficult to implement with clients so deep in conflict that they can discern no positive attributes in the other, but has an advantage in terms of a value of stressing strengths and positives rather than weaknesses and negatives. Furthermore, it is probably best to supplement the first strategy with the second, since there is evidence that positive interaction does not automatically replace conflictual or negative interaction (S. Johnson, Bolstad, and Lobitz, 1976; Vincent, Weiss, and Birchler, 1975). With both these strategies, a particularly useful form of specific task is the reciprocal task, in which separate but related actions are carried out, for example, John (husband) will not nag about Betty's cooking, and Betty will cook at least two "old favorites" during the week. In determining both behaviors to be changed and appropriate actions for reciprocal tasks, it is important that there be reciprocity, i.e., that both parties feel that the exchange is fair.

A third strategy with interpersonal conflict is to focus on the interactive sequence that leads to overt conflict rather than on the conflictual behavior itself. All communication and conflict can be conceptualized as an uninterrupted sequence of interactions where the definition of "who started it" is a matter of irrelevant punctuation (Watzlawick, Beavin, and Jackson, 1967). The intent in this strategy is to locate a point in the sequence which is susceptible to change, for example, before a quarreling couple lose their tempers and begin throwing things (Reid, 1978). In some cases, the focal point for intervention may be particular communications, with more appropriate, less conflict-inducing communications substituted, as in teaching husband and wife how and when not to interrupt (Thomas, 1977; Tolson, 1977) or parent and adolescent how to respond to each other with the other's point of view in mind (Robin, 1979). In other cases, the focal point may be specific circumstances which can be modified or avoided, for example, selecting appropriate places or times to initiate controversial topics (C. Taylor, 1977; Thomas, 1977).

A fourth strategy with interpersonal conflict is to resolve the specific issues at question through joint problem solving or task action. This strategy is appropriate only when the issues at conflict are fairly clear and delimited (even though they may be longstanding). For example, many cases of marital conflict revolve around finances, and a frequent strategy is to focus on resolving the financial problems and teaching the couple fiscal responsibility (Fortune, 1976).

Dissatisfaction in social relations includes problems where the client perceives deficiencies or excesses in her interactions, for example, loneliness, shyness, or rejection. It also includes overt conflict which is perceived by only one person, i.e., problems which would be classified as interpersonal conflict if both parties defined a conflict.

The first factor to be considered in dissatisfaction in social relations is whether the client has the knowledge and skills to perform as she desires socially and, if not, how to acquire them. There are any number of specialized treatment packages to correct social skills deficits that practitioners may borrow or adapt, for example, assertiveness training (Gambrill, 1977), social problem solving (Spivack, Platt, and Shure, 1976), dating anxiety reduction (Pendleton, Shelton, and Wilson, 1976), etc. If such "packages" are borrowed, however, the practitioner must take care to adapt them to the individual client and to involve the client in the process of selecting appropriate components.

A second strategy, assuming the client has or is learning the requisite skills, is to involve the client in social interactions of increasing complexity, intensity, or threat, i.e., an incremental task plan (Reid, 1978). Here, it is important that the steps be gradual and not beyond the client's limits of self-confidence or social skills. Often sessions will include planning alternative client responses or reactions should the others to be involved in tasks not respond as the client wishes or expects.

Within the strategy of increasing social interaction, a frequent approach is to involve a shy or isolated client in social groups. Several cautions are appropriate: (1) It is often more effective to initiate social interaction through instrumental activities rather than social activities, that is, through a hobby or interest club rather than a group expressly for socializing or meeting others. In singles clubs or senior social groups, the public spotlight on interaction may undermine the client's already shaky confidence, whereas in activity clubs the social interaction takes place around mutual interests that are of more concern to the participants than social skills. (2) The practitioner should avoid specially created groups or projects of short duration, as clients often revert to isolation when the group ends (Stafford and Bringle, 1980). (3) Treatment groups are very appropriate for meeting people with similar problems, learning new social skills, and practicing skills (see Garvin, Chapter 2, Macy-Lewis, Chapter 4, and Toseland and Coppola, Chapter 5, this volume). However, they should include focus on translating social skills to other environments and should not substitute for other social activities.

Another approach to increasing social interaction is to focus initially on the client's interaction with a few specific individuals—boyfriend, coworker, etc. To ensure that the client is able to use social skills in more general situations and after treatment is completed, later tasks should vary circumstances and, if feasible, persons involved, in order to maximize the client's ability to use and apply social skills (Emshoff, Redd, and Davidson, 1976; Garcia, 1974; Koegel, Egel, and Williams, 1980; Marholin and Touchette, 1979).

A third general strategy with dissatisfaction with social relations is to deal with the internal obstacles to social interaction, e.g., fear of rejection or being a fool (Reid and Epstein, 1972; Reid, 1978). Depending on the practitioner's theoretical stance, this may involve cognitive-behavioral approaches (A. Beck, 1976; Ellis and Grieger, 1977) or psychosocial approaches (Ewalt, 1977; Wise, 1977). However, a strategy which focuses on internal obstacles should be combined with another strategy. The task-centered model emphasizes action, and there is evidence that approaches which combine task activity with focus on internal process are more effective than those which focus only on cognitive processes (Berlin, 1980; Fuchs and Rehm, 1977; Pendleton, Shelton, and Wilson, 1976).

The third problem category, *problems with formal organizations*, includes difficulties the client is experiencing with an organization or an individual in his organizational role, for example, problems with receiving entitled social security benefits, or dealing with a school principal to get suspended children reinstated. Here, the initial question is, again, does the client have the necessary knowledge and skills to resolve the problem? If providing such information and assistance in dealing with the organization does not help the client, or the organization is so bureaucratic (or hostile) that the client cannot negotiate it herself, then the practitioner's second strategy is to act as mediator, initiating contact on the client's behalf, sitting in on meetings between client and organizational personnel, etc. Often the practitioner's professional status, status within the community, and knowledge of persons and policies in other service organizations will enable resolution of problems where individual client effort cannot. However, as Hashimi (1981) points out, the client should be involved in the planning process and in as much of the task activity as possible, in order to develop skills to cope with organizations on her own.

A third strategy in problems with formal organizations, if the first two fail, is for the practitioner to act as advocate on behalf of the client or a group of clients, attempting to change agency policies or procedures. This strategy is often neglected but equally often crucial (Grinnell, 1973).

Frequently, when problems with formal organizations exist, the difficulties are aggravated by the client's attitudes or behavior toward the individuals with whom she must interact in the organization. In such instances, the practitioner may consider an approach to changing the client's behavior using one of the strategies outlined under dissatisfaction in social relations. However, this should be undertaken only if the client agrees that her behavior is contributing to the problem, and should be subsidiary to the primary goal of resolving the specific difficulty.

Difficulties in role performance include problems related to carrying out a social role such as spouse, parent, student, employee, or patient. For example, academic problems fall into this category, but marital conflict is included only when the primary conflict is about roles as husband or wife.

In difficulties in role performance, the first strategy is to clarify expectations of roles, i.e., what the client is expected to do either by societal or situation-specific norms. For example, a very upset elderly woman was calmed by an explanation of what was expected of her as a hospital patient (Dierking, Brown, and Fortune, 1980). Role norms should not be imposed on the client, but the norms must be clarified so that the client may understand what others expect of her and can with that knowledge determine the extent to which she wishes to conform to those expectations.

The second strategy assumes that the client knows role expectations but does not necessarily have the skills to perform them, and involves assisting the client to learn and implement those skills. For example, a child with academic problems may learn to schedule and concentrate on his homework, or to behave appropriately in the classroom, depending on where the skill deficit lies.

Decision problems include difficulties in making specific decisions, often related to major life changes such as divorce, marriage, or career choice. Although the core of decision problems is the client's need to make major decisions, focus on "making a decision" as a primary strategy is generally ineffective. A more effective strategy is to employ a problem-solving approach, clarifying the options available, the steps involved in carrying out each option, and the consequences of both the steps and the options themselves. Tasks often involve completing preliminary steps, and the client may carry out steps for several options simultaneously, "trying them on for size." For example, a woman undecided on whether to leave her husband, find a job, or return to school (or some combination) completed concurrent tasks to reduce quarrels with the husband, assess her employment skills, and explore local educational opportunities. By the end of treatment, she had decided to stay in the marriage and was enrolled at a community college.

Once a decision is made, if the client wishes, the focus of treatment may shift to making the transition into the new role involved (or improving performance in an accustomed role) and to the strategies suggested under difficulties in role performance that are appropriate. For example, a pregnant woman decided not to have an abortion. After the decision was made, several sessions were spent securing prenatal care and preparing for her new role as mother.

Reactive emotional distress includes problems where the client is concerned with her feelings (anxiety, depression) rather than events precipitating them, but those events can be pinpointed (death, separation, illness, unemployment, etc.).

There is much literature on normal and abnormal reactions to crises to which the practitioner can turn. For example, the typical stages of reaction are known for various illnesses (B. Anderson and Auslander, 1980; Brodland and Andreasen, 1977; Hinton, 1977), surgery (Kimball, 1977), divorce and remarriage (Kleinman, Rosenberg, and Whiteside, 1979; Wallerstein and Kelly, 1979), rape (Burgess and Holmstrom, 1974; Katz and Mazur, 1979; Lukton, 1982), and death of a spouse (Parkes, 1972). Knowledge of crises and stages can serve the practitioner in two ways: (1) recognizing the reactions and being able to assure the client that they are "normal" for people in her situation can reassure both client and practitioner, and (2) typical stage reactions can give the practitioner general guidelines both to what the client is capable of doing now and the direction in which to move.

The strategies depend somewhat on the stage the client is in (with the caution that such stages are typical, not normative, and do not characterize every client); for example, some grief work or catharsis may be necessary before the client is ready to take action. Tasks may relate to increasing client understanding of the precipitating event and her reactions, or to rechanneling feelings about it (Reid and Epstein, 1972). At a later stage of reaction, the major strategy is to address what the client can do to reestablish a normal active life within the context of stage and future activity. For example, a newly bereaved widow may complete tasks related to settling her former husband's finances with the dual purpose of permitting appropriate mourning and preparing for handling her own financial affairs.

The seventh problem category, *inadequate resources*, includes lack of tangible resources such as a job, housing, money, or child care. The first and most important strategy is to get the lacking resource (Reid and Epstein, 1972), either directly through agency resources or practitioner intervention or indirectly through assisting the client to plan and secure acquisition. Only when the problem is resolved, and with the client's consent, should the practitioner consider a second strategy, assisting the client to prevent the problem from recurring. For example, a couple with severe financial problems were assisted in securing a consolidated loan and then learned financial planning to avoid future overspending.

The final category, *psychological or behavioral problems not else-where classified*, includes problems which do not fall into other categories, such as phobias, addictive behaviors, bed-wetting, self-image problems, etc. Because of the catch-all nature of the category, it is difficult to suggest general strategies beyond taking concrete steps to control or minimize the difficulty. The literature on specific problems can often suggest effective approaches, for example, thought stopping to control hallucinations or obsessive thoughts (Gambrill, 1977), or in vivo systematic desensitization for phobias (Brown, 1977).

Task Planning and Implementation

The middle phase of task-centered practice is devoted to planning and implementing specific tasks (also called operational tasks) for client or practitioner to carry out between sessions. Criteria for tasks are: "the action must be: (1) planned and agreed on with the practitioner; (2) capable of being worked on by the client (or practitioner) outside of the treatment session" (Reid, 1978: 139). Tasks may be concurrent (carried out more or less simultaneously) or sequential; mental ("to think about Lisa's [wife's] strengths") or physical ("to go to the unemployment office"); unique or one-time actions ("to join the volleyball team") or repetitive ("to get up on time each morning"); unitary ("to call the doctor") or complex ("to call the doctor and, if he feels it is necessary, make an appointment and attend the appointment"), shared ("Robert and Lisa will balance the checkbook") or reciprocal ("Robert will keep receipts for his purchases and Lisa will balance his checkbook"). Tasks may stand alone, unrelated to other tasks, or they may be incremental actions in an overall task plan, each successive task building on previous tasks and representing a step toward the goal. The crucial factor in task planning is not the type of task but that the task be within the client's capability to complete (with assistance from the practitioner) and have a good chance of reducing the target problems. Completion of tasks is the single greatest predictor of problem alleviation (Ewalt, 1977; Reid, 1978).

Activity during sessions of the middle phase follows a problem-solving process. The steps are: generating alternatives, task agreement, planning details of implementation, summarization, establishing incentive and rationale, analysis of obstacles, simulation, guided practice, and task review. The order of the steps as presented is logical; although there are some patterns in practice, the typical practitioner–client pair "jump around" among steps with no apparent loss of effectiveness (Fortune, 1978, 1979b).

Task Review. Each interview in the middle phase should begin with a review of effort and progress on the tasks formulated in the previous interview (task review) and of the impact of completed tasks on the target problems. If tasks were not successfully completed, why (analysis of obstacles) may be discussed before turning to possible new task actions (generating alternatives). Unsuccessful tasks may be dropped altogether, repeated, or revised in light of new information from analyzing obstacles. Successfully completed tasks become the basis for next steps in progress toward the client's goals.

Generating Alternatives. Generating alternatives is the process of finding ideas for task actions. Sources of ideas include the client's own experience, the practitioner's expert knowledge, and the practitioner's experience with similar cases (L. Epstein, 1980). D'Zurilla and Goldfried (1971) suggest that the quantity of ideas generated is important to selecting an effective solution (here, task), and recent research indeed suggests that the more ideas generated the better (D'Zurilla and Nezu, 1980; Nezu and D'Zurilla, 1981). The various possible courses of action are then evaluated by practitioner and client for feasibility, desirability, and client motivation (Reid and Epstein, 1972). Considerations in determining which task to pursue include positive and negative consequences of doing or not doing a task, the relation of client effort to client benefit, and the effect of the task on other problems and other people (Reid, 1978). Nezu and D'Zurilla (1979) also suggest personal criteria such as time involved; effort; emotional cost or gain; consistency with morals, ethics, and values; physical well-being; idiosyncratic personal effects; and social criteria such as effects on family, friends, and community, and consequences to one's community standing and reputation.

Task Agreement. The client's agreement to attempt a task is crucial. Who initially suggested a task is unimportant compared to the client's willingness to work on the task (Reid, 1978). Task agreement may be implicit, as when the client eagerly moves into discussion of how to carry out a task, but it is generally wiser to ascertain explicit commitment, to avoid the practitioner inadvertently imposing her notions of "good" tasks on the client.

Planning Details of Task Implementation. Planning details for implementation involves the nitty-gritty of how the task will be carried out. Reid (1978) suggests beginning by "breaking the task down into sequences of operations that may be required to carry it out" (144). Questions that need to be answered include where and when the client should carry out the task, whether she has the resources or skills to complete it, and what to do if the first attempt fails or backfires. It is often useful at this point to analyze *potential* obstacles to plan ways to avoid them. For example, if a wife is to approach her husband to ask him for a larger household allowance, what happens if he is grouchy? When is he most likely to be receptive? What can she do to put him in a better mood? What phrases can she use? What should she do if he misunderstands or says no?

The process of planning details of task implementation is often time consuming, but lack of clarity or of careful planning are frequent causes of failure of task efforts, and it is surprising how often practitioners overlook important details. For example, one young inner-city couple was very highly motivated to prevent further lead poisoning of their four children; they agreed to purchase and install a plywood panel over the peeling lead paint in the children's bedroom. Several weeks went by without task accomplishment, although the parents were obviously concerned. Eventually the practitioner discovered that the couple did not have a car and could not afford a taxi to the distant lumber yard. The task was changed to purchasing nonleaded plaster (which was cheaper and could be carried on the bus) and the wife (who enjoyed such things) would replaster the entire room. The new task was completed that evening.

Summarization.   Summarization involves summarizing the task, including essential details of task plans and why it should be done. Normally, summarization is done at the end of the interview (especially if there are several tasks), but it may also be done earlier, if the discussion of a task has been complex or there have been digressions. Ideally, the client should summarize, since the point is client clarity and understanding. Many practitioners also provide a written copy of the tasks (including practitioner tasks). Written copies are especially useful with children (who often enjoy writing them themselves), retarded or confused adults, families, and in any complex case with a large number of tasks.

Establishing Incentives and Rationale.   Establishing incentives and rationale for task completion involves motivating clients to complete a task and providing reasons for it. The most important incentive is the belief that the task is worthwhile and will alleviate the problem. Discussion may include some of the factors already mentioned in evaluating alternatives: the benefits and dangers of completing or not completing a task, social benefits, how the task relates to the problem, etc. (Reid, 1978). Practitioner praise and encouragement are also important but should not be used in lieu of a clear explanation of why a task is relevant or beneficial.

Behaviorally oriented practitioners may use tangible reinforcers such as candy, tokens, or special events as incentives and rewards for task performance (Reid, 1978). Such use is appropriate within the task-centered model, but extreme care must be taken to ensure that behavior does not become contingent on those rewards alone; there is a great deal of evidence that clients do not continue improved levels of functioning after the practitioner and the rewards have "disappeared" unless attention is paid to maintenance (Conway and Bucher, 1976; Fishman and Lubetkin, 1980; Keeley, Shemberg, and Carbonell, 1976). Some strategies to enhance maintenance when structured, tangible reinforcement programs are used include: (1) changing the form of reinforcement to something naturally available, e.g., from candy to praise or social interaction (Ban-

dura, 1969; Conway and Bucher, 1976; Wildman and Wildman, 1980);
(2) changing the frequency of reinforcement until the client can no longer
tell when she will be rewarded and consequently occasional unpredictable
rewards will reinforce the behavior (Bandura, 1969), or until the type and
frequency of response approximates real life (usually immediate negative
feedback but postponed and erratic positive feedback (Corson, 1976));
(3) changing the locus of reinforcement from practitioner to significant
other (teacher, parent, spouse) (Bandura, 1969) or to the client (self-
reinforcement) (L. Anderson, Fodor, and Alpert, 1976; Kanfer, 1979;
O'Leary and Dubey, 1979). Many effective maintenance approaches include combinations of these strategies, for example, teaching children to
elicit praise from adults when their behavior is appropriate (Seymour and
Stokes, 1976; Stokes, Fowler, and Baer, 1978).

   Analysis of Obstacles.   Analysis of obstacles has already been alluded
to in terms of examining potential obstacles while planning tasks; it also
occurs as a client-practitioner activity when tasks have failed. An obstacle
is anything that prevents task accomplishment or problem alleviation but
that can be modified through careful task planning, through tasks directed
at removing the obstacles, or through in-session activity such as discussion
of irrational beliefs or role-playing to gain self-confidence. Epstein (1980)
suggests six common types of obstacles: (1) When the client lacks resources
to complete a task, the resources should be obtained (see the strategies
suggested for the target problem category Lack of Adequate Resources);
if resources are not available, alternatives will be necessary. (2) If the
client lacks social reinforcement for task completion, the practitioner may
undertake facilitating tasks to involve significant others (Epstein, 1980),
select or create environments for task action that will support the client
(Marholin and Touchette, 1979; Price, 1979), or help the client learn to
elicit reinforcement (Cantor and Gelfand, 1977; Stokes, Fowler, and Baer,
1978). (3) When the client lacks skills, the practitioner may assist her to
learn them (see suggested strategies under dissatisfaction with social
relations), engage in modeling or role-play, or refer the client to experts in
those skills (Epstein, 1980). (4) If the client's adverse beliefs such as low
self-evaluation interfere with task completion, approaches include factual,
realistic discussion (Epstein, 1980) and cognitive-behavioral approaches
(Reid, 1978). Also useful are tasks which are set up to succeed and which
demonstrate clearly to the client that her beliefs are unfounded. (5) If the
client lacks the capacity—for example, is too young or physically debilitated to learn necessary skills to perform a task—the tasks should be
scaled down to her ability or others involved in assisting her (Epstein,
1980). Indeed, whether the client lacks capacity or not, an important
consideration in analyzing unsuccessful tasks is whether the task was too
large a step for the client at that particular time, and, if so, whether

smaller, incremental steps should be attempted. (6) Finally, practitioners themselves may be biased or lack skills. Practitioners should be alert to those possibilities and take steps to remedy them, through further experience, training, reading, or reference to a resource person (Epstein, 1980).

Simulation. Simulation is the task-centered term for trying out new behaviors or tasks in the interview, i.e., role-play, rehearsal, and modeling (Reid, 1978). It is particularly useful when the client lacks skills and is learning new skills, or if she simply lacks confidence and wishes to "try it out."

In addition, the practitioner can use role-playing diagnostically, for example, noting obstructions to husband–wife communication that neither spouse could have described in words; and to help clients visualize reality, for example, by the practitioner role-playing a strict teacher rather than the totally acquiescent teacher the child fantasizes. Simulation is not useful when the client already possesses the skills or feels too inhibited to "perform" (Reid, 1978); perhaps for these reasons, it has been used considerably less often with adults than with children (Fortune, 1979b).

Guided Practice. Guided practice involves actual work on a task, in the practitioner's presence. It has been used primarily in children's cases, for example, reading out loud as practice for a similar task. However, Tolson (1977) notes its use with a marital couple practicing hand signals when they wished to speak, and it is appropriate whenever the client is learning new skills that the practitioner may coach, as in learning relaxation techniques.

Termination

Termination in task-centered treatment actually begins as soon as there is contract agreement, when the number of sessions is set (Reid and Epstein, 1972). At some point in each of the middle interviews, the practitioner reminds the client gently of the stage in treatment: "This is the fifth of our ten interviews," or "That was our eighth meeting; we've got four more to go." The reminders serve as notice of progress and are intended to enhance the goal-gradient effect. Reference to time limits and to the client's ability to resolve problems within those time limits also reduces dependency on the practitioner so that the client is better able to deal with termination as a normal and growth-inducing process.

The termination phase has several purposes beyond simply marking the end of treatment. It is simultaneously an assessment of current status, a recapitulation of treatment and the treatment process, and an effort to generalize and maintain the client's problem-solving capacities, no matter how limited. The termination procedures normally take place in the last scheduled interview, but in cases with complex problems or if difficulty

in termination is anticipated, the termination procedures may begin in the next-to-last scheduled interview. The final interview involves: (1) review of tasks formulated in the preceding session, (2) review and assessment of progress toward alleviating client's target problems, (3) planning directions for further client work on the target problems, if they are not fully alleviated, or maintaining gains, if the problems are alleviated, and (4) assisting the client to see how the task-centered problem-solving steps can be applied to other problems in living (Reid, 1978).

Task Review.   The termination interview, like middle-phase interviews, begins with review of tasks formulated in the previous session. Reid suggests the last tasks be "repetitions or modest extensions of previously successful tasks" (Reid, 1978: 179). In many cases, particularly those involving a change in behavior or way of interacting by the client, repetition of new behavior or slight variation in the behavior (for example, being assertive in a new situation) is important to enable the client to "overlearn" or stabilize new behavior (Fishman and Lubetkin, 1980; A. Goldstein, Lopez, and Greenleaf, 1979) and to generalize it to new settings (Emshoff, Redd, and Davidson, 1976; Marholin and Touchette, 1979). In other instances, however, the last tasks may be new ones which are the final steps in an incremental task strategy. For example, with a target problem of unemployment, final tasks would appropriately involve beginning a job or enrolling in a job-skill-building program. In any case, the final tasks are reviewed with particular emphasis on the client's accomplishment and ability to carry out the action.

Final Problem Review.   The second step of the termination interview, final problem review, includes a description of the current status of the target problems, the client's perceptions of the problems, of changes in the problems, and of her current situation overall, including new problems or those not worked on. The final problem review should be similar in detail and specificity to the initial problem review.

The final problem review has three purposes. First, it provides data for a relatively accurate evaluation of progress on the case, useful to the client, the practitioner, and often, the agency. After involvement in intensive problem-solving efforts, client and practitioner are apt to forget "how it was in the beginning" and to paint an overly rosy or dreary view of current conditions. Reviewing the problems in terms similar to the initial problem review helps reduce "recall" or forgetfulness difficulties and puts progress in the context in which it should be perceived in task-centered practice, the context of client's acknowledged problems.

The second purpose of the final problem review is to provide the information from which the practitioner can realistically praise and encourage the client for her achievements, that is, it serves as the basis for making the final interview a positive, competence-oriented experience.

The assessment must be realistic, not glossing over areas in which work remains to be done, but at the same time the client's accomplishments are emphasized. The intent is to bring about "positive feelings of mastery or achievement" (Parad and Parad, 1968). In most cases, there will be considerable improvement in at least some areas, so it is not difficult for the practitioner to find areas for realistic praise. A different aspect of encouragement relates to attribution of problem change. There is evidence that clients who attribute change to their own efforts, or who feel that they are in control of their behavior, are better able to maintain improved functioning or deal with new problems (Davison and Valins, 1969; Rodin and Langer, 1977; Sonne and Janoff, 1979). Consequently, to the extent possible, the practitioner should underline the client's own contributions to problem change, reinforcing her ability to take action on her own behalf. Even when much of the effort has been by the practitioner, for example, in negotiating a complex bureaucracy for the client, the client's new knowledge of negotiating procedures can be emphasized.

The third purpose of the problem review is to provide information for discussion in the remainder of the termination interview. Obviously, one cannot plan for maintaining or furthering change unless one knows the current status of target problems. Too often, however, practitioners in the later parts of termination interviews get caught up in planning for the future without reference to the efforts made during treatment. The client's past successful efforts should be included in discussion of the future, as examples, just as much as during the problem review.

Planning for the Future.   The third step of termination interviews is planning directions for further client work on the target problems, either improving further or maintaining desirable changes. Considerations to be discussed with the client include what the client can do to continue working toward a goal on her own and what she can do in the future to ensure that there is no relapse.

If the problem is not totally alleviated but a successful incremental task strategy has started, planning in the final interview may involve a discussion of the next steps in the strategy. For example, a lonely woman had attended several social activities; it was clear that the next step was to become more involved in the club that interested her most. In this instance specific tasks (e.g., joining the ski club) were appropriate, with discussion of potential obstacles and consequences. However, too many specific tasks may defeat another purpose of the termination interview, generalizing the client's problem-solving skills, since formulation of multiple specific tasks implies that the practitioner is needed to assist the process. Therefore, it is often more appropriate to formulate general strategies or organizing tasks which, when combined with review of the problem-solving steps, will enable the client to determine on her own the concrete actions necessary in the future when the practitioner is unavailable.

Ways to maintain improvement or ensure that the client continues to cope with the problems after termination should also be discussed. Practitioner and client may review strategies or tasks that have been effective in alleviating problems. For example, with a mildly depressed woman, the practitioner might review tasks that helped reduce the depression—staying active in her church, and saying no to unreasonable requests rather than acquiescing and then feeling guilty because of her anger at the imposition. Fishman and Lubetkin (1980) also advocate what they call "fail-safe planning" or anticipating things that might interfere with current functioning, and planning what to do about it, that is, looking at potential obstacles in the future and at ways to overcome or avoid them. For example, the no-longer depressed client might predict situations likely to reactivate the depression—a rift with her boyfriend or quarrel with her boss—and plan ways to cope with those situations. Even if specific suggestions for coping are not made, client and practitioner can review the problem-solving process to demonstrate how it is applicable in the future. Here, as elsewhere throughout the final interview, the client's ability to cope and to control her situation should be emphasized.

Generalizing Problem-solving Ability.   The final step of the termination interview is assisting the client to see how problem-solving steps can be applied to other problems, or attempting to generalize the client's problem-solving ability (Reid, 1978). In actual practice, this effort is usually spread throughout the final interview; for example, discussion of maintaining treatment gains may include review of the problem-solving process. However, at some point in the interview, the practitioner should describe the problem-solving steps in a clear, nontechnical way. In addition, the practitioner should illustrate the process using a brief example from the client's own experience in treatment. In most cases, the client will have experienced enough improvement to use a successful problem-solving effort as an illustration, but it is often useful to include a failed task as an example of assessing impact and revising strategies instead of "giving up." The review of the client's problem-solving experience may be done by the client with the help of probes from the practitioner, rather than didactically.

Often it is appropriate to include a third review of problem solving. If there are acknowledged problems not worked on in treatment, the client may outline how the problem-solving steps could be applied to those problems. Applying the steps to new problems may be particularly helpful in generalizing problem-solving ability since flexibility in use of coping skills is often more important than having *all* skills or knowing use of skills for specific situations (Karoly, 1980).

The purpose of the problem-solving reviews is, of course, to give the client skills to resolve problems other than those which were dealt with directly in treatment. Preliminary evidence from one task-centered study suggests that task-centered treatment alone does not increase ability to use problem-solving skills either on other problems (generalization) or at a later date (maintenance), but combining task-centered treatment with explicit instruction in problem solving does increase general problem-solving ability (Brown, 1980). Research in other areas also indicates that teaching coping and problem-solving skills either as a general treatment approach or in conjunction with focus on presenting problems leads to better maintenance or longer-term coping ability than other forms of treatment (Glogower and Sloop, 1976; Richards and Perri, 1978; Urbain and Kendall, 1980). Furthermore, review of basic principles—whether problem-solving, other treatment methods, or simply taught concepts— increases the individual's ability to retain and apply those principles (Glogower and Sloop, 1976; A. Goldstein, Lopez, and Greenleaf, 1979; Gruber, 1971). Consequently, clear review of the problem-solving steps is an important part of the final interview; with clients who may not have experienced much reduction in target problems, the review of problem-solving steps may be the most important, useful part of the final interview.

Extending a Contract and Recontracting

Extensions involve continuing work on the same target problems for up to 4 sessions; recontracting is making a new contract, usually for different target problems, and follows the same principles as an initial contract, i.e., acknowledged problems, specific times limits (6-12 sessions), etc. Basically, requirements which must be met before extending or recontracting are (1) the client desires to continue, *and* (2) there is a reasonable expectation of a significant improvement in problems with further work, *and* (3) a specific purpose or goal and a specific time span are set.

Although about one-quarter of clients say they would have liked a few more interviews, clients rarely request extensions or have serious reservations about brevity of service (Reid, 1977b, 1978). Usually it is the practitioner who has reservations and wishes to continue treatment, whether because of agency expectations for long-term service (Ewalt, 1976), unrealistic goals of "cure" for clients (H. Levinson, 1977; Maluccio, 1979), their own fears of separation (Rosenberg and Klein, 1980; C. Shapiro, 1980), or because their own needs are gratified by clients (Firestein, 1978; Goodyear, 1981). For all these possible reasons, the practitioner must be doubly careful not to suggest extensions or recontracts inappropriately or without a clear need and client desire.

Ambivalence is a normal reaction to separation, in both client and practitioner (Moss and Moss, 1967; Reid and Epstein, 1972; Rosenberg and Klein, 1980; Schiff, 1962). While it is important to acknowledge and explore the client's ambivalence, the practitioner should focus on the positive reactions as much as on the negative, and expressions of ambivalence should not be misinterpreted as requests for extensions.

Nevertheless, extensions or recontracts are appropriate under a number of circumstances, assuming the criteria are met. For example, extensions should be considered if a near-future event will have a major impact on target problems. A new contract is appropriate if the client wishes to work on new problems or problems which were set aside as "low priority" during problem specification. Successive contracts may also be used when a problem is so complex that only aspects of it, or subgoals, can be worked on within the time limits specified by the task-centered model.

Short-term Service within a Long-term Context

For the typical voluntary or semivoluntary client at an outpatient facility, planned short-term service is as appropriate and effective as long-term service (Butcher and Koss, 1978; D. Johnson and Gelso, 1980). However, service delivery systems are often structured to provide primarily long-term service; prevailing social work opinion leans toward long-term service; and some clients are indeed in need of long-term care. This section will discuss use of task-centered practice in two long-term care contexts: when the practitioner is responsible for a substantively or temporally limited segment of service, and when the practitioner is responsible for mandated long-term service.

Clients in Transition

Frequently, the practitioner is responsible for providing service while the client is in one sector of a service system but will be transferred to another. Examples include psychiatric patients who will return to the community, medically ill hospitalized elderly who will move to nursing homes, and children in short-term residential treatment programs. Implementation of a task-centered treatment contract poses few problems within these settings. Several studies have shown short-term, goal-oriented treatments similar to the task-centered model to be effective with psychiatric patients both during and after hospitalization (Hart, 1978; LaFerriere and Calsyn, 1978; Willer and Miller, 1976). However, when negotiating the task-centered contract, care must be taken to avoid imposing institution-defined problems on the client. It is also important to ensure that target problems and new behaviors are relevant to and reinforceable in the situation to which the client will transfer as well as to the institutional setting (Wildman and Wildman, 1980). The time limits and goals of the contract can be adjusted to anticipated length of stay and "natural" time limits can be used to increase the goal gradient effect.

In some settings, the practitioner is responsible only for assisting the client's transition, as in medical hospital discharge planning. Here a contract can be set up around the transition itself, with effort devoted to locating an appropriate placement and preparing the client to function in that placement. If the family is involved, treatment may include joint or concurrent family contracts, for example, determining appropriate care for a physically debilitated elderly parent through specifying needs, examining options, and arriving at alternatives acceptable to both family and patient (Jackson, 1979). When contracts focus on problems of transition, it is often useful to plan the initial contract length to include one or two sessions after the client has made the transition, to ensure continuity for the client and to aid adjustment to the new setting.

Long-term Treatment in a Single Agency

In many social service agencies, once the client is in the system, the system assumes that it has a long-term obligation. Examples include probation, protective services, welfare services, rehabilitation services, psychiatric aftercare or community care, and some family agencies. There is some evidence that an overprotective stance can lead to deterioration and chronic dependency rather than to these services' espoused goal of support and independence for the client (Blenkner, Bloom, and Nielson, 1971; Langer and Rodin, 1976; Rodin and Langer, 1977). Nevertheless, these systems exist and continually pose practical and ethical dilemmas for practitioners implementing short-term treatment.

Task-centered practice can be used in a number of ways when longer-term service is required. In some mandatory settings, client supervision is indeterminant but dependent on certain, often unspecified, goals being reached. Task-centered contracts can be used to specify goals and time limits within which to accomplish them. If the mandatory problems are too complex or great to be alleviated in a single two- to four-month contract, successive contracts can be used to work on parts of the problem or interim goals, in a "shaping" process. Task-centered practice has been used in this way to assist mothers to retain or have returned children threatened by court removal (Rzepnicki, Chapter 10, this volume; Salmon, 1977) and to aid delinquents to avoid extension of probation (Hofstad, 1977). Major difficulties in implementation of task-centered practice in such situations include "imposing" of mandated problems on clients and negotiation with third parties such as courts to respect goals and goal-accomplishment, particularly when the third-party standards for termination of supervision are unclear. Nevertheless, both Salmon (1977) and

Hofstad (1977) report that the clarity of expectations derived from involving clients in negotiating goals and the clarity of goals themselves were well received by both clients and courts.

A second strategy, suggested by Reid and Epstein (1972), is to use task-centered practice at specific points within long-term, relationship-oriented treatment, for example, at crisis points or points of transition in the client's life. While this approach is feasible, it poses a number of difficulties, not the least of which is mobilizing both client and practitioner to take a more problem- and action-focused stance when their previous work and expectations have been for a "talk" therapy. Fortune and Rathbone-McCuan (1981) suggest transition or "socialization" interviews when converting from open-ended to task-centered treatment. The idea of active, time-limited attempts to resolve problems is introduced clearly, but the structure and focus on the outside-the-session activities of task-centered practice is introduced gradually over several sessions, to reduce the discontinuities and potential resistance clients may experience in a sudden switch of treatment modalities.

A variant is to use task-centered practice as an adjunct to other treatment approaches. Newcome (1979, Chapter 3, this volume) describes task-centered groups as an adjunct to medication and day care for psychiatric patients. Other forms of treatment were used to minimize psychiatric dysfunction, with task-centered practice addressing specific problems in living and coordinating other treatments in a modified case-management approach.

A fourth strategy, when continued service is necessary, is to use short-term task-centered contracts with the case placed on a "monitoring" status between contracts when intervention is not warranted. This approach reconciles the effectiveness and dependency-limiting effects of short-term treatment with ethical or legal requirements to maintain ongoing contact with clients. In Chapter 11 of this volume, Rooney and Wanless describe such a system for organizing Adult Protective Services, interspersing crisis intervention, task-centered practice, monitoring, and termination according to the client's problems and needs at the time.

The Rest of the Book

This chapter has outlined the basic premises and processes of the task-centered model and discussed their rationale. Much of the work from which this review was drawn focused on treatment of individuals. Recently, however, the task-centered model has been extended to work with larger client units. The remainder of this book focuses on those developments with families, groups, and organizations. In the sections on groups and families, the first chapter highlights general background material (group dynamics and family life cycle); the second offers details of the task-centered approach with groups or families; and the remaining chapters examine application and adaptation with specific populations. The final section offers a glimpse of new directions, teaching task-centered practice, and use of task-centered principles to inform service delivery management.

Working with Groups

1 Treatment Groups

Anne E. Fortune

Group treatment for individual problems is increasingly popular. Although groups are not more effective than individual treatment, they can reduce waiting lists and make more efficient use of practitioner time (Copeland, 1980; J. Taylor, 1980). However, conducting group treatment requires knowledge and skills beyond those necessary for individual treatment. This chapter highlights selected issues in short-term group treatment, including when to offer group treatment, whether a group should be ongoing or closed-membership, group-member roles, and the stages of group development. The details of forming and running task-centered groups are taken up by Charles Garvin in the next chapter.

Group Versus Individual Treatment

Group treatment differs from individual treatment because of the presence of others and the potential for interaction among clients. This adds several "therapeutic mechanisms" which are not available in individual treatment: (1) acceptance, or feelings of belongingness, (2) spectator therapy, or learning from others, (3) universalization, or learning that others have problems, (4) reality testing, or using the group to test and correct one's own perceptions, (5) altruism, or helping oneself through helping others, (6) socialization, and (7) imitative behavior (W. Hill, 1975).[1] Despite these additions, however, group treatment does not appear

[1]W. Hill (1975) summarized the therapeutic mechanisms from his own, Yalom's (1975), and Corsini and Rosenberg's (1955) work. Additional therapeutic mechanisms which are shared with individual treatment are (1) ventilation, or catharsis, (2) intellectualization, or insight or imparting information, and (3) instillation of hope. Research on the therapeutic

to be more helpful than individual treatment. The characteristics of those who are successful in group treatment are the same as those who do well in individual treatment: they have better interpersonal skills, have high but realistic expectations, are moderately but not severely disturbed, are psychologically minded, and can define treatment goals for themselves (Baekeland and Lundwall, 1975; Garfield, 1978; VanDyke, 1980; Woods and Melnick, 1979). Comparisons of group and individual treatment with the same populations suggest also that group treatment is not substantially more effective than individual treatment (Bednar and Kaul, 1978; Parloff and Dies, 1977). Additionally, group treatment, like individual treatment, can lead to casualties or severe deterioration in some individuals (Bednar and Kaul, 1978; Dies, 1979; Lieberman, Yalom, and Miles, 1973). Thus research provides few guidelines for when to offer group treatment. An agency which wishes to offer group treatment must consider primarily practical matters: are there enough clients with similar problems and interest in group treatment to ensure a stable group? Is there appropriate physical space available at a time attractive to clients? Will group treatment, which requires more preparation time, indeed be more cost-effective than individual treatment? Can groups also serve a secondary purpose, such as diagnostic screening for other forms of treatment? Are there practitioners with group leadership skill? Or a need for training of practitioners or students through co-leadership of a group?

In deciding whether to offer group treatment to a client, the practitioner must consider whether family members should be involved (see Chapters 6 and 7 this volume), how well the individual will respond to a group, and whether the group may serve an additional purpose for the individual, for example, meeting others as in Macy-Lewis' group of single parents (Chapter 4). Garvin (Chapter 2) also recommends group treatment when peer influence is strong, when problems include interpersonal skills which could be practiced in a group, or when the intimacy of individual treatment is too threatening. Finally, the practitioner must consider how compatible the individual will be with others in the group, as isolation or deviancy in a group is associated with dropping out and with poor outcome (Koran and Costell, 1973; Lieberman, Yalom, and Miles, 1973; Woods and Melnick, 1979; Yalom, 1975). Ultimately, however, the client should make the final choice of group, individual, or family treatment based on her own preferences.

---

mechanisms is equivocal, with some consistent results about what clients perceive as important (Long and Cope, 1980; Sherry and Hurley, 1976; Yalom, 1975) but questions about validity, universality, and relationship to outcome still remain (T. Butler and Fuhriman, 1980; Rohrbaugh and Bartel, 1975).

Open Versus Closed Groups

In "open" groups, members may be added (or terminated) at any time, with other members remaining; "closed" groups do not change membership during the life of the group. In planned short-term treatment, the most common forms are closed-membership groups with all members beginning and ending treatment at the same time, and open groups in which the group continues but an individual participates for a short period of time. Macy-Lewis' closed single-parent group, for example, was planned for six sessions, and all members were aware of the closed membership and time limits before the group began (Chapter 4). Newcome's group of psychiatric outpatients, by contrast, was open, with individuals contracting initially to attend a specified number of meetings, but membership changed as individuals entered, dropped out, or returned to the group (Chapter 3).

Closed short-term treatment groups are more likely than open groups to develop cohesion, stable norms, stable roles, and influence over group members, and to devote more time to therapeutic work (Cartwright and Zander, 1968b; Douglas, 1979; Northen, 1969). Open groups, while hindered by changing membership, may also provide more role models and greater incentive for change (Copeland, 1980; Waxer, 1977; Yalom, 1975). Since both have advantages, whether to offer a closed short-term group or an open, ongoing group depends on several pragmatic factors: (1) Agency policy, staffing, and intake determine feasibility. For example, in a psychiatric hospital with a limited number of beds, open groups are appropriate because there are not enough patients with similar expected stays at any given time to form closed groups. In an outpatient agency where a limited number of clients are identified as potential group members, a closed group is appropriate. (2) The expected length of time to resolve client problems (or that clients will be available) can influence whether groups are open or closed. Where client availability is unpredictable as in hospital observation wards, or if groups are used during "waiting list" periods, open groups are more appropriate. Similarly, if client problems will take differing time periods to resolve, open groups may be more appropriate. (3) It is sometimes difficult to get a stable closed group because of high dropout or erratic attendance during beginning phases (Rooney, 1977). In such instances, groups may be open, or may be open through the initial stages, then closed once stable membership is attained. (4) Closed groups may be easier to conduct than open groups (Imber, Lewis, and Loiselle, 1979). Consequently, the practitioner's comfort and skill in conducting open or closed groups should be considered.

If new members are added to a group, several steps can be taken to assist their assimilation. First, since anticipation improves assimilation, the group should be prepared for new members through discussion of the change and of old members' own feelings when beginning the group (Cartwright and Zander 1968b; Northen, 1969). Second, newcomers are more easily accepted if two or more are introduced at a time or, if that is not possible, an old member is assigned to sponsor or orient the newcomer to group process and norms (Crandall, 1978; Waxer, 1977; Yalom, 1975). Third, since new members' anxious reactions can retard their assimilation, they should be prepared carefully not only for group treatment in general but for entering that particular group. Preparation may include discussion of stresses encountered in entering the group, reassurance that anxiety is normal, and assistance in verbalizing appropriately to make a good first impression (Crandall, 1978; Yalom, 1975).

Group Functions and Member Roles

All groups evolve a structure or organization which is influenced by and influences communication patterns, member status, and member roles. There are two basic functions in any group: achievement of the group goal and maintenance of the group (Cartwright and Zander, 1968a; Northen, 1969, 1982). In treatment groups, the goal (sometimes called task) is individual change; activities directed toward therapeutic change are goal-oriented functions. Maintenance functions (also called socio-emotional functions) keep the group together and make it attractive to members. Often the two functions conflict. For example, confrontation about a member's behavior, sometimes necessary for therapeutic change, can frighten group members into dropping out.

A balance between goal-orientation and maintenance functions must be developed for a group to function successfully, although the ideal balance is unclear. Usually, maintenance is a primary concern in early stages but of lesser concern in middle "production" phases, when members are comfortable with the group, their roles in it, its norms, and its therapeutic goal function.

The goal and maintenance functions of a group may be carried out by any member. In most treatment approaches, learning leadership skills is considered part of the therapeutic process; consequently, the professional leader encourages group members to assume such roles rather than attempting to fill them herself. In task-centered practice, group members are expected to contribute substantially to the group goal by helping each other formulate and carry out tasks, and sessions are often structured around teaching and engaging in these skills.

Members may specialize and establish regular roles as task or socio-emotional leaders.[2] Factors which influence who takes what roles include communication patterns within the group; members' personal characteristics, expertise, and information available; and the importance of the group to the individual (Cartwright and Zander, 1968a). However, it is not clear that it is appropriate for an individual to specialize in a function for any length of time. Some consider clear, interrelated roles as essential to well-functioning groups (Caple, 1978; Sarri and Galinski, 1974), while others stress flexibility of roles (Garland, Jones, and Kolodny, 1973). In one study, group members' goal or maintenance roles were unrelated to individual outcome, but decreases over the life of the group in goal-oriented leadership correlated with poorer outcome (Lieberman, Yalom, and Miles, 1973). Probably, role differentiation which aids group functions but does not place the individual in a stereotyped, limited, or isolated situation is appropriate. For example, if one individual has been acting as socioemotional supporter, others should be able to assume that role while the group focuses on treatment-oriented changes for that individual.

Stages of Group Development

Group development refers to changes in group social organization, activities, functions, decision-making procedures, and norms as a result of interaction over time (Sarri and Galinsky, 1974). Table 1.1 outlines the major characteristics of stages of group development following the life-cycle model of Lacoursiere (1980) but synthesizing contributions of other prominent theorists. The table includes group member behaviors common (but not inevitable) in each stage; the developmental tasks the group must accomplish to continue as a productive group and to move into the next stage; leader interventions which enhance group development and processes in any group (indirect interventions); and additional leader or member activities specific to task-centered groups (direct interventions).

As the table indicates, there are changes in member behavior as the group develops, shifts in roles needed and assumed, shifts in the goal

---

[2]Numerous subfunctions or subroles have been proposed. For example, the goal-oriented function includes doctor's assistant, initiator, information seeker, evaluator, and clarifier, and the maintenance function includes harmonizer, tension-releaser, clown, and encourager. Unfortunately, there is little research on these subfunctions and little agreement on which are crucial. A review of just four authors (Angell and DeSau, 1974; Hare, 1976; Hartford, 1972; Northen, 1969) found 43 different roles mentioned. Even within a single author, so many roles are identified that it is doubtful that so many specialized roles could develop within a single group.

Table 1.1. Stages of Group Development, Characteristics, and Leader Interventions

Developmental Stage and Tasks[a]	Characteristic Member Behaviors	Leader Process Interventions	Additional Task-Centered Interventions
Orientation 1. Attract members to group 2. Establish (a) realistic expectations, (b) consensus on group goals, (c) group norms (B. Hill, Lippitt, & Serkownek, 1979; Sarri & Galinsky, 1974)	Positive expectations but anxiety; testing members and leader; search for common ground; "approach avoidance" (Garland, Jones, & Kolodny, 1973; Lacoursiere, 1980)	1. Increase attraction through refreshments, prestige, activities, importance of membership (Feldman & Wodarski, 1975) 2. Explore common values, experiences, concerns, expectations (Garland, Jones, & Kolodny, 1973) 3. Model warmth, empathy, open expression of feeling, trust (Larsen, 1980; Northen, 1969) 4. Explain and reinforce therapeutic norms (Larsen, 1980) 5. Provide structure appropriate to type of group (Crews & Melnick, 1976) 6. Increase understanding of stage (Lacoursiere, 1980)	1. Identify and specify individual members' target problems 2. Explain and reinforce group norms and expectations including: attendance, confidentiality, helping each other, working on tasks outside sessions; use of formal leader modeling, consulting pairs, or buddy system 3. Formulate initial task(s), often to further specify problem 4. Negotiate contract (if not done in pre-group meeting)
Dissatisfaction 1. Reconcile expectations with reality	Disappointment from unrealistic expectations; conflict over power, control and leadership; challenge	1. Nothing different from preceding unless dissatisfaction impedes group. Then (a) clarify difficulties and	1. Continue problem specification and goal setting 2. Begin teaching task planning and implementation activities *(continued)*

Table 1.1. (continued)

Developmental Stage and Tasks[a]	Characteristic Member Behaviors	Leader Process Interventions	Additional Task-Centered Interventions
	leader; high dropout rate (Garland, Jones, & Kolodny, 1973; B. Hill, Lippitt, & Serkownek, 1979; Lacoursiere, 1980; Tuckman & Jensen, 1977)	power struggles, (b) discuss events as a stage of development (Lacoursiere, 1980)	through leader modeling, consulting pairs, buddy system, or role-playing 3. Plan and implement tasks
Resolution 1. Differentiate member roles and interrelationships 2. Begin sense of cohesion, purpose, and identity with group (Lacoursiere 1980; Sarri & Galinsky, 1974)	Decreased animosity; consensus on norms for interpersonal behavior; clarified role structure, purpose, and identification with group (Caple, 1978; Garland, Jones, & Kolodny, 1973; Lacoursiere, 1980)	1. Teach and reinforce skills for group maintenance and goal functions, e.g., accurate interpersonal interpretations, decision-making procedures, supportive, confrontational motivational roles (Larsen, 1980; Sarri & Galinsky, 1974; Tuckman & Jensen, 1977) 2. Clarify individualization (so not lost in growing cohesion) (Garland, Jones, & Kolodny, 1973) 3. Assess and support or restructure norms and leadership structure (Garvin, Chapter 2; Sarri & Galinsky, 1974)	1. Continue teaching task planning and implementation; focus on obstacles and avoiding them 2. Continue formulating, implementing, evaluating, and reformulating individual tasks, reviewing impact on target problem

(continued)

Table 1.1. (continued)

Developmental Stage and Tasks[a]	Characteristic Member Behaviors	Leader Process Interventions	Additional Task-Centered Interventions
		4. Be flexible; permit group as much responsibility as possible but be directive when necessary (Sarri & Galinsky, 1974)	
Production 1. Maintain group stability and productivity	Cohesion; mutual interdependence and supportiveness; enhanced morale; free and intimate communication; clear but flexible and functional member roles, structure and norms; focus on personal problems, resolution of those problems, and roles outside group, established "routine" for conduct of meetings (Caple, 1978; Feinberg, 1980; Lacoursiere 1980; Yalom, 1975)	1. Assist group to run itself, to act, and to make decisions (Lacoursiere, 1980; Northen, 1969) 2. Help clarify and modify individual and group goals if necessary (Garland, Jones, & Kolodny, 1973; Northen, 1969)	1. Continue task planning and implementation 2. Begin planning for maintenance and generalization through tasks which use new skills repetitively or in new situations
Termination 1. Evaluate individual progress and meaning of group 2. Build bridge to	Ambivalence: pride in progress vs. regression; review or recreate previous group events vs. denial, resistance, and flight; dependence on	1. Stimulate, identify, and discuss ambivalent feelings (C. Johnson, 1974; Northen, 1969; Wayne & Avery, 1979) 2. Encourage reflection on	1. Assess current status of target problems 2. Plan for further progress and for maintaining gains through discussion of specific tasks,

(continued)

40

Table 1.1. (continued)

Developmental Stage and Tasks[a]	Characteristic Member Behaviors	Leader Process Interventions	Additional Task-Centered Interventions
other and future activities, "let go" (Garland, Jones, & Kolodny, 1973; Sarri & Galinsky, 1974)	group and leader vs. individual autonomy and orientation outside group. Irregular attendance, termination rituals, evaluation of group (Lacoursiere, 1980; Lewis, 1978; Garland, Jones, & Kolodny, 1973)	success, pleasure, resolved conflicts (Northen, 1969) 3. Reinforce member self-concept through discussion, repetition of successful activities, or new activities where success is likely (C. Johnson, 1974; Wayne & Avery, 1979) 4. Increase emphasis on individually-oriented activities and on outside-group roles and behaviors (Feldman & Wodarski, 1975; Garland, Jones, & Kolodny, 1973)	general strategies, and problem-solving steps 3. Generalize problem-solving ability through review of problem-solving steps and applications to other or future situations 4. Evaluate group experience

[a]The titles of stages of development are from the group life-cycle model summarized by Roy B. Lacoursiere, *The Life Cycle of Groups: Group Developmental Stage Theory* (New York: Human Sciences Press, 1980).

41

versus socioemotional balance, and increasing assumption of direct interventions by members. The stages are not inevitable: a group may never "get off the ground" if sufficient members are not attracted to the group at the orientation state. One group may dissolve in conflict at the dissatisfaction stage or, if expectations were totally realistic, a group may skip the dissatisfaction stage altogether (Hare, 1976; Lacoursiere, 1980). Similarly, the characteristic behaviors refer to the group as a whole; individual members may not go through the stages of development or show the behaviors characteristic of each phase (Lacoursiere, 1980; Northen, 1969). For example, some individuals may be cheerful during the dissatisfaction stage, while others are hostile throughout without retarding the group's progress (Babad and Amir, 1978).

Several factors may affect how a group develops and the pace it takes through various stages. The orientation phase may be short if the task is clear and skills are available, or long if the task is ambiguous (Lacoursiere, 1980). In task-centered groups, the structure of the task-centered model, pre-group interviews to prepare members for the group experience and homogeneous target problems which increase commonalities among members (see Garvin, Chapter 2) help to reduce the time necessary for orientation. The same factors also help establish appropriate group norms, enhance development of cohesion, and increase likelihood of good individual outcome (Crews and Melnick, 1976; Lacoursiere, 1980; Leak, 1980).

A second factor in development of stages is whether member skills and group structure and norms necessary for the current phase are available or were acquired in preceding phases (Caple, 1978; Lacoursiere, 1980). Careful group composition—including members with a range of skills necessary for goal and socioemotional functioning—facilitates movement through early stages to the "production" stage (Bertcher and Maple, 1977). Several approaches for developing member skill in task-centered problem solving are described in this volume. For example, leader modeling and consulting pairs or groups teach problem specification in early interviews and task planning in middle interviews (Garvin, Chapter 2; Macy-Lewis, Chapter 4). Newcome (Chapter 3) introduces variants for chronically mentally ill with limited functioning: a "Dear Ann Landers" exercise to establish rapport and aid problem-specification; and a role-play "game" whose roles of "player," "helper," and "observer" simultaneously accomplish task planning, teach the task planning and implementation steps, and permit marginal group members to be involved without overly threatening commitment. Obviously, skill-teaching vehicles vary with the level of individual and group functioning and may not be used at all, as in Toseland and Coppola's elderly group (Chapter 5).

A third factor in development of group stages is the experience of members with similar treatment groups. Groups with some experienced members move through initial stages to the cohesive production stage more rapidly than those without (W. Hill and Gruner, 1973). Rooney (1975, 1977) "seeds" adolescent groups with "junior leaders" who have successfully completed a task-centered group and who act as role models and peer influence in development of therapeutic norms. This may also facilitate recruitment and attraction of new members through word-of-mouth about success of a peer.

Finally, the professional leader's skill and to a lesser extent personal style can enhance or retard group development (Angell and DeSau, 1974; Lacoursiere, 1980). Important skills include ability to make the direct and indirect interventions mentioned in Table 1.1; timing of such interventions, including differentiation by stage of group development; ability to analyze and modify one's own behavior to fit varying circumstances; and skill in implementing the treatment approach, in this instance, task-centered practice (Garvin, 1981; Rose, 1977). If two leaders are used (which is not more effective than one leader), the leaders should be selected for complementary characteristics, not similar ones, and should routinely conduct post-session meetings for feedback and planning (Davis and Lohr, 1971; Schlenoff and Busa, 1981; Yalom, 1975).

Task-Centered Work with Groups

Use of the task-centered model for individual problems within a group context began shortly after the task-centered approach was used with individuals. Initially, the application to groups was viewed as straightforward, but with continued clinical trials, techniques became more sophisticated and diverse, especially in using group processes and dynamics to enhance likelihood of individual success. Some of the adaptations of the model to group treatment included:

1. Increasingly careful attention to group composition, to make members' target problems and tasks as similar as possible (Garvin, 1977).
2. Use of group as well as individual tasks, including (a) identical tasks for each individual, relevant either to group norms ("Be on time to meetings") or to a common purpose ("Each locate one resource to use for child care by members"), and (b) tasks which members carried out as a group ("Visit the Senior Center to find

out what it is like") (Conyard, Krishnamurthy, and Dosik, 1980; Crousby, 1979; Rooney, 1975).

3. Use of visual aids including posters about group norms, "work sheets," task-report sheets, and cartoons illustrating steps in problem solving, all intended to clarify procedures and maintain a goal orientation (Garvin 1977; Rooney, 1975, 1977).

4. Additional individual work with group members, to help them make better use of the group or to assist them with particularly difficult tasks (Larsen and Mitchell, 1980; Rooney, 1977).

5. Use of various meeting formats or rituals intended to provide structure, teach appropriate skills, and make meetings more attractive and interesting to members. These include leader modeling, consulting pairs, buddy system, formal consensual decision-making procedures, and role-playing (Garvin, 1974, 1977; Garvin, Reid, and Epstein, 1976; Larsen, 1980; Reid, 1978; Rooney, 1975, 1977).

The adaptations, of course, vary with the needs of particular groups and group members. Consulting pairs, for example, do not appear appropriate for children, although the buddy system to help each other complete tasks is useful with youngsters. These procedures are detailed in the next chapter (Garvin, Chapter 2), which includes these adaptations to the model as well as newer material. Several chapters in this volume also report other adaptations for specific populations, for example, Macy-Lewis' extension of consulting pairs to consulting groups (Chapter 4) and Newcome's "games" (Chapter 3).

Clinical trials of task-centered group treatment include groups of children and adolescents with school and peer problems (Garvin, 1977; Garvin, Reid, and Epstein, 1976; Rooney, 1977), physically ill adolescents (Conyard, Krishnamurthy, and Dosik, 1980), institutionalized delinquents (Larsen and Mitchell, 1980), adult psychiatric outpatients (Garvin, 1977; Newcome, Chapter 3), single parents (Macy-Lewis, Chapter 4); and frail elderly (Crousby, 1979; Evans and Jaureguy, 1981, 1982; Toseland and Coppola, Chapter 5). These clinical trials suggest that task-centered group treatment can be adapted for diverse populations in a range of institutional and community settings.

2 Practice with Task-Centered Groups

Charles Garvin

This chapter presents details regarding procedures to facilitate task-centered groups. These procedures have been described for all task-centered practice in a general way by Fortune in the introductory chapter of this volume. Fortune indicates that task-centered practice is divided into three phases: problem specification, task planning and implementation, and termination. We shall describe the activity of the practitioner and the expectations the practitioner holds for clients during each of these phases. In addition, we shall discuss the actions of the practitioner during a fourth phase that, in task-centered group work, precedes the others—the pre-group phase.

The procedures we describe here utilize a range of research findings on the types of people and problems for which a group approach is appropriate; on the impact on group functioning of setting, space, size, composition, and the way members are prepared; on how group norms emerge; and on how members respond during phases of group development.

In addition to our discussion of the procedures used in each phase of practice, we shall discuss some principles we use to train group workers to engage in task-centered practice and to supervise their subsequent work. The chapter concludes with information on the effectiveness of task-centered group work from evaluation of outcomes.

The Pre-group Phase

Agency Conditions

The likelihood that members in task-centered groups will attain their goals as well as the types of groups that are created are heavily determined by conditions existing in the agency. We have discussed these elsewhere (Garvin, 1981) and draw from that formulation to identify how such conditions affect task-centered group work. One such condition is the *purpose* the agency holds for its services in general, as well as the more specific purpose it establishes for working with groups. Some purposes are conducive to task-centered work while others inhibit it. Those that are conducive are a focus on specific and immediate concerns of clients and on enhancing the skills clients possess to cope with their situations. When agencies view their purposes primarily as enabling basic changes in client personality, providing resources (money, recreation), or as offering long-term supportive or custodial services, task-centered work may be seen as peripheral. It is possible, in these instances, to offer a task-centered program as a special component of agency services, but a full range of agency supports for this service is less likely to be made available.

Practitioners who are employed in settings conducive to task-centered work can secure support for the development of this service by pointing out to agency colleagues that this service is clearly related to agency purposes and is an obvious extension of them. Practitioners in less conducive settings may have to work to change agency purposes as a first step in initiating a task-centered program. This can sometimes be accomplished by raising cost and effectiveness questions with the agency as task-centered work with its short-term focus and its established effectiveness poses a clear challenge to many agencies to alter their purposes.

Another agency condition that can affect task-centered group work is its *physical and social environment*. Physically, an agency that offers group services must make available rooms that are suitable for group meetings. These must be large enough to accommodate a group without too much crowding; the chairs must be comfortable and movable so that members can sit in a circle or form pairs, depending on the physical requirements of the particular session. As we shall describe later, some task-centered groups (such as those with adolescents) may require members (as well as the practitioner) to list their tasks and progress in accomplishing them on large sheets of paper that can be taped to the wall. The group room should allow for this kind of usage. Members will sometimes prepare for tasks by role-playing and this activity also requires space. Members will keep records related to tasks, and files or cabinets where these can be stored and to which members will have access should be provided, preferably in the group's meeting room.

The group and its members individually will also be affected by the social environment, namely interactions with professional staff members, other clients, and other types of agency personnel. If members are also served on a one-to-one basis, or even in other agency groups, their participation in the group will be affected by the support other practitioners give to their work in the group. Members will be affected by how they are greeted in the agency and directed to their meeting room. The practitioner should ensure that the task-centered group session is free of interruptions and that staff at all levels are supportive of the events that occur in the group and the group's use of the agency facilities and resources.

The agency's attitude to service *ideologies and technologies* will also affect the task-centered group. This has two dimensions: how the agency regards task-centered work and how it regards any group service. Task-centered practice, as is amply demonstrated in this volume, is a social work technology that emphasizes specificity regarding goals, practitioner procedure, and level of attainment of outcomes. If the agency is not committed to these ways of viewing practice, it may not supply the forms, resources for keeping records, and staff time that good task-centered practice requires. If the agency also does not recognize the value of group approaches, it may not provide the resources required for a task-centered group. Some agencies retain an outmoded set of views that individual approaches are more powerful or that people will not divulge personal information in groups or that groups emphasize recreational activities.

Another major impact of the agency on task-centered groups is *the process utilized in the agency to refer members.* As we shall describe later, task-centered groups are often composed of clients who have similar problems and who are motivated to work on them in a focused, time-limited way. This requires that the agency have a procedure at intake that identifies applicants for service who meet these criteria. All too often, agencies refer to groups people who are rejected by practitioners who offer one-to-one services because the applicants are unmotivated, inarticulate, or hostile. While such people can sometimes be helped in task-centered groups, they present the same problems there as they do in any other type of service.

A final agency condition that affects task-centered group work is the *status of the practitioner in the agency.* As the preceding discussion shows, the practitioner must be in a position, when necessary, to affect agency purposes, the allocation of agency resources, the agency's attitudes toward service technologies, and the agency's internal referral processes. The practitioner, therefore, must be viewed as a fully empowered member of the service team and not as a person who performs some less valued or tangential service. If the latter is the case, the worker should adopt a strategy of changing his or her status in the agency before seeking to change the agency's service pattern. This can be accomplished as the practitioner demonstrates competency and a serious investment in solving the agency's problems.

Recruitment of Members

The three sources of recruiting group members are other social workers, professionals in other disciplines, and the population of potential members itself. Each of these groups requires some variations of a basic format which includes information on the potential purpose(s) of the group, the nature of task-centered work, and the way task-centered groups are structured.

Purposes. We believe that when members have a commonality of purpose, their ability to help one another formulate and accomplish tasks will be greater than when they do not. Some examples of purposes of task-centered groups in different settings are the following: *school setting* —to improve educational performance, to improve relationships with peers; *medical setting*—to enhance rehabilitation from a handicap, (for a significant other) to learn to appropriately support a handicapped person with whom one has a close relationship; *family setting*—to learn effective approaches to child rearing, (for young adults) to move toward independent living. The practitioner must determine a purpose which is within the purview of the setting and which is likely to interest sufficient clients to form a group. She or he must then communicate that purpose to agency staff, to prospective group members, and to other individuals who can help recruit group members.

Nature of Work. Information to any audience on task-centered work should focus on the following ideas: (1) increasing people's competence for living involves learning how to select and carry out tasks in order to cope with problems, (2) the task-centered group practitioner helps members to *help one another* to do this, and (3) the service is a short-term one in which goal attainment is monitored.

In presenting this basic information to any one group, the issue is usually raised as to whether one should join (or be referred to) a group as compared to one-to-one or family contexts. We believe that the most important decision is whether or not to involve the family. A family approach is essential either when the family must supply the resources for the task-centered work or when the family dynamics present serious obstacles to such work (see Chapter 7). Beyond this principle, we know of no clear-cut evidence that either one-to-one or group work is better for different types of problems or tasks.

Assuming that a suitable pool of group members is available, therefore, we recommend that client preferences be considered in referring the client to an individual or group experience. A "catch" in this principle is that clients might make a choice based on incomplete or inaccurate information. We recommend, therefore, that in the initial interview the practitioner conducts with clients a presentation should be made on the nature of both group and individual task-centered work (even if they are slated for a group). This might take the form of playing excerpts from audio-tapes of sessions with individuals and groups.

Beyond individual preferences, we have found that there are circumstances when a group is preferable. These include the following:

1. At some stages of the life cycle, peer influence is a major source of support and change. Task-centered groups for adolescents are, for example, a "natural" for this age-group (Garvin, 1977).

2. For problems in which a strong component is deficiency in interpersonal skills, the group can be very beneficial. This is because a group offers many opportunities to simulate and practice tasks associated with such skills.

3. Some individuals are more anxious in one-to-one helping situations than in groups because of the intimacy or the high demands for participation promoted in the former. A group allows *either* for intimacy to develop between members *or* for members to temporarily withdraw from such intimacy. Similarly, in individual task-centered practice, the client must continuously interact with the practitioner, while in a group the individual can observe other individuals interacting.

We do not find that there are many situations in which an individual approach is essential. One exception is when issues of confidentiality are so compelling that the individual is unlikely to work on his or her problem in a short-term group. Another is when the individual's need for support and feedback is greater than that which can be supplied in a group, when sharing of time must take place. In the latter instance, however, a "buddy system," to be described later, can be employed to increase such supportive responses.

Structuring Groups.   In recruiting members for groups, the *practitioner* will also indicate the time and frequency of sessions, their number (usually around 12), the desired size of the group, and a brief description of typical meetings.

Recruitment Variations.   When seeking referrals from other professionals, we have employed a task-centered group work referral form. This form requests the following: demographic information (age, sex, family composition); a brief description of the problem; the type of help the person requested, if applicable; a description of previous group experiences; and the way it is anticipated the individual will behave in a task-centered group. Sometimes such professionals are more likely to provide referrals if they are offered the opportunity either to view groups or to receive a report on results, or both.

We have also directly recruited task-centered group members from such populations as high school and college students, people attending parent-education classes, and inmates of prisons. In each case, we publicized in newsletters distributed in the relevant institutions and included some of the problems and tasks that can be worked on in task-centered groups.

Preparation of Members

There are two aspects to preparing people for task-centered groups: the first is to prepare them for the group experience in general; the second is to begin the process of task-centered work so as to expedite the group process. Several well-executed pieces of research have demonstrated that members who are prepared for groups act more responsibly in the group and relate more quickly to group purposes than those who are not prepared (Meadow, 1981; Yalom, 1975).

The points that we cover in our general introduction to task-centered groups are as follows: people can be helped to resolve problems by selecting and carrying out tasks related to the problem; a group will be convened in which the members have similar problems and life situations so that they can help one another to provide important details regarding the problem as well as suggest tasks to one another; some members may already have begun to carry out tasks so that they can give "pointers" to others on ways of doing this; because members have some similarities in their lives, they can understand the difficulties each other faces and give support to one another.

We also state that there are difficulties that people experience in task-centered groups and we hope that, knowing this, the prospective member will be able to surmount them. One difficulty is being open and honest with other members; since all members will work together to remove this barrier, problems in giving information and feedback to others will gradually be reduced. Second, the initial phase of working out the details of problems and selecting tasks may seem to go slowly as members catch on to what task-centered work is all about. After this period, when tasks are being implemented, some of the initial frustration of not knowing what "this is all about" will also vanish. Finally, we discuss the individual's past experiences in groups as these relate to this experience and his or her expectations of the practitioner.

Depending on the nature of the prospective member, we will go over the above points at different paces. In all cases, however, we suit the language to the culture of the individual and we provide relevant examples. We also pause for questions after each point. For some groups, we have written the points on cardboard so that an idea can be kept in front of the client while it is discussed.

When the above material has been covered and if the practitioner and client agree to proceed with the plan for task-centered group work, the next step is to help the client select a problem(s). We recognize that when some clients actually attend a group session, they may change their decision. This can occur because of a shift in their actual situations; because the reality of the other group members convinces the client that some problems are too sensitive for presentation; or even that the readiness of other members to risk convinces the client that a problem he or she thought was too sensitive is "O.K." In any event, the experience of learning how to state a problem in some detail is important. Also, if the client retains the problem, the group process will move more rapidly than if each member has to make a start at deciding on a problem and selecting the details to be presented to others.

The process of helping the client to select a problem can be initiated in several ways. One is to ask the client about the situations in which he or she is uncomfortable. In a school setting, for example, a student said that he was failing in his history class. In a prison, an inmate stated that she did not "get along" with her work supervisor. Another way is to ask the clients about goals they are having trouble achieving. In a school setting, a student said she wanted a friend while a prison inmate said he wanted to have an early parole. Often several problems are elicited and we must help the client to prioritize them in order of either urgency, client readiness, or relationship of problems to each other.

Details of the problem are elicited. These include how long the problem has been in existence, who else is affected by the problem, what the client hopes can be attained with regard to the problem, and what the client has previously done to solve the problem. These questions not only have relevance for what the client will be encouraged to tell other group members, but they help the practitioner to assess how the client will function in a task-centered group and what tasks might ultimately be selected.

When the client tells the details of the problem, the practitioner either indicates that this kind of description is appropriate to share with group members or helps the client to consider other things he or she will say about the problem to them. We rarely find that the client wishes to withhold information from other members, but sometimes he or she requires help in how to offer a clear and succinct statement of a problem.

After the client has chosen the problems to be presented in the task-centered group and has specified them, the practitioner explains the concept of task. While we usually wait for the group session to select tasks, it is helpful for the members to be clear about what a task is. If the member is ready, some illustrative tasks in relationship to the chosen problem might be generated. We usually review the task concept again in the group, but for some people it takes a while to think in terms of tasks, so this concept is explained at every opportunity.

A final stage of the pre-group interview is to tell the member about the plans for the first group meeting. Rooney (1975) suggests that the interview might even be held in the room in which the group will meet. He also shows the prospective member a chart of the agenda of the first meeting as well as a sample of a task chart he uses to record tasks and monitor progress on them. He assigns tasks for the first meeting, such as to come on time and to know group rules. This kind of preparation was established for an adolescent group in a high school, but this degree of specificity is also appropriate for many other types of task-centered groups.

Assessment Issues

A task-centered approach does not require a traditional psychosocial assessment, yet the practitioner must assess aspects of the client and the client's situation that bear on the appropriateness of a task-centered approach and the feasibility of the tasks. During the pre-group interview, the practitioner assesses the motivation of the prospective member for a task-centered group experience, the capacity of the individual to select and work on tasks, and the resources and barriers the individual will experience for this kind of work.

Motivation is assessed in part by determining the likely benefits the individual perceives he or she will achieve if the problem is resolved as compared to the costs of not solving it. In addition, since the problem must be resolved by the individual accomplishing tasks, the practitioner assesses motivation by ascertaining the likelihood that the member will undertake and carry out tasks. This is determined by finding out whether the individual has sought to solve problems through his or her own efforts as opposed to expecting others to take action. As the clients describe their expectations of the group experience, the practitioner can observe for evidence on these matters. Clients with low motivation can be worked with in task-centered groups, but the practitioner must then plan for a rich array of reinforcements—rewards for coming to meetings, for making even small gains in selecting and working on tasks, and for reaching out to help other members.

The capacities to be assessed for task-centered work are the client's ability to select and define problems, to choose tasks, and to carry them out. In addition, in a task-centered group the member must be able to take help from peers as well as offer it to them. These attributes are assessed by observing the kinds of questions the client poses, as well as his other responses, as the practitioner describes the task-centered process. It is again possible for the practitioner to assume responsibility in some of these areas if the client lacks competence, but unless the client has some ability to participate in the process of selecting problems and tasks (even if these are largely suggested by the practitioner), the essential qualities of task-centered work will be absent. Task-centered work should not be reduced to the client responding to a set of behavioral mandates established by the practitioner.

The presence or absence of resources for task accomplishment are also assessed. These include the following: the degree to which relevant individuals and institutions will supply money, equipment, and other resources for task accomplishment; the extent to which they will offer encouragement or discouragement to the member as he or she carries out tasks; the existence of opportunity structure related to tasks such as job and educational career possibilities. Of particular relevance here are the barriers to opportunity often experienced by women and members of oppressed ethnic groups (these issues will be discussed later).

Planning the Group

In concert with the task of preparing individuals for a task-centered group, the practitioner must decide on the composition and size of the group, as well as the number of sessions to be held. These decisions may precede the process of preparation of members or may follow it, but, in any case, these two activities are interwoven. The practitioner's ideas on group composition will affect the preparation of members, and the pre-group interview with individuals will affect final decisions on these group plans.

As a general rule, we compose task-centered groups so that they are homogeneous with regard to the problems experienced by the members. Examples of some of these types of problems are those of elderly people who seek to engage with others, students who experience learning difficulties, parents who wish to use appropriate discipline, and handicapped people who desire to improve their functioning. The reason for this homogeneity is that the dynamics created by the short-term nature of these groups can best be facilitated when members are sufficiently similar in problems and tasks so that one person's progress facilitates that of others.

At times, the size of the potential pool of members is too small to compose a group of people with similar problems. Groups have been successful when members have problems in relationship to a single role such as student, parent, or handicapped person. Nevertheless, problems of these people can be quite different so that members have difficulty in identifying with one another. We have sought to compensate for this by reducing the size of such groups or extending the length of time they meet.

Ideally, the practitioner should consider other member attributes in order to create a group to which members are attracted and, consequently, express attitudes of caring for one another. Attraction is enhanced when members are similar in age, sex, ethnicity, social class, and other descriptive characteristics (Bertcher and Maple, 1977). This should not be regarded as a strict rule, however, and an identification with others with a similar problem can be stimulated by the practitioner in most circumstances regardless of descriptive characteristics.

The practitioner can also use common sense in determining other factors to consider in composition. Thus, in forming an adolescent group, a practitioner considered sexual sophistication and athletic interests. In forming a group in a prison, another practitioner considered length of sentence remaining and degree of antisocial and pro-social attitudes. In the latter case, the practitioner wished to have a mixture of attributes present among group members so that motivation to carry out tasks might be enhanced as a result of conflict around social norms expressed in the group.

We recommend five to seven members for task-centered groups. This number appears to guarantee that the group is small enough for each member to receive the individualized help he or she needs while large enough to allow for sufficient diversity of inputs and for a minimum number of members to be present at every meeting. However, task-centered groups have been successful with larger numbers if the group is composed of members who are not in crises, can postpone immediate gratifications, and are able to use a device such as the consulting pairs technique when immediate feedback is required.

Almost always, we recommend that members contract with the practitioner for 12 sessions. It usually takes about 4 sessions for members to understand the model, settle on a problem, and plan a task or sequence of tasks. Another 4 or 5 sessions are spent carrying out tasks and the final sessions are spent reviewing task accomplishments, planning future actions in the light of these, and terminating the group. As is true of most task-centered work, hedging with regard to the time limits encourages members to postpone actions they should take and weakens the entire structure upon which this approach to practice is based.

Solutions to Pre-group Problems

One of the most frequent problems encountered in any kind of work with formed groups is a lack of sufficient members. In order to overcome this we have used people who are interested in the group to recruit others; we have contacted other agencies with an offer to jointly sponsor a group; and we have begun a group with fewer members than we wished and subsequently added members who were helped to catch up to the group through individualized coaching sessions.

Another problem is related to an anticipated delay before members are likely to be ready to undertake tasks because of either motivational or capacity problems. Task-centered practitioners have successfully experimented with seeding groups with members who have completed a full cycle of task-centered group work but wish to use the group for support for another set of tasks, often related to a different problem. While these members are likely to find the group formation period unnecessary, they can be asked to volunteer as models or as coaches for other members during this period (Rooney, 1975). They can enter into role-plays or can be paired with new members for this purpose.

While going through a second round of task-centered work contradicts our statement above regarding firm time limits, the possibility of successive task-centered experiences has not been rejected by the theorists of this approach. This, in our opinion, is likely to be desirable when members are known to the agency for a long period as students, inmates, or patients and when task-centered work is set apart from the long-term services the organization offers.

Group Formation

First Group Meeting

At the first group meeting what Fortune refers to as the orientation phase begins (Chapter 1). The specific practitioner tasks in reference to this phase at the first meeting are as follows:

1. Help the members get acquainted with each other and discover sufficient commonalities to want to help one another.
2. Provide an explanation of task-centered group work so that members can clarify or reinforce the understanding they received, during the pre-group interview, of this approach.
3. Contract with the members regarding group rules and norms with regard to confidentiality, meeting attendance, and behaviors

they are expected to exhibit toward each other, the practitioner, and the agency.

4. Facilitate the members' telling one another about problems they will bring to the task-centered group and formulating individual goals.

5. Formulate tasks for the next meeting. Depending on how much the members accomplish in the first meeting, these may include ranking problems, identifying an example of a problem, or listing possible tasks.

6. Explain the buddy system at the first meeting (and create it at the second), when this approach is to be utilized.

7. Handle feelings about group beginnings.

Getting Acquainted.   The techniques used by task-centered practitioners to help members get acquainted are the same as those used by other group leaders. Members are invited to provide their names and such information as occupation, marital status, or area of residence. Members are also encouraged to tell other group members additional information about themselves that they think is relevant to getting acquainted. If members wish to, and time allows, they ask each other questions about this introductory information and this interaction can enhance the development of group cohesiveness. Practitioners have also used the device of having members interview each other and on the basis of the interview "introduce" each other to the group when they perceive that members are reluctant to introduce themselves to others. The practitioner also introduces himself or herself and provides information that is intended to model desirable behavior in this getting acquainted process.

Explanation of Task-Centered Work.   Since the practitioner has already provided an explanation of this approach during the pre-group interview, he or she may ask members to tell each other what they had heard and understood about the group. This serves to reinforce their understanding of task-centered work while allowing the practitioner to correct misunderstandings. The practitioner will also relate this information to the activities of the first few meetings.

Initial Contract.   The practitioner will seek to build group norms that help the members to begin to trust one another, such as confidentiality and the responsibility to help each other. As in other groups, members usually agree that they can discuss their own experiences freely with others outside the group but not the statements and experiences of other members. Because of the short-term nature of the group and its focus on concrete tasks, members are not usually asked, as in group psychotherapy, to report to the group relationships they form with each other outside the group. In fact, when this occurs, it usually has the effect of enhancing group cohesiveness and a task orientation. This becomes a problem only if members become critical of some aspect of the group experience and talk about this outside the group rather than during group sessions, where solutions can be found. If this happens, norms regarding how to handle criticisms of the group should be created quickly.

In addition to these types of norms, rules regarding attendance and behavior in the group and the agency are stated. Members are asked to commit themselves to attend all meetings. If unexpected absences are necessary, the member is asked to call the practitioner and, if a buddy system is used, the buddy. This allows the practitioner to arrange for the individual to accomplish whatever tasks are required by the phase of work occurring at the time. This is also necessary in short-term groups as it is possible for the member after an absence or two to think that he or she is far behind and should drop out.

Decisions on Problems and Goals. The members should have identified a problem(s) they would like to work on in the group during the pre-group interview. When they are confronted, however, with the reality of who the other group members are, some members change their mind. They may decide either that they are uncomfortable presenting their problem to the others or that a problem they were uncomfortable presenting is actually "safe." These redecisions are rare, however, and members usually retain the problem focus they had selected earlier. When they become gun-shy in the group, they sometimes can be helped to overcome this by imagining the worst consequences of presenting information and realizing that these are really not so bad.

Typically, therefore, members tell each other about their problems and through this process become more committed to working on them in the group. Through questions members pose to each other, they also become clearer on the dimensions of the problem. During this process, especially when members bring several problems to the group, they discover commonalities among each other with regard to some problems. This leads to prioritizing problems, and members usually give a higher ranking to those that are shared with others. This process of discussing problems should produce enough detail about them to facilitate task specification. Depending on the capacities of group members and the complexity of problems, this procedure may not be completed in the first meeting and it thus becomes a major activity at the second (or even third) session.

Another task is to determine *goals*, which are statements about the changes that are sought in relationship to the problem. Some goals are fairly obvious and do not take long to formulate; these may be chosen at the first session. Thus, for a problem of unemployment, the goal is to find a job; for a problem of low school grades, the goal is to attain higher grades. (Such goals are, of course, stated more specifically in terms of a particular type of job, a particular level of grades.)

Other goals require more thought. Thus, an adult member who saw his problem as being too dependent on his parents discussed his situation with other members for two sessions before he decided that his goal was to visit his parents no more than once a month and to no longer seek his parents' advice on how to spend his money.

Because members have similar problems and roles, they usually ask each other appropriate and helpful questions and make useful suggestions in regard to the selection of problems and goals. The insight they have into each other's situation leads to ideas that are usually realistic. When this is not the case, the practitioner's intervention with regard to one member will have relevance to the others.

The practitioner will help the member to record his or her goal so that this can be referred to by the member and others as the work proceeds. Since the ultimate measure of task-centered work is whether the client's tasks enable him or her to attain goals, it is important to maintain a goal focus and to evaluate whether goals are accomplished. In task-centered work, we have frequently used the Goal Attainment Scales as a means of evaluation (Kiresuk and Sherman, 1968).

Task for Next Meeting. As we stated above, some (or all) members may not have provided enough detail regarding their problem to choose appropriate tasks and they consequently take on the task of preparing this detail for the next meeting. A fully specified problem includes information regarding who the other people involved in the problem are and the behaviors of the group member as well as these others. The member can be helped by describing an example of a situation in which the problem occurred. Practitioners further facilitate this by examples or role-plays. If this specification process has occurred, the members are asked to think of goals for presentation at the next meeting and are given examples of these.

The "Buddy System." Usually in advance of the first meeting, the practitioner will have determined whether to introduce a buddy [or consulting pairs (Rooney, 1975)] system. When this approach is employed, members choose (or are sometimes assigned) another member as a "buddy." At subsequent meetings, part of the session will be devoted to interactions within pairs. Buddies will interview each other and help each other to specify problems, choose goals, select tasks, and solve problems in carrying out tasks. The practitioner will conduct training in how to be a buddy through discussion and role-play and will be available to pairs when consultation is required.

A buddy system should be used when the group is too large or the members' problems are too different to afford members the kind of week-to-week help they require to make satisfactory progress. Even when these conditions are absent, adolescents usually prefer the buddy system because of the way it parallels typical friendship patterns of that age. In any situation where members want a good deal of support, a buddy system can provide this and can be used between meetings while members are actually performing tasks as well.

In some groups, a buddy system is contraindicated. Members may find pairing threatening either because of the degree of intimacy it requires or because of fears of with whom they will be paired. Pair composition can be changed, however, whenever this is desirable. Other members may wish to have the multiple inputs that are possible when all time is spent within the whole group. In still other circumstances, especially with children, the ability or motivation of the members to function in pairs may be lacking and the presence of the practitioner during all interactions is essential.

Feelings about Beginnings. Members usually feel some ambivalence as a new group experience begins. On the one hand, members are likely to look forward to alleviation of their distress through this experience. On the other hand, they are likely to fear failure or, even worse, harm at the hands of the leader or other group members. In all groups, at least an acknowledgment of this ambivalence should be offered, and the topic can be reopened if it proves to be a barrier to accomplishing individual and group purposes. In some groups, a more extended discussion is required, particularly in involuntary groups.

Subsequent Orientation-Phase Meetings

Depending on the size of the group, the capacity of the members, and the complexity of their problems, anywhere from one to three meetings after the first one are devoted to completing the formation process. The second meeting will usually begin with a discussion of member reactions to and questions about the first meeting. Following this, the practitioner helps the group pick up where it left off on prioritizing and then specifying problems. If the buddy system has been chosen, this will be the first time in which it is used, and the practitioner may demonstrate it through a role-play or through a volunteer pair meeting in front of the group.

It is valuable to record the way that each member has specified the problem, so as to help the member formulate goals and tasks. Some practitioners have accomplished this through tape-recording this information. In some groups, the practitioner will summarize the details of the problem as a way of making sure that there is agreement and understanding among members and with the practitioner as to each person's concern.

The formulation of individual goals should follow closely upon problem specification. They should be recorded on a form available to the member. This form also displays tasks and progress on them. Rooney (1977) used for this purpose large sheets of newsprint, which were posted in the group's meeting room. Rooney has also used this device to record tasks assumed by the practitioner such as to secure information, help individual group members, and contact people outside of the group on behalf of members. This, particularly in adolescent groups, helps to decrease social distance between practitioner and members as well as to model the use of the recording format.

Task Selection. The task-centered practitioner in groups utilizes the same concept of tasks as all other such practitioners. As Fortune indicates in the introductory chapter, there are many types of tasks differentiated by whether they are unique or repetitive, mental or physical, unitary or complex. The problem this array presents in groups is that members can become confused when their tasks are of different orders. While the practitioner who works with the task concept over and over again comes to find it a simple one, members do not have the same experience.

For this reason, the practitioner should first seek to help members state tasks at a general level and then more specifically. Thus, in a group in a prison, all the men described their general tasks as selecting and engaging in activities in order to earn a parole. The practitioner subsequently employed a buddy system to help the members choose the activity in which they would enroll (specific tasks). Several of the men chose classes offered in the prison, one chose to enroll in group therapy, and another chose to ask for a new work assignment through which he could demonstrate his ability to handle more responsibility.

In some groups, practitioners have created subgroupings of two to four members to help each other make their tasks more specific after general tasks have been chosen (for example, see Macy-Lewis, Chapter 4, this volume). If general tasks are very similar, it may not make much difference what system is used to generate such subgroups. On the other hand, when there are substantial differences in general tasks, these groupings should bring together members with similarities. An example of this was a group of six members formed in an adult day treatment program. Two different types of general tasks emerged in this group: one was to change housing arrangements; the other was to improve relationships with people in the housing situation. Two subgroups were formed with three members in each. At times the practitioner's presence was required simultaneously in both groups, and to alleviate this problem, a social work student was recruited to assist the practitioner.

Problems during the Orientation Phase. One problem encountered during this phase occurs in involuntary groups. Task-centered group work has been employed in settings where the service is either mandated by law (probation, for example) or strongly pressed upon the members (some school settings, for example). This issue has been discussed in the task-centered casework literature and Epstein (1980), for example, suggests that the client might contract with the practitioner and the group to work on two sets of problems—those mandated and those chosen by the client. In many instances, these two would merge.

However one views the situation of involuntary clients, there are dilemmas related to the highly voluntary nature of task-centered work and the concept of involuntary service. We prefer, therefore, to ultimately respect the right of the client to choose the problem to be worked on, including the choice not to work on any. We recognize that some agencies may legitimately press services on clients but believe that other service approaches should be employed for this rather than a deteriorated use of task-centered work. (See my concept of social control groups, Garvin, 1981.)

A compromise is that involuntary clients can be asked to "try out" the process with their first task to determine whether they wish to make use of the task-centered group work service. Using this plan, we have seen involuntary clients reverse their opposition to working in such a group. The fact that task-centered groups are highly focused and time limited has recommended them for such mandatory service settings. We further believe that many so-called involuntary clients are often "created" because we offer them services that are inappropriate in terms of goals or methods.

We have already implied the solutions to other orientation-phase problems, particularly those dealing with diversity of member problems and goals. At times, however, one or more members feel isolated because of dissimilarity to other members. To offset this, practitioners may alter composition after the group has begun by adding members to a group or transferring a member to another group.

A final problem is related to a lack of motivation in some members to make the series of choices task-centered work requires or to carry out tasks. With children and developmentally disabled adults, to name a few, we have used behavioral principles to select and use reinforcements at all stages of the process when these are necessary (Rose, 1972). Children, for example, have been given tokens with which to "purchase" items when they engage in such behaviors as helping other group members and carrying out their own tasks.

The Contract

As in task-centered practice in general, during the first session we negotiate either a written or an oral contract with group members. As in the individual approach, the contract states the target problems, specific goals, member tasks, practitioner tasks, duration of service, dates of group sessions, and a general statement of the process (task selection, implementation, and so forth). In addition, however, we add the stipulation that members will offer help to, and accept help from, other members when this is necessary to generate and carry out tasks.

Task Planning and Implementation

The group may properly be thought of as ready for task accomplishment when its members have made a commitment to work on specific problems by taking help from the group to accomplish tasks, when members recognize responsibility to help others in the group, and when problems have been adequately specified and general tasks have been selected as a result. Task accomplishment activities are to specify a task or sequence of tasks and to complete these tasks. In this section of the chapter, we shall describe how the members and practitioner work together so that these activities are satisfactorily undertaken.

As Fortune states (Chapter 1), after a group completes its orientation phase, it proceeds through a dissatisfaction phase, a resolution phase, and a production phase. Our experience has been that these phases, when they occur, do so during the period when members are accomplishing their tasks. Although small-group research and theory predict that these phases are likely to occur in groups, we know of no research that has examined the presence or absence of these phases in task-centered groups, and this type of inquiry should be given high priority.

In our experience, however, some task-centered groups have shown clear evidence of these phases. A dissatisfaction phase often occurs as members begin to either specify their tasks or carry them out. The dissatisfaction is expressed in a number of ways: members state that the process is too difficult, that the barriers to task accomplishment are too great, or that the practitioner or other members are not helpful. Members may indicate that they are considering dropping the group, choosing another form of help, or that they wish for a different group composition or practitioner. As group theory predicts, this phenomenon occurs in many groups, and practitioners should not assume that the task-centered group will consequently fail. Rather, practitioners should be empathic and supportive during this phase, should reevaluate the kind of indigenous leadership that has emerged in the group and, when necessary, help members who have been too underactive or overactive to modify their behavior. Practitioners can also tell group members that this kind of feeling occurs in groups and is a result of the fact the "honeymoon" period is over and members are getting down to business.

A result of successfully weathering the dissatisfaction phase is that group participation becomes more evenly distributed; the practitioner will have developed a more diversified series of inputs; new ways of conducting meetings to increase member satisfaction are also often created. This represents the emergence of the resolution phase and prepares the way for "production" in which members invest their energies in their tasks.

The above formulation regarding task accomplishment and associated group phases has been fairly general. Therefore, we now turn to a more detailed examination of the group processes and practitioner behavior that occur related to task accomplishment.

Specific Tasks

Work on some types of problems requires the members to accomplish several specific tasks. An example of this is a high school group to improve the members' academic performance. One member of the group formulated the following specific tasks for himself: to do homework three times a week; to ask the teachers to give him feedback at least once a week, and to arrange for a tutor for his science class.

During this phase of the group, members help each other to select specific tasks when these are required in order to reach individual goals. Members with similar general tasks may have different specific tasks. In the school group in the previous example, another member who had the same general task chose the specific tasks of attending a remedial reading class; picking a buddy to study with for examinations; and also doing homework three times weekly. The advantage of group membership for choosing specific tasks is that the tasks chosen by one member can help another member to conceive of tasks, and the very act of choosing tasks in the presence of each other can encourage members to invest their energies in this activity.

Supports and Barriers

After members have chosen their general tasks and specific tasks, the practitioner directs their attention to accomplishing them. At this point, the practitioner states that members are likely to encounter support from others as they work on their tasks; they are also likely to come upon some barriers. Rooney (1975:20), in his work with adolescents, introduced this subject with a cartoon "of a man standing on a road, scratching his head, as a great boulder stands in his way." Below the cartoon he lists the following questions:

1. What got in your way? What blocked you?
2. What did you try to do to get around it? What part worked? What didn't work? Why didn't it work?

3. What ways do you have of getting around the roadblock? Can someone else help you?
4. What would be a good step to take in getting around the roadblock?

We begin consideration of support and barriers with a discussion of support members might find in performing general or specific tasks. We do this because it places an emphasis on the positive, while at the same time identifying resources that can be drawn upon to overcome barriers. Depending upon circumstances, we emphasize internal resources as well as external ones. The former might include how the individual has completed difficult tasks in the past, has used help, or has been able to generate solutions to problems. The latter might include support that can be obtained from family, friends, teachers, employers, other professionals or agencies. We also discuss the kinds of resources the members can expect to gain from the group such as the use of buddies; encouragement from all members; suggestions as to how to overcome barriers; concrete help such as tutoring; and the active participation of the practitioner.

We have been careful not to generate too long a list of potential barriers so as not to discourage members. Nevertheless, it is important to remind members that these can occur so that they do not become discouraged when they do, in fact, encounter a "roadblock." One way that Rooney (1975) does this is to use one of his own tasks related to facilitating the group. He identifies a barrier that confronts him and asks members to help him find a way to overcome it. When this is not desirable or possible, we have used either the buddy system or the group as a whole to identify a barrier that at least some members expect to encounter as they begin to accomplish their tasks. Ways to cope with this common barrier are then generated in the group.

Some of the barriers members mention frequently are that they are distracted by others from performing their tasks, that others fail to provide them with the rewards or other resources they require, that others punish them for tasks, and that they lack the skill to perform the task. Since throughout this middle phase of the group much of the work of the group is devoted to overcoming barriers and facilitating task accomplishment, we now provide details on the resources for this available through the group.

Practitioners use four systems to help members overcome barriers to completing their tasks. These are with members on a one-to-one basis, subgroups, the group as a whole, and people outside of the group. In discussing interventions, we note that a shift has taken place in task-centered practice theory regarding the practitioner's interventions. As Reid states (1978:177-178):

In our first version of the model (Reid and Epstein 1972), the practitioner's contribution was viewed largely in terms of such techniques as exploration, structuring, encouragement, direction, and explanation. While this structure has been retained and revised . . . it has become secondary to the present system of activities.

Activities are given greater emphasis than techniques for two reasons. First, the activities spell out the basic and distinctive strategies of the task-centered approach in its present form. . . . Second, activities express the collaborative spirit of the model—what the practitioner and client do together to achieve common ends. This emphasis helps us move away from a view of helping in which the practitioner acts through techniques, procedures, and so on, and the client reacts by accepting or rejecting the practitioner's offerings.

This distinction has relevance to task-centered group work as most of what Reid calls activities are enacted in the group and involve several or all members along with the practitioner. What he calls techniques are often used by task-centered practitioners not only in their interactions with a member but also to *model* for all members ways that one individual can facilitate the work of another and thus how members should *help one another*. We shall now discuss levels of interaction and how this distinction between techniques and activities informs practice.

One-to-One Interactions. As we have suggested above, remarks that the practitioner directs to a member of the group may have the same form as a remark delivered when only a practitioner and a client are present, but the effects can be different. This is because other members can echo the practitioner's sentiment, can express the same ideas to each other, can elaborate on the practitioner's ideas, or can even disagree with them. The practitioner's decision to use a technique will also be affected by his or her awareness of the effect it will have on other members. We shall illustrate this with four practitioner techniques (Reid, 1978) and the issues raised by their use in group situations.

1. *Exploration* (such as questions used to elicit information). The practitioner should demonstrate to members that there are a variety of ways to secure information from each other and that continual use of direct questions is aversive. These ways include paraphrasing the final thought in a statement or making an empathic response. In group situations, practitioners should be aware that members may be fearful of giving too much information to others because of fears of rejection or ridicule and that this may have to be dealt with in the group at the time that exploration takes place.

2. *Encouragement* (such as praise or approval). These kinds of statements are all too infrequently available to social work clients and constitute one of the most important things a practitioner can model for members. Sometimes it is very difficult for members to accept encourage-

ment and they will discount it by denying they have done anything worthwhile or by turning a compliment into a criticism. ("You only recognized that I went for the interview but not how I handled it!") Some practitioners have introduced an exercise under these circumstances in which members in rotation offer each other compliments. Feedback is then provided by the group on how well compliments were offered *as well as received* (Lange and Jakubowski, 1976).

3. *Direction* (such as advice). In group situations, whenever a practitioner gives direction to one member, others are likely to vicariously experience the advice as directed to them also. Further, they are likely to jump in and also offer advice. The group practitioner, therefore, has to consider these effects and either promote them or discourage them as the situation warrants. In particular, the practitioner may have to support a norm of individual choice of action if the group members become too directive about action that may not be in an individual's interest.

4. *Explanation* (such as efforts to promote the members' awareness of aspects of themselves or their situations). This technique can have some of the same effects as "direction" in that members will "take" explanations offered to others and apply these to themselves or they will add on their own explanations. It is important for the practitioner to state that explanations that apply to one member may not apply to others. Thus, when members offer explanations, there is a chance that they may be assessing their own situations (projection) rather than that of the member in question.

Subgroup Interactions. As we have indicated, the practitioner will frequently divide the group into pairs (or even threes or fours) so that members can help each other with the task-centered process. Under this arrangement, the practitioner will use techniques to promote the functioning of such subgroups. These include the following:

1. *Communication training.* This involves helping members to listen to each other and give each other feedback. One specific technique is to require members to paraphrase the comments of the speaker and to give feedback on the accuracy. Another is to point out some common barriers to good communication such as attributing intent which has not been stated, placing value judgments on the acts of others, and assuming that a concept used by another means the same as when the listener uses it (Rose, 1977).

2. *Mediation.* At times, members will argue with each other in an angry fashion. The argument may have many sources including a disagreement as to who should help whom. The practitioner is frequently called on to mediate in such situations. Sometimes, communication train-

ing solves the problem; at other times, the work helps members to express anger or disagreements constructively. This involves being specific about what has made one angry and being open to negotiation. For the person who is the target of the anger, this involves being willing to take appropriate responsibility for one's acts while being assertive in rejecting inappropriate attributions.

3. *Problem-solving training.* Much of the interaction in subgroups involves problem solving such as deciding which problem to solve first, what goal to select, what task to establish, and how to overcome barriers to task accomplishment. In engaging in this process, members may make many common errors in problem solving such as acting with insufficient information, too quickly closing off a listing of alternatives, or choosing one alternative without adequate evaluation of others. Since this is so common, in almost all groups we offer training in problem solving. This can be accomplished by explaining the model of problem solving (that we describe later), by demonstrating the model through a role-play, or by giving members feedback on the adequacy of their problem-solving efforts.

Group Interactions. The feature that distinguishes task-centered group work from other task-centered work is how it uses group forces. The ways that practitioners draw upon these are embedded in how the practitioner plans the agenda for the sessions and intervenes in group structures and group processes. We shall discuss each of these in turn.

AGENDAS FOR MIDDLE SESSIONS. As in other forms of social group work, the agenda for the sessions should be generated jointly by the practitioner and the members. Nevertheless, in task-centered groups a similarity of meeting content usually occurs during the middle phase. The group opens with routine matters such as attendance, announcements, change in meeting arrangements, and so forth. Either in the whole group or in subgroups, members report progress on task accomplishment and, with the help of others, identify barriers and look for ways of removing them. Some members will have completed tasks and will consult with other group members on a subsequent task. Other members may find that the task they chose cannot be completed and they will seek alternative tasks. In some, hopefully rare, instances members will ask to change the problem they are working on.

At times, the members can be helped to overcome barriers through participation in a group experience such as a role-play. The practitioner and the members may inject this type of learning at any point in the agenda that it appears appropriate. When these experiences are complex and time consuming, they may be planned for the next meeting when most of the time may be devoted to them.

The meeting usually ends with a brief evaluation of the session. Following this, members join with the practitioner in planning the agenda of the next session. If there has been a problem of a group nature such as lack of attendance, poor member motivation or progress, or obstructive member behavior, the practitioner will ask the members to reserve enough time to discuss the issue.

MODIFYING GROUP STRUCTURE.   The group's structure consists of the pattern of relationships among the members. By the middle phase of the group, such a pattern has usually emerged and is seen in whom members talk to, choose for partners, and seek to influence. Task-centered practitioners in groups must assess whether these aspects of structure enhance or impede the task-centered process.

In reference to communications, the practitioner will observe whether members volunteer to tell of progress on tasks, whether they are listened to by others, and whether the responses members make to each other are well distributed in the group. When members fail to communicate or when others do not respond to them, the practitioner will take remedial actions. These include the following:

1.   Inform the members of the communication problem and ask them to substantiate the practitioner's assessment and to seek a solution to the problem if they agree that there is one.
2.   Provide some reinforcement (praise, tokens, and so forth) for appropriate communications.
3.   Suggest that members pick a buddy (or simply assign this role to the adjacent member), who will either reinforce communication (perhaps with a pat on the back) or restrain it (through a touch on the wrist).
4.   See if there is some other group condition inhibiting communication such as lack of trust or the presence of resentment.

In reference to the pattern of attraction and rejection among members (so-called sociometric structure), the practitioner will be aware that the emergence of differential association is a natural one. It becomes a problem only if subgroups protect members from the constructive input of others, reinforce members to obstruct the group, clash severely with each other, or exclude individuals who then become isolated. The kinds of actions the practitioner can take in this situation are:

1.   Construct different subgroups than the ones that exist by assigning members to pairs or subgroups that are different from the existing pattern.

2. On a temporary basis, the practitioner "pairs" with an isolate (and this sometimes raises the isolate's status).
3. The practitioner can alter interactions between subgroups by assigning tasks that require cooperation or that change the status of one subgroup. For example, a practitioner asked a subgroup to help one of its members solve a problem in accomplishing his task. Another subgroup, antagonistic to the first, was asked to observe this interaction and to make constructive suggestions regarding the ways the subgroup helped the member. This intervention initiated a series of positive interactions among the members of the two subgroups.

In reference to the power relationships among members, the practitioner should make note of occasions when members either fail to secure the help of other members or offer appropriate help which is rejected. This is often indicative that the member possesses inadequate power to influence group members in ways that are constructive to both self and others. The obverse situation is when a member makes inappropriate suggestions to another that the latter is likely to enact. In this situation, a member possesses too much power.

Even within the time constraints of a short-term group, the practitioner can act to equalize the power distribution. The following are some techniques for accomplishing this:

1. A norm of support for every member's contributions can be suggested to the group.
2. The influence of a member can be increased by coaching that member to make constructive comments, by praising such comments, and by assigning to the member tasks that are viewed by the group as prestigious (for example, representing the group at an agency function). In addition, recognition of a member's creativity or persistence in overcoming obstacles is likely to increase that member's prestige in the group.

MODIFYING GROUP PROCESS.   Group process consists of the sequence of interactions among group members. This is embedded in the activities that occur in the group. Two types of activities that we shall discuss here because of their importance are problem-solving and structured programs.

Virtually every writer on interpersonal helping includes *problem solving* as a major activity and there is almost complete agreement on the stages of the problem-solving process (Compton and Galaway, 1979;

H. Goldstein, 1973; Northen, 1982; Perlman, 1957). We follow these stages in facilitating problem-solving in task-centered groups and also train the members in using them through charts, presentation of examples, and coaching them in their problem-solving work. The stages are:

1.   Identify and specify the problem. This involves stating the specific problem under consideration at the time and providing details of the problem such as who is involved, how each person views the problem, what each person does, and what the member does. This suggests the conditions that must be considered for an adequate solution.

2.   Generate several alternative actions the member can take in relationship to the problem. This often involves "brainstorming" in which the member and others involved in the discussion suspend any evaluation of the alternatives until a reasonable number are listed.

3.   Evaluate the alternatives. The types of questions that help in an evaluation are whether the alternative can be enacted by the member with his or her existing competencies or whether new competencies will have to be acquired; how the alternative will affect significant others in terms of costs and benefits; and the likelihood that the alternative will actually solve the problem. Such factors as time and energy must also be considered.

4.   Choose an alternative. Based on the information produced in stage (3), the member is helped to choose the "best alternative." This can sometimes be facilitated by actually listing the negative and positive features of each alternative and assigning these weights.

5.   Develop a plan for carrying out the alternative. This should be done in detail and involves what the client must do, what others must be asked to do, and when each act of the member or others must occur.

6.   Carry out the alternative and evaluate the results. The member should be informed that additional "problems" may emerge as he or she carries out the plan developed in (5) and, therefore, the other group members should be kept informed of the details of the enactment. The member should also be helped to state a criterion as to whether the problem-solving action does, in fact, accomplish what was intended.

Structured programs include any planned activity in the group that is introduced by the practitioner or others to help members to define or accomplish tasks. Such activities are likely to include the following:

1.   The client *simulates* proposed task behavior through role-play, practitioner modeling, and client rehearsal. Simply asking the client to

indicate what he might say or do under particular circumstances is Planning Details of Implementation. Simulation involves a more extensive "dry run" of the client's performance.

Simulation is a "natural" for group work because the presence of a number of members allows for a reconstruction of almost any social situation. This can be done in a variety of ways such as having the member play himself or herself to practice a task or having the member observe others in order to benefit from modeling.

2. *Guided Practice.* Reid distinguishes this from simulation in that the member actually engages in a task rather than rehearsing it (Reid, 1978). Thus, if a task is to make direct requests for help rather than acting helpless, this can be enacted in the group; if students are to complete school assignments, this can be an appropriate group activity.

Environmental Modification. In our model of task-centered group work, environmental modification is an important part of the service and occurs under two categories: when the group leader undertakes this activity, it falls under the heading of practitioner tasks; when the client undertakes it, it falls under client tasks. As we have stated elsewhere (Garvin, Reid, and Epstein, 1976:260):

1. The worker may collaborate with other persons and organizations to create opportunities for tasks to be performed.
2. The worker may ask relevant others to supply reinforcement to the client for task performance.
3. The worker may have to utilize whatever legitmate authority is possessed to change situations which prevent clients from fulfilling tasks.

The member's tasks to change his or her environment may include any of the following types (Garvin, 1981):

1. Request a change in the social or physical situation. A member requests a change in assignment to a classroom.
2. Interpret behavior of self or other as the basis for seeking a change in the latter. A member explains to a teacher that when he becomes drowsy in class it is because he has failed to take his medication on time and he wishes the teacher to remind him of this.
3. Educate others. A member of a group of ex-offenders develops a plan to explain to prospective employers the benefits of hiring an ex-offender.

4. Use of influentials. A member resolved to ask her employer to intervene with her supervisor whom she accused of sexual harassment.

5. Confrontation. A member resolved to assertively state to her supervisor that she was opposed to sexual harassment and if he did not stop, she would make a formal complaint.

It is also possible for the entire group to act together to change an environmental situation that is detrimental to some or all of the members' task accomplishment. In a task-centered school group, the members wished the school's library to be open longer hours so that they could more easily fulfill their homework tasks. They petitioned the principal to change this and their recommendation was accepted.

Assessment

During Task Planning and Implementation, the practitioner will employ a number of assessment tools. We have used the same instruments for assessment of group member activities and outcomes that have been employed in individual task-centered work. Reid (1978), for example, presents a recording format for individuals that includes problem statement of client and others; target problems and their specification; problem, client, and situation characteristics; problem assessment and planning; contract and task scheduling (including achievement ratings); and final problem review.

We have employed, in addition, a recording form for group meetings that includes the meeting agenda, the kinds of interactions among members, the names of members and the activities in which they engaged during the session, and the nature of group-level activities. We have also introduced *ad hoc* instruments in which members have evaluated the degree to which the practitioner has been helpful; the degree to which members are helping each other; and how purposeful and involved the member believes he or she has been during the session.

Gender and Ethnicity

We do not have any systematic evidence on the ways members of different ethnic groups might experience task-centered group work, but we have some impressions based on our experience. Many poor people and members of oppressed groups like both the short-term and peer helping features of the model. The former conforms to a desire for fairly immediate results around goals that one has picked for oneself rather than had imposed. The rationale behind task-centered groups can easily be understood, thus giving members a sense that they have control over what happens in the group. The latter overcomes the negative features of cultural differences between helper and helped. When all members of the group come from the same ethnic background, the group has the added possibility of enhancing one's ethnic identification.

There are also features of the model that may positively or negatively affect its use in specific cultures. The model does not emphasize extensive examination of emotions or a demand for self-disclosure beyond that required to choose and work on tasks. In cultures where one has not been socialized to display these behaviors with relative strangers, the model has much to commend it. On the other hand, the model does have an individual goal/problem focus. In some cultures where the welfare of the community is emphasized or where one is expected to relate one's problems only within one's family or "tribe," the model, if used at all, will have to be employed with those systems.

Our awareness in the human services of the different needs and experiences of men and women and the implications for our work of the oppression experienced by women because of their sex is growing. This has several implications for task-centered group work. First, in groups with women as members, we must be careful not to sexually stereotype either problems or tasks. In some groups we have observed women being maneuvered into defining their desire to move into new roles as the problem rather than the barriers they experience. Second, task-centered groups, like all others, when composed of both sexes can fall prey to the domination of women and to an increase in competition among men. The practitioner must be sensitive to these and other gender-related issues so that task-centered groups can serve to liberate members to choose and pursue courses of action that genuinely conform to their wants.

Termination

Fortune (1981; introductory chapter) has indicated the activities that constitute the termination phase of task-centered work and these, with some additions, are also used in groups. As she indicates, in task-centered work the issue of termination is considered from the beginning because the work is time limited, and members are reminded at each session how many meetings remain. This ordinarily mobilizes the members to work at a pace that ensures that the work is done in the time allowed.

In the final session, however, specific activities include task review, final problem review, evaluation of treatment, client encouragement and other maintenance strategies, and future planning. In addition to these, for group purposes we include dealing with feelings about termination and "bidding farewell." In some groups we also close with a ceremonial event such as a party.

The process of task review and problem review will employ the same instruments and format that have been used at earlier sessions. The difference at the last session is that members will have to consider the implications of having tasks that are not complete when the group ends or problems upon which more work should be done.

The evaluation of treatment should incorporate feedback to the practitioner on how members have evaluated task-centered work, the techniques employed by the practitioner, the way group members interacted, and the effort expended by each individual. In some groups this information can best be secured by members' completion of a questionnaire. The data on the questionnaire can be summarized to the members for their comments and clarifications.

Maintenance strategies are developed in several ways. Members can be given encouragement by the practitioner and others in the group; feedback can also be secured and used for this purpose from others such as parents and teachers. The task-centered process can also be reviewed so that members can try to use it on their own. In some cases the group is small enough or there is time enough for members to perform repetitive tasks one more time as a way of reinforcing performance. If a buddy system has been utilized, members sometimes agree to call one another to check up on how things are going.

Future planning might involve applying for other types of services such as those offered by educational, recreational, or mental health agencies. Members might also indicate problems they plan to work on using what they have learned about task-centered methods.

Groups come to represent powerful emotional forces in the lives of people, especially if their impact has been beneficial. Members of task-centered groups, consequently, may have feelings of loss and sorrow on terminating even if there is also pleasure that goals have been accomplished and that the time spent in the group is now available for other things. Unless members have a chance to express these feelings, they may block out some of the valuable learning that has taken place in the group. Members, for this reason, often ask for a chance to mix with each other to reflect on the group experience and to say good-bye. Even a modest presentation of refreshments at this point facilitates this exchange.

Training and Supervision

We have found that training for task-centered group work can be most effective when it combines three elements. The first element is a didactic one in which the trainees read and discuss articles such as those included in this book in order to gain a thorough understanding of the principles of the approach. This can best be accomplished if examples through tapes or other recorded material accompany this presentation.

At the same time, or following this introduction, we strongly recommend that trainees have a task-centered group experience. The problem and tasks they choose can be of the sort that can appropriately be used in an educational environment and thus are not too "sensitive." Problems, for example, in one's role as a student or employee are quite appropriate.

Following this phase the trainee should begin supervised work with a task-centered group. We recommend that a careful recording of each group session be maintained, one which indicates the actions of the practitioner-trainee and thus helps ensure conformity with the model. Innovations of, or departures from, the model are often appropriate in practice and these should be documented and justified. Some trainers have developed recording guides in which there is space for the supervisor to note whether activities are properly in phase, whether techniques have been appropriately applied, and whether deviations are adequately justified. Tolson's material in Chapter 13 is an example developed for task-centered work with individuals which could easily be adapted for group work.

The practitioner-trainee should also discuss with the supervisor the group conditions that emerge, namely the structures and processes we described earlier. When trainees are not well versed in group-level analyses, we have recommended that they seek out experiential group learning opportunities that are geared to helping participants understand group processes and their relationship to them.

Research

In the close to ten years between the time we published the first paper on task-centered group work (Garvin, 1974) and now, several pieces of research have evaluated the effectiveness of this technology. Garvin, Reid, and Epstein (1976) reported on outcomes in groups conducted by graduate social work students in an adult outpatient setting and in three inner-city schools. Of the nine school groups, members in three achieved their tasks at a rating of substantial or better, members in another three achieved their tasks at a level of partial task attainment, and in the remaining third, members accomplished minimal task attainment. The members in the high achieving groups were more likely to have specific behavioral target problems, tasks that consisted of verifiable public acts, and structured programs. A tenth group was conducted in an outpatient setting and consisted of women who had reactive depression. They viewed their problems dissimilarly and the tasks they chose were poorly specified.

While several members achieved substantial progress on tasks, others did not.

Newcome (Chapter 3) reported on the outcome of task-centered work in an adult day treatment program in which a major outcome measure was the Goal Attainment Scale (Kiresuk and Sherman, 1968). The experimental group showed an improvement in their score of 27.06 while the control group had an improvement of only 20.3. During the six month follow-up period, clients in the experimental group were rehospitalized 7 times, those in the control group 15 times.

Toseland and Coppola (Chapter 5) reported on task-centered group work with older people. They do not present quantitative findings but their qualitative report indicates that they met with success when they adapted the model to conform to the needs of this age-group. Evans and Jaureguy (1982) used a task-centered group approach with the visually impaired elderly through a telephone conference call medium. On several scales used to measure outcomes, the experimental group did better than the control group (on one at the $p < .10$ level of significance; on the other, in the right direction but without statistical significance). Behavioral measures of outside social activities and household chores also changed in a positive direction in the experimental group.

Conyard, Krishnamurthy, and Dosik used some aspects of a task-centered group approach in work with adolescents suffering from sickle-cell anemia. While they do not present data, they state that "The task oriented group method used in this study was more successful than individual casework or a discussion group" (Conyard, Krishnamurthy, and Dosik, 1980:25).

Larsen and Mitchell (1980) worked with delinquents committed for observation to a state correctional facility. Experimental boys received an adaptation of task-centered group work which included group decision making by consensus and individual work with members to help them to make better use of the group. At the end of treatment, on four of eight categories of the Tennessee Self-Concept Scale (Basic Identity, Physical Self, Moral-Ethical Self, and Personal Self), the experimental group had a higher self-concept than the control group, who did not receive task-centered group work. The experimental boys also had higher performance rating by institutional staff in areas such as response to supervision and personal hygiene.

All of the above studies display weaknesses that reflect the current stage of development of this approach and the research designs associated with it. The exact ways in which task-centered group work was implemented were not well specified; measures of outcome vary from study to study; and problems exist in the nature of the experimental and control conditions. Nevertheless, a beginning has been made in demonstrating the usefulness of the approach and groundwork for more rigorous testing has been accomplished.

Summary

In this paper, we have identified the procedures to be employed at all phases of the task-centered group work process. We described activities in the pre-group phase related to establishing appropriate agency conditions, recruiting members, and preparing members for the group experience. We elaborated on the events that occur during the group formation phase as members become familiar with the model, form relationships with each other, and choose problems and tasks.

The task accomplishment phase was described as consisting of help offered the members in choosing subtasks and accomplishing them. During this phase the practitioner helps the members to focus on overcoming barriers to task accomplishment while working with them to create a facilitative group environment. The practitioner also establishes means to evaluate both the process and outcomes of the group experience.

The next section of the chapter described termination activities as including an evaluation of task accomplishments and problem reduction, as well as activities to maintain gains, separate from the group, and to generate future plans. The utilization of the task-centered group approach must respect ethnic- and gender-related issues brought by members, and some of these were described. The chapter concluded with comments on training and supervising task-centered group practitioners and a summary of research findings related to this approach.

Task-Centered Group Work with the Chronically Mentally Ill in Day Treatment

3

Kent Newcome

The possibility of short-term, goal-oriented treatment approaches with the chronically mentally ill has sometimes been overlooked because of the severity of interpersonal problems, debilitating nature of mental illness, and necessity for long-term care and rehabilitation. However, short-term, task-centered practice can be effectively adapted for the chronically mentally ill and integrated into a holistic long-term treatment approach. This chapter describes the use of task-centered group treatment in a community-based day treatment program for the chronically mentally ill and handicapped.

A major goal of the community mental health movement is maintenance and rehabilitation of the chronically mentally ill in the community. A traditional approach to community-based treatment is the day hospital (Herz et al., 1971). Partial hospitalization programs often originated as extensions of state mental institutions (Steiman and Hunt, 1961) and consequently functioned as combination crisis-intervention networks and babysitting services. In the 1960s and 1970s, the population of day hospitals had spent years in psychiatric hospitals and were thoroughly institutionalized; thus, this type of programming was often adequate.

Recently, however, the approach to day treatment has been changing. Institutions discharging mentally ill and handicapped are implementing new programs and procedures to prepare clients for community placement (Boettcher and Schie, 1975; M. Stone and Nelson, 1979). An increasing number of outpatients are not bewildered newcomers to the community with long and close ties to an institution, but are natives of the community with few or no previous hospitalizations. Often these clients are quite young with fewer episodes of illness and closer ties to families, jobs, friends, and schools (Newcome, 1978). Clients who were discharged

10 to 15 years ago, when deinstitutionalization began, are now already a part of the community. Consequently, the chronically mentally ill and handicapped of the 1980s have needs, goals, opinions, attitudes, and behaviors different from those of the 1960s and 1970s.

The Day Treatment Program of the Madison County Mental Health Center, Inc., Alton, Illinois, is an example of such changes in institutional clientele and policies. The Program originated in 1965 as an extension of the Alton Mental Health Center (formerly Alton State Hospital). Its initial population was clients newly discharged from the state hospital, residents of the hospital, and those in a "revolving door" pattern of discharge and readmission. Programming was the milieu treatment frequently described as "hospitals without beds" (LaCommare, 1975; Peck, 1962).

As the community's mental health system effectively reduced return rates and unwarranted admissions, referrals from the State facility to the Day Treatment Program dropped drastically (Newcome, 1978). Community hospitals, shelter-care homes, physicians, vocational rehabilitation programs, and agencies replaced the hospital as the major referral sources. The population became more varied with myriad social, emotional and vocational problems as well as a broader range of psychiatric disorders. Economically, the population remained low to low-middle income; however, community clients were more likely to have recent employment histories, to complain of unemployment and disability as a source of discomfort, and to actively seek employment. They were more likely to be involved in concurrent programs for vocational rehabilitation, training, or school. Community clients, therefore, were less likely to accept public assistance and psychiatric disability as a permanent condition and often presented high expectations of themselves and of the results of treatment. Community clients also maintained ties to family members, friends, and social groups more than deinstitutionalized clients, who had often lost touch with these social units. In sum, the Day Treatment Program's population shifted from a clientele with a singular set of needs and one overriding goal to a multi-problemed clientele.

In 1978, the Day Treatment Program expanded the "hospital without beds" concept in response to the changing characteristics of its clientele. Innovations included training in attending or listening skills to improve social skill (Bradshaw, 1982); individualized treatment planning in place of uniform programming; and problem-solving groups. This chapter focuses on task-centered problem-solving groups for chronically mentally ill.

Psychiatric patients may differ from normal individuals in problem-solving ability and require a specialized problem-solving approach (Platt and Siegel, 1976; Platt, Siegel and Spivack, 1975; Platt and Spivack, 1972, 1974; Siegel and Spivack, 1973; Spivack, Platt, and Shure, 1976). The use of undefined group problem solving has not been effective for aftercare schizophrenics (Parloff and Dies, 1977). Sociobehavioral, cognitive, and social role theory has been applied to group problem solving with the chronically mentally ill with greater apparent success (Churchill and Glasser, 1974; Rose, 1977). These task-oriented, role transition, and skill training groups illustrate attempts to improve problem-solving ability (Boettcher and Schie, 1975; Fairweather et al., 1969; Goldsmith and McFall, 1975; A. Goldstein, Sprafkin, and Gershaw, 1976; Hersen and Bellack, 1976; Olson and Greenberry, 1972).

Such approaches demonstrate effectiveness in changing topographical features and self-reports of anxiety (C. Wallace et al., 1980). However, the author's experience with these approaches indicates that the client's presenting problem(s) often remain unaddressed or unresolved, resulting in little substantial difference in how the client perceives his quality of life. Since problem-solving behavior, like other interpersonal skills, often does not transfer to the natural environment or generalize from one situation to another, an approach was needed that promotes the occurrence of actual problem-solving behavior within a context both therapeutic and meaningful to the client (Goldfried and D'Zurilla, 1969; A. Goldstein, Heller, and Sechrest, 1966; Rose, 1977; Shepherd, 1977, 1978).

The goal of the Day Treatment Program was to develop a structured group problem-solving process for chronically mentally ill and handicapped and to incorporate the approach into a traditionally milieu-oriented day hospital program. The task-centered system was selected as the structured problem-solving model (Epstein, 1980; Reid, 1978; Reid and Epstein, 1972, 1977). Task-centered practice has been used previously with psychiatric outpatients (Brown, 1977; Hari, 1977) and specific group guidelines are provided by Garvin, Reid, and Epstein (1976), Garvin (1974), Rooney (1975), and Larsen and Mitchell (1980). This chapter reports the adaptations, guidelines for implementation with psychiatric and handicapped outpatients, and evaluation of the Day Treatment Program's problem-solving groups.

Adaptations of the Task-Centered Model

Chronic mental illness and disability have common behavioral characteristics regardless of specific diagnosis. Chronically mentally ill individuals suffer more than necessary. Not only do they struggle with illness and disability which totally disrupt and impoverish their lives and the lives of significant others, but they appear to passively watch their lives slip by. Many face progressively worsening physical and mental conditions, the reality of several psychiatric illnesses. This, coupled with social and financial breakdown, results in a flood of problems in living that over-whelms them during their periods of remission.

The time dimension of chronicity lends itself to repeated condition-ing. Chronic mental illness can be viewed as a learned set of behaviors. During periods of relapse, abnormal behaviors replace normal ones tem-porarily. As relapses are repeated, it becomes more difficult to revert to "normal" behavior patterns during remission. Thus, chronicity means that the individual's life-style increasingly reflects the course of the illness: the individual displays more ill behaviors and fewer healthy behaviors. Since chronically ill individuals experience extended periods of inactivity and debilitation, these periods create sequences of behavior-environmental consequences which support passivity as a conditioned response. Even when the overt symptoms of the illness are contained, these passive responses persist.

In addition, the chronically mentally ill and handicapped are extraor-dinarily vulnerable to stress (Ellis, 1978). Minor problems in living can create extreme dysphoric states of anxiety and depression with a possibility of reactive psychotic symptoms. The benefits of activity, socio-education, skill development, recreational, and socialization groups are lost to clients overwhelmed by the stress stemming from a particular problem.

The psychosocial ramifications of chronic mental illness—continuous chemotherapy, disability and unemployment, dependence on others, ex-tended and at times unnecessary inpatient hospitalizations, the potential for regression and relapse—all reinforce and maintain a distinct orienta-tion to time and a belief in passivity that leads to reactive, instead of proactive, behaviors.

In applying a task-centered group approach to the chronically men-tally ill, a major adaptation involves recognizing the client's concept of briefness rather than adhering rigidly to the two- to three-month guide-lines of the task-centered model. With the chronically mentally ill, the sense of briefness may vary from a few minutes to four weeks, even though realistically the problem in living may take considerably longer to alleviate. It is the practitioner's responsibility to orient his sense of time to that of his particular client and to focus on the client's immediate goals even though he recognizes that full goal accomplishment may take longer than the client realizes. The client's definition of briefness can be adopted even when at odds with the practitioner's since what is important is that the *client* perceive the time as brief.

A second major adaptation of the task-centered group model was its use for case management. As the group progressed, the group leader spent increasing time in case management techniques of assessment, case planning, advocacy, linkage, and monitoring. Supplemental individual interviews and group activities and tasks were also used to coordinate client involvement in other treatment modalities available at the Day Treatment Program. Thus, the group served both to treat members' problems in living and to coordinate clients' entire treatment programs.

Format of Group Sessions

Group composition may be homogeneous or heterogeneous on sex, age, diagnosis, and presenting problems. The more important criteria for selection of group members appears to be some degree of remission from the active phase of psychiatric illness and the client's expressed desire to attend. Experience suggests that the task-centered group be an open, ongoing 90-minute weekly component of partial hospitalization programming or psychosocial rehabilitation services. The client initially contracts with the group leader to attend a specific number of sessions. The client is, however, assured that he may drop out of the group at any time without prejudice and rejoin the group at a later time if desired. A group member may also recontract for additional sessions when his original contract expires. Recontracting is conducted by the group itself, rather than between practitioner and client only. The emphasis in composing and recomposing the group is firm yet flexible boundaries for membership, insistence on expressed desire to attend, and an explicit agreement concerning group rules, traditions and rituals.

Group structure attempts to maximize client focus. Facilitating focus on the problem-solving sequence is the group leader's constant and unremitting task. This requires firm yet gentle leadership skills. With the chronically mentally ill, as with other clients, the leader uses systematic communication to encourage focus on the problem-solving sequence (Reid and Epstein, 1972). Adherence to a standard format each session can also improve the group's ability to focus. The lack of ambiguity in a highly structured, flexibly bounded, time-limited supportive group is often described by these clients as comforting and reassuring. The general format used in the Day Treatment Program's group sessions is outlined in Table 3.1.

The content of each session varies depending upon the ability of current members to focus, proportions of new and old members, and success in rapport-building efforts. Rapport building can be accomplished using either general group discussion or a structured warm-up exercise intended to enhance task-centered problem specification. An example of this is the "Dear Ann Landers" exercise. Group members read real letters to an advice columnist, generate responses to the problems, and then compare their responses to the columnist's advice.

Table 3.1. Task-Centered Group Format

Phase I	Rapport Building A. Structured group exercise. B. Open discussion.
Phase II	Problem Specification A. Search for members who need group time. B. Defuse potential disruptions. C. Probe for emotional responses and action tendencies. D. Probe for events and situations. E. Quantify feelings and action tendencies. F. Explore reinforcers, consequences, and costs. G. Summarize the problem in concise, concrete terms.
Phase III	Goal Setting A. Discuss client "readiness" for goal setting. B. Determine area of preferred change. C. Estimate nature and amount of change desired. D. Estimate amount and duration of effort to achieve change. E. Summarize in written contract.
Phase IV	Role Assignment A. Encourage volunteers. B. Assign each group member role as "player," "helper," or "observer."
Phase V	Task Planning and Implementation A. Structure implementation to begin immediately upon task formulation. B. Encourage "players" to utilize "helpers." C. Intervene in only those areas that facilitate task accomplishment.
Phase VI	Task Review and Session Termination A. Summarize remaining tasks. B. Review "leftovers" (tasks not completed). C. Suggest "helper tasks." D. Consult "observers." E. Link tasks to other concurrent treatment if appropriate.
Phase VIII	Practitioner Tasks Outside Group A. Case management. B. Concurrent individual sessions as needed. C. Work with significant others as needed.

Once rapport is established, specification of individual target problems can be facilitated by using problem checklists or by constructing Goal Attainment Scales (Kiresuk and Sherman, 1968). Examples of target problems identified by group members include medication misuse; difficulties with parents, landladies, or others; unemployment; anxiety; hygiene; and impulse control.

A problem specification sequence can be ritualized by asking three questions of each group member. First, the leader asks each client whether he or she needs time to discuss any pressing issue or crisis. This is referred to as "looking out for powder kegs." After locating and defusing potential disruption and recognizing individual needs for group time, the leader then asks each member for a word or phrase that describes how he or she has been feeling or acting during the past week. A chart with feeling words facilitates this step. The leader then asks each group member for "reports" on what events or situations are occurring in his or her life. This exploration of "what's happening" attempts to connect the events to emotional responses and action tendencies. Action tendencies are the individual's general behavior patterns, often attack or withdrawal, which usually interfere with realistic assessment of and appropriate responses to the situation.

Further details of events, situations, emotional responses, and action tendencies are then gathered to provide data for goal setting. The leader helps members measure duration, intensity, and magnitude of emotions and action tendencies. The leader also facilitates client exploration of environmental or attitudinal conditions that reinforce the emotional responses and action tendencies. The consequences and costs of continuing to respond as described or to passively accept a problem are grapically outlined. This discussion intends to lead group members to examine their habitual problem-solving behavior and distorted perceptions. For example, John, diagnosed schizophrenic in remission, reported feeling sleepy all week. He connected this to the breakdown of his automobile. Further probing revealed that his father had not helped out with the breakdown, John had not been assertive in requesting assistance, and John's anger at his father had led to withdrawal, depression, and sleepiness.

Prior to beginning goal setting, the leader helps each group member summarize in a clear, concise statement the salient aspects of his situation, emotions, action tendencies, and attitudes. In John's case, the summary statements to help John identify his dysfunctional patterns were:

> *What happened:* I asked dad to help with my car and he refused.
> *What I think about it:* He should help me, but since he won't then I'm no good.
> *How I feel:* Angry at dad and myself; sad and depressed.
> *What I do:* Withdraw and sleep.

Critical leader activities during this stage include accurately reflecting feeling and content, remaining focused on salient aspects, and reframing and relabeling distorted perceptions.

While rapport building and problem specification engage the entire group, goal setting is optional for those who wish to improve their current situations. The leader discusses briefly with each group member his readiness to focus on goal setting. When maintaining focus is difficult, the practitioner avoids confronting the group. If no one is ready for goal setting, the leader can use the time by: (1) encouraging responsive communication among group members; (2) suggesting role-play or other group activity; (3) selecting consulting pairs; (4) teaching skills; (5) presenting didactic material; (6) using probing questions; and (7) respecting the clients' right to decline rehabilitation by ending the group session.

For members ready for goal setting, the following four steps are outlined to members and then carried out: First, the member decides what aspect of the problem—the situation, emotions, action tendency, or attitude—is the preferable focus of intervention. Second, the area selected is again quantitatively described with an estimate of how much change is desired. Third, the member is asked to estimate the duration and amount of effort needed to result in the desired change. Fourth, a written contract summarizing the above is completed.

At each step of the goal-setting process, the practitioner encourages group input and comment. The practitioner legitimizes the client's definition of the problem (although he may not agree), recognizes client distress, and encourages the client to set limits on the time and energy to be utilized in problem-solving efforts.

In the example above, John decided that he wanted to be more active and less withdrawn. Although the practitioner preferred to help John assert himself with his father, John was reluctant and chose to "forget it" and to work on increasing his pleasurable activity. Describing that in more detail, John discovered that early evenings were his most troublesome time. He decided to increase his participation at the local YMCA's evening sports program. John estimated that he could accomplish this goal in a week. Since the Y activity replaced his usual joyriding in his car, John felt he was also solving his original problem with his father's refusal to help him with his broken-down car.

The next phase is assignment of roles for the problem-solving activities which take up the remainder of the group time. Members are encouraged to volunteer, but usually the leader must assign roles. The "player" role is reserved for those members who have set goals during the previous stage. The "helper" role is assigned to those who were not ready for goal setting or who have target problems well on the way to solution through work in previous sessions. The "observer" role is for those not yet ready or willing to participate actively. The technique of role assignment emphasizes role transition and role performance as well as facilitates group interaction. The assignments of roles clarify members' functions and duties and give permission to those remaining passive to continue to do so while simultaneously modeling for them a more active orientation toward problems.

Most of the remaining session time is devoted to task planning and immediate task implementation with "helpers" and "observers" supporting and encouraging the "players'" task accomplishment. The practitioner helps plan the tasks that can be implemented while the group is still in session. Depending on the target of change, the group members' activity may vary from assisting the leader in teaching and coaching the "players" in cognitive coping skills through modeling and role-playing to develop more productive action tendencies to locating resources, gathering information, and accompanying the "player" to outside agencies. In John's case, a "helper" accompanied him to the Y to sign up for the evening Physical Fitness program. The "helper" also signed up and agreed to accompany John to the sessions, thus simultaneously assisting John and himself becoming more active.

Removing obstacles to task completion can be accomplished through the same interventions as in other forms of task-centered practice (Epstein, 1980; Reid, 1978). When subjective distress is an obstacle, the leader's task is to help the client reduce the distress only to the point that task accomplishment proceeds. A lasting change in emotional makeup is unnecessary for task accomplishment or problem resolution.

Toward the close of the session, the leader reviews and summarizes the remaining tasks for each "player," checks on task accomplishments from previous sessions (known as "leftovers"), and encourages those with remaining tasks to complete them as soon as possible. The more proficient at task accomplishment a group member becomes, the more the leader encourages task implementation outside the session. To facilitate the transition from in-session implementation to out-of-session implementation, the leader suggests "helper tasks" to reinforce prompt task accomplishment outside group. These shared tasks are left for discussion among "players" and "helpers" as the group session ends. "Observers" may also be involved in helping "players" carry out remaining tasks. Thus, even those who are not ready to work on their own goal setting may increase their action tendencies and learn to cooperate with others outside the immediate group environment.

For those in other forms of treatment at the Day Treatment Program, attempts are made to link treatment modalities and use of treatment through tasks. For example, John returned from signing up at the Y anxious about being able to "keep up" with the other Y participants. The group referred him to the Day Treatment Program's recreational aides for practice sessions to increase his skills and confidence in sports and exercise. Thus, both task-centered group treatment and recreational therapy were used to resolve an obstacle. Such tasks also help the chronically mentally ill to learn to use other groups and resources for their own benefit. The individual's problem-solving activity outside the group is also coordinated through case management functions.

Therapeutic Guidelines

Task-centered group work with chronically mentally ill and handicapped attempts to maximize elements thought to facilitate gradual improvement in social functioning. Therapeutic guidelines for this approach include:

1. An ecological orientation to time that accepts the client's definition of briefness in establishing time limits (Germain, 1976).
2. Recognition of the client's definition of a problem in living as valid though not necessarily correct.
3. Flexibility in establishing group boundaries that respect the client's right to decline rehabilitation without prejudice.
4. Emphasis on social functioning and community adjustment rather than on the individual's psychopathology *per se.*
5. A structured problem-solving format that maximizes client participation, understanding, and desire; focuses on concrete mutually set goals; and utilizes group process through the assignment of roles to enhance individual goal accomplishment (Garvin, Reid, and Epstein, 1976).
6. Beginning task implementation within the group session.
7. Acceptance of the probability of regression and relapse, but
8. Valuing the client's effort to receive support by making maintenance of current functioning a legitimate goal for problem solving (Nelsen, 1980).
9. Focusing leader intervention on only those client behaviors that obstruct task accomplishment or are necessary for task completion.
10. Incorporating other concurrent treatments into the tasks.

These features embody a humanistic, holistic orientation which recognizes the heterogeneity and unique needs of the chronically mentally ill (Lamb, 1979a,b). The approach also serves simultaneously as a form of group treatment and a means of case management (Newcome, 1979). Integrating long-term case management functions with shorter-term, limited-goal problem-solving treatment also contributes to a holistic approach to the rehabilitation and maintenance of the chronically mentally ill and handicapped in the community.

Evaluation

To determine the efficacy of task-centered groups with chronically mentally ill, a research study was conducted with clients attending the Day
Treatment Program between January and July 1980. The purpose was to
assess the effects of a task-centered group on problem-solving effectiveness and community adjustment. Twenty-nine clients volunteered for the
experimental group. This group received the task-centered group work
approach combining brief, structured group problem solving with case
management functions as described above. Clients were involved concurrently in day hospital program activity and treatment. The control
group consisted of 29 clients randomly selected from all other clients and
received the same concurrent program activity and treatment except for
exposure to the task-centered model. The experimental group included
more males (23 compared to 13 in the control group) and more individuals
under 26 years (13 to 6), but diagnoses were similar, with the majority
suffering schizophrenic disorders.

Goal Attainment Scales (Kiresuk and Sherman, 1968) were developed
for each client as an aid in developing treatment plans and as a mechanism
to measure problem-solving effectiveness. Goal Attainment Scales scores
and other data were gathered monthly in short interviews with each
client.

Table 3.2 presents the Goal Attainment Scale scores from beginning
and end of treatment. Overall average change indicates a slight advantage
for the experimental group (+8.9 to +4.5). More experimental clients
(52%) improved than did control clients (28%), and the average change for
improved clients only was greater among experimental clients (+27
compared to +20). On the other hand, three experimental clients deteriorated and their average deterioration was −25 compared to −13 for

Table 3.2. Comparison of Goal Attainment Scale Scores [a]

	Experimental Group (n = 29)	Control Group (n = 29)
Average score: January 1980	−25.65	−29.30
Average score: June 1980	−16.80	−24.82
Average overall change	+ 8.85	+ 4.48
Change in GAS scores		
Improved	15 (52%)	8 (28%)
Unchanged	11 (38%)	19 (65%)
Declined	3 (10%)	2 (7%)

[a] Range of scores: +80 to −80

the two control clients who deteriorated. Two of the three experimental decliners attempted suicide during the test period. Both suffered from multiple physical and psychiatric handicaps and abused alcohol episodically.

Indicators of community adjustment also suggest differences between the groups. In vocational training and employment, two clients in the experimental group began two training programs; one dropped out of one, and one voluntarily withdrew from another, while three control clients enrolled in school or training programs. Six experimental clients obtained some type of employment; one control client obtained employment while another lost a job. In community living, four experimental clients but only one control client moved into more independent living while two from each group moved to more restrictive environments. Finally, the clients in the experimental group were hospitalized half as many times as control clients (7 times—6 for psychiatric, 1 for medical reasons—compared to 13 psychiatric and 2 medication-adjustment hospitalizations for the control group.) Thus, the experimental group was slightly more active and successful in obtaining employment and moving to more independent community living and considerably more successful in avoiding hospitalization.

The types of problems the experimental clients selected to work on in the task-centered group are indicated in Table 3.3. Clients identified an average of 3.5 problem areas. The most frequent problems were (1) vocational problems such as enrollment in school or training, linkage with vocational rehabilitation services, job hunting, and problems on the job; (2) treatment issues such as attendance and participation in the program, acceptance of handicap, and medication; (3) psychopathological problems such as delusions, bizarre thoughts, intense anxiety, or depression; (4) interpersonal relationships; and (5) lack of interests and involvements.

Although the numbers in each category are small, it appears that improved Goal Attainment Scale scores were most likely when the problem was a specific relationship problem, personal appearance or hygiene, impulse control, and lack of interests and involvements. In contrast to the success with specific relationships, general communication problems showed very little improvement. Other areas showing little or no change over the six months included medication problems and those in the "other" category: responsibility taking, attention concentration, substance abuse, and physical complaints.

These results suggest that brief, structured group problem solving using the task-centered model combined with case management functions may be helpful in the coordination and treatment of the chronically mentally ill and handicapped in the community. The approach was applied to a wide range of problem types and clientele. The superior performance of clients participating in the group may be due to motivation

Table 3.3. Problem Areas Identified by Experimental Group

Problem Area on Goal Attainment Scale	Number of Clients Identifying Problem Area	GAS Score Improved	GAS Score Unchanged or Declined
Treatment issues			
Attendance/participation	9	4	5
Medication	5	1	4
Psychological problems[a]	14	5	9
Lack of interest/involvements	12	7	5
Interpersonal relationships			
Specific relationship problem	4	4	0
General communication problem	10	2	8
Vocational/employment	17	9	8
Housing	8	4	4
Personal appearance/hygiene	3	3	0
Impulse control/anger	7	5	1
Guilt (dwelling on past mistakes)	1	1	0
Self-confidence	2	2	0
Other[b]	8	0	8

[a]Includes delusions, anxiety, depression, etc.
[b]Other includes two problems each in the categories physical complaints, responsibility taking, substance abuse, and attention concentration.

or other personal characteristics coinciding with the selection of volunteers, but it is clear that task-centered group work, with adaptations, is feasible and even encouraging with this difficult population.

These results, however, do not suggest that task-centered group work will successfully rehabilitate chronically ill clients and help them to avoid rehospitalizations altogether. For a few clients, readmission to hospitals for inpatient treatment was an aspect of their problem solving. Many problem areas remained the same. Other clients, although able to improve in some problem areas, still had negative scores in others. However, given the comparatively lower rehospitalization rate among experimental clients, it may be that the model functions to help clients maintain current functioning. At times, a task-centered sequence was employed to deliberately maintain and stabilize a deteriorating situation.

The results also suggest that some problem areas are more amenable to change than others. The least change occurred with suicidal, substance abusing, and multiply-handicapped mentally ill. Although the sample is too small for a definitive statement of contraindication, the model, as applied in this setting, appears inappropriate for these situations. The greatest change occurred in the areas of employment, increasing involvements, controlling impulses, and lessening readmissions to hospitals.

4 Single-Parent Groups

Jane A. Macy-Lewis

A Task-Centered Single-Parent Group: An Overview

Providing a group experience for single parents within the framework of a public social service agency is a challenging and creative process. The challenge is to provide a short-term group which successfully combines educational and supportive components and in which members experience both a gain in knowledge, skills, or abilities and a positive peer-group experience. The creative aspect is present throughout as the group practitioner juggles the balance between educating, teaching, and facilitating support, discussion, and interaction among group members. One approach that seems to successfully address these issues is that of a task-centered group.

The Setting

The single-parent group described here was conducted under the auspices of Dane County Social Services (DCSS), a public welfare agency serving a population of approximately 305,000 people centered primarily around the metropolitan Madison, Wisconsin area.[1] DCSS's Educational Services unit is responsible for providing educational group services for the agency's

[1]The co-leaders were the author and Ms. Sue Sutton. The author would like to gratefully acknowledge the valuable contributions of her co-leader, as well as the wise and patient guidance of Dr. Ronald Rooney in the design and implementation of this group.

clients and low-income persons in the county. A wide variety of groups have been sponsored, including GED Preparation, Teen Assertiveness, and Social Skills for Developmentally Disabled Adults.

While the recent cutbacks in human service funding have made it difficult to sponsor single-parent groups on a regular basis, in the past they were a popular choice, with a group being offered approximately once every three months. While the format varies, groups normally run from four to eight weeks, meeting once a week for one to two hours in a community building such as a church, school, or community center. Participation in groups is voluntary with the rare exception of someone court-ordered to participate in a particular type of group. Members of DCSS's single-parent groups seem to be evenly divided between those who are referred by an agency practitioner and those who are self-referred after reading about the groups in the agency newsletter or in a local newspaper.

The Members

Members for the task-centered group were recruited on the basis of a common status (Garvin, 1974, Chapter 2, this volume; Reid, 1978), that of single parent, with no distinctions among types of single parents (never married, divorced, separated, or widowed). The literature on single parents suggests that the status of single parent may yield similarity in problems, with financial problems, parenting and childrearing concerns, social life and personal relationships, child care, and personal problems as recurring issues regardless of the reason for being a single parent (Bequaert, 1976; Brandwein, Brown, and Fox, 1974; Granvold and Welch, 1977; Mendes, 1979; Raschke, 1977; Schlesinger, 1978; Wattenberg and Reinhardt, 1979; R. S. Weiss, 1979a,b). Group members were recruited through notices in the agency newsletter and local newspapers, as well as a memo to agency practitioners requesting referrals. The group, called Single Parent Problem-Solving, was set up to run for six weeks, two hours per week, during April–May, 1980. Free child care at the group site, a local church, was provided. The co-leaders were two MSSW students placed at DCSS, one of whom had previous group facilitation experience.

The Agenda

Prior to the beginning of the group, a tentative agenda for the sessions was organized following guidelines for task-centered groups (Garvin, 1974; Reid, 1978; Rooney, 1975, 1977). Included were the use of a pre-group interview, consulting pairs, lecturettes, presentations, and group discussions. Large charts and posters were developed to outline the presentations and provide direction for the members' work on tasks, and an evaluation questionnaire was developed to provide feedback and input to the leaders during the course of the group.

The Group Process

Pre-group Interviews

Eleven people initially indicated interest in the group. Telephone contacts with each included a brief overview of the group and an invitation to an individual pre-group interview at the site of the group. Six people, five females and one male, followed through on the interviews and wished to join the group. The group rules, which were explained during the interviews, included coming to each group on time, working on accepted tasks, helping others with their tasks, and maintaining confidentiality. Members were also asked to list one or two problem areas that they might want to work on during the group. Their concerns included child management issues, social relationships, financial pressures, child–parent interactions, and relationships with ex-spouses.

Sessions

The group ran for six sessions, as planned. Following the basic framework of the task-centered approach, the group focused on problem specification during the first session. This was done through work in consulting pairs, after the group leaders had presented a brief overview of the hows and whys of problem specification. Written instructions were also posted. Some members were able to clearly specify target problems: One member was new to town and wanted to become more familiar with the social activities and child-care resources for single parents. Another member disliked her interactions with her children, describing herself as "irritable and distracted." She wanted to be able to set aside times when she could focus on her children and give them her undivided attention. Other members decided on a general problem area but were unable to further specify a problem focus. An example was the member who had a difficult time dealing with her teenagers as she started to date a new man. Further problem specification may have been difficult for some because the work in pairs required them to share personal information with a person they had met just minutes before.

As the whole group discussed the specification process at the end of the meeting, it was decided that all members would gather information about their particular problem before the next meeting. The co-leaders went through each person's problem area and demonstrated how that problem might be baselined. If a target problem was clearly specified, the co-leaders gave specific suggestions for baselining. For the woman who wanted to increase the time she spent doing activities with other adults, the leaders suggested that she keep a chart, day by day, of the kinds of activities and amount of time spent doing those activities at present. For individuals who had not yet clarified their target problems, examples of possible baselining tasks were given using potential problems as examples. This gave them an idea of what the next step might look like for themselves, as well as highlighting generally how the specification of a target problem leads to baselining tasks.

The second session was spent further specifying target problems, reviewing previous baselining tasks, and developing initial tasks to attack the problems. After some group discussion aimed at helping them specify their target problems, several members decided that their primary concern was their lack of interaction with other single parents. For them, attendance at group meetings was part of the problem resolution. Other members were now more able to specify their problems clearly. For them, new tasks included further gathering of baseline information and development of initial tasks.

Development of individual tasks was done in the large group, with the co-leaders modeling skills related to task development. The co-leaders asked individuals what they thought they could do as a first step in resolving the target problem. If the response seemed too large a step, the co-leaders would ask additional questions until an achievable, realistic first task was decided upon. The group members each had the opportunity to go through this process with a co-leader, as well as the opportunity to watch the development of initial tasks with the other members. The group members also contributed suggestions and advice to each individual.

The third session began with a presentation: What is a task? Where do tasks come from? Why do tasks? Who does tasks? The co-leaders incorporated examples from the members' problems to help illustrate tasks. Also presented were task do's and don'ts and questions that might aid task development. The task do's and don'ts included the following:

DO
1. Do start with *small* steps.
2. Do pick tasks that make sense in reducing the problem.
3. Do choose tasks that you will complete.

DON'T
1. Don't pick tasks that are too large or too vague.
2. Don't force your own advice or solution.

3. Don't continue to attempt a task if it isn't working.
    (Be on the lookout for obstacles!)

The questions to aid task development included asking what specifically would you like to see different? What have you tried? How has that worked? What are some first steps you could take to reduce the problem? What are you willing and able to do?

Following the presentation and discussion, one co-leader and one member went through the steps for task development in front of the group while the other co-leader made comments, highlighted significant components, and clarified the steps' relationship to the general model. This "role-play" situation gave members a chance to see the process as it happened. After this, the group worked with one individual at a time, developing tasks. The co-leaders usually started the questions and members added to this, asking questions, making suggestions, giving advice. By the end of the session each individual had received group time and help and had developed a task for the week.

The format of the fourth session was much the same as the third. The leaders made a presentation on roadblocks and obstacles to tasks, a role-play was done with a member who was experiencing difficulty in task accomplishment, and then each individual received group time in going over his or her task from the previous week, analyzing any obstacles, and developing a new task. It is important to mention that members "signed-in" on task sheets each week, making comments about task accomplishment, obstacles, their feelings, and anything else related to their tasks. From this base, in each session tasks were reviewed and new tasks developed. During each of the presentations, examples related to members' problems were used to illustrate the steps being discussed. For example, the discussion of obstacles included as an illustration the member who wanted to spend more time in social activities with other adults but who had a difficult time finding a reliable babysitter. Additionally, the co-leaders emphasized throughout the presentations, discussions, and task work the relationship between the work each member was doing individually and the general problem-solving model that was being used. This was explained in terms of two levels: one level was learning a model that could be applied to many situations and the second level was the actual work on their specific problems.

The fifth session was also similar, but the group began work toward termination. The presentation during this meeting dealt with planning for continuing work on the target problem each had identified during the group. The group engaged in a brainstorming activity, generating eight to ten suggestions for each member to continue work on his or her problem after the group was over. For example, for the group member who wanted to spend more enjoyable time with her children (and who by now had set aside two to three hours one afternoon a week just to be with them), the group suggested a number of activities she might enjoy doing with them, suggested switching the time slightly, so it did not interfere with any of the children's regular activities, rehearsed with her what to do if she ran into a time conflict herself after she had promised to be with the kids, and suggested ways she might involve the kids in planning their time together.

During the sixth and final session, emphasis was placed on reviewing the group's progress, the progress made by each individual, and the steps in the general problem-solving model. Each individual discussed his or her perceptions of change in target problems. The group also discussed steps each would be making individually after the group. The group members were supportive of each other and enthusiastic about the progress that they had made. On the final evaluations, many members wrote that they appreciated the support, encouragement, and warmth they felt from the other single parents.

Discussion

Group Dynamics

Between the second and third session the group seemed to "gel" and become a cohesive unit. Members became increasingly more able to do task review and develop steps with each other, with less input from the co-leaders. As the group continued, members also made statements linking their own actions to the general problem-solving model. For example, one woman commented that it was "just like climbing a ladder . . . you go one step at a time, slowly, and don't try to skip steps." Members were better able to generate their own tasks, and input from other members was more in the form of appropriate suggestions than advice giving. By the third session, all made some progress in their problem areas, some more than others. This difference was caused by the number of obstacles individuals encountered. For example, the group member who wanted to locate child care and social activities for single parents was able to compile an impressive list of resources and began to check some of them out. However, the member who wanted more pleasurable times with her children had set aside the time but was still working on making that time enjoyable for both the children and herself.

The format used during the third session became the pattern for the rest of the sessions. Each session began with a presentation by one of the co-leaders related to the task-centered stage, followed by task review and development done individually but within the context of the large group. Initially, a co-leader started with one member, and then members gradually became more actively involved. This format appeared very useful because it allowed members to be involved in the task work of five other individuals as well as their own. By the end of the sessions, the group had a smooth-running rhythm to its meetings. The feedback obtained from members after each session consistently stated that one of the things members enjoyed most was the work in the group itself, with the active input by other single parents.

Group Formation: Common Status versus Common Problem

This group used a common status, single parenthood, as a formation point. However, single parents are as diverse as any other group and present a wide variety of concerns as appropriate target problems. The diversity poses a difficulty in very short-term groups: the varied concerns require more time for the group to address than common target problems; the group must switch gears, as it were. Because of this, the six weeks set for the group described appeared too short. Although all members experienced reduction in target problems, many could have fruitfully continued for several more weeks.

On the other hand, there are advantages to having single parents together as a group. One of the strongest is their own desire to participate with other single parents. All of the single parents who participated in a pre-group interview specified that they wanted a group in which they could meet and interact with other single parents. The common status of participants helps establish group cohesion rapidly and also makes fellow members more credible as advice and support givers who have shared similar experiences.

With these concerns in mind, I would recommend either of two approaches for other such groups. The first is to have a single-parent group formed on the basis of common status but with increased duration to accommodate the variety of concerns. Eight to ten weeks appears appropriate for a group of similar size (six members). The second approach is to form a single-parent group which would focus on one particular area determined in advance. Recruitment would focus on parents who saw that problem area as one they would like to work on. In effect, this would be a group with a common status and a common problem focus. As mentioned earlier, there are several major themes that occur with single parents—difficulties with finances, childrearing, child care, social life—and any of these might be a focus of a task-centered group. Of course, each individual's specified target problem would have its own unique characteristics, but there would be a common theme and purpose for the group.

Techniques and Methods

Consulting Pairs and Task-Work Groups.   Consulting pairs, a technique used successfully with adolescents (Rooney, 1977), was not adequately tested in this group. The format which developed during this group suggests another possibility: subgroups of three or four members and a co-leader can function as "task-work groups" and do what is usually done in pairs. This still allows each member to receive individual time from a small group, but increases the "help" available to them and is not so isolating as pairs can be. The leaders are also better able to ensure that the subgroups remain on task, since there are fewer subgroups than pairs to receive practitioner input. Also, each member can become more familiar with several others in the group, an especially important plus for single parents whose goals include interaction with other single parents. Further trials of task-work groups are needed, including tests of when pairs versus groups are appropriate (see also Garvin, Chapter 2).

Role-Plays.   The format for this group included a co-leader verbally going through the steps involved in part of the model (often with visual aids), and then the co-leader and one group member working through these same steps in relation to that individual's specific problem situation in front of the group. This served more as a model for group members than a role-play, although leaders and members called them role-plays. Members used questions and statements similar to those of the co-leaders more frequently after one of these demonstrations, and rapidly became more adept at asking the questions themselves, going through the steps with one another. The modeling/role-playing technique may have helped members feel more confident about what they were supposed to do, and they were also able to see the end result (a new task) being developed successfully. This method serves as a bridge between a leader explanation in general terms and members' own attempts to work on an individual level.

"Two-Level" Approach.   Although the primary goal for this group was the successful completion of task work with subsequent target problem reduction, a second goal was to teach members the steps involved in general problem solving (Fortune, introductory chapter, this volume). Throughout the group, references were made to two levels: learning the general problem-solving model of task-centered treatment and the specific individual work that each member was doing. One of the possible benefits

of the task-centered model may be the generalization of problem-solving skills that can take place along with actual problem reduction actions. Members seemed to work well on both levels and could illustrate the relationship between the two. With a variety of concerns being addressed in the group, the applicability of the general model to various situations was clearly demonstrated to members. At the end of the group, members requested handouts listing the general steps involved in the task-centered model.

Summary

The experience of this group suggests that task-centered groups are of value to single parents. The most important indication of this was the general overall satisfaction expressed by the group members themselves. When asked on their evaluations to comment on how they felt about the group overall, five members stated "good or very satisfied," while the sixth said she felt "fair" about her experience. The task-centered model proved to be a simple and straightforward means of helping this group of single parents alleviate a target problem and enjoy a positive peer group experience. Several techniques including task-work groups, modeling role-plays with a leader, and explicitly teaching general problem-solving skills appeared particularly useful but need further testing and refinement.

5 A Task-Centered Approach to Group Work with Older Persons

Ronald W. Toseland
Mary Coppola

This chapter examines the use of the task-centered model in working with a group of older persons. As mentioned in previous chapters, the task-centered model has been applied in a wide variety of settings with many different client groups (Garvin, Reid, and Epstein, 1976; Reid and Epstein, 1977). It has not, however, been used extensively in work with older persons (Dierking, Brown, and Fortune, 1980). This may be due, in part, to the general lack of attention which has been given to the mental health needs of older persons in our society (R. Butler, 1975).

In recent years, there has been a growing recognition of the under-utilization of mental health services by older persons and an increased effort to serve this population through individual and family treatment (Harbert and Ginsberg, 1979; Herr and Weakland, 1979; Keller and Hughston, 1981; Lowy, 1979; Sherman, 1981). These efforts have included the use of task-centered individual and family treatment (Cormican, 1977; Dierking, Brown, and Fortune, 1980; Fortune and Rathbone-McCuan, 1981; Rathbone-McCuan, Travis, and Voyles, 1983; Stafford and Bringle, 1980).

There has also been an increased effort to treat older persons in groups. Much of this effort has been focused on work with activity groups and socialization groups utilizing program activities and group discussion within a group-centered, mutual aid treatment model (Gordon, 1955; Shulman, 1979). It has also included work with reality orientation and remotivation groups for severely impaired older persons (Burnside, 1978; Stabler, 1981; Weiner, Brok, and Snadowsky, 1978). Although no applications of task-centered group work with older persons have been reported in the literature, there have been several closely related applications of a task-focused, problem-solving model of group treatment with older persons (Toseland, 1977, 1980; Toseland and Rose, 1978).

In this chapter, the strengths and weaknesses of the task-centered model for working with frail, socially isolated older persons in groups will be explored and a case example presented. The case example highlights adaptations of the task-centered model which are particularly appropriate when working with frail, socially isolated, older persons.

Strengths of the Task-Centered Model

There are several strengths of the task-centered model in working with older persons in groups. One of the major strengths of the model is its emphasis on structure, or specific procedures, steps, and rules to organize the treatment process. Older persons respond well to this structure. It helps them to orient themselves to the treatment process and to understand what is expected of them in their roles as group members.

A second strength of the task-centered model is its emphasis on members' wishes and motivations concerning what tasks to work on in the group. As Tobin (1982) notes, a major task of old age is to maintain the self. By encouraging older persons to select tasks that are unique to their own developmental needs and life history, the task-centered model helps older persons maintain a sense of self-sameness in the midst of age-related deterioration in physical, psychological, and social functions.

A third strength of the task-centered model for working with older persons is its planned short-term duration. A fixed number of sessions apprises older persons about the duration of their commitment to a particular group. It also helps to emphasize the accomplishments they can achieve in a brief time period. This is particularly important for older persons because their orientation to time is often reduced when they no longer have work, marital, or child care roles to keep them aware of a particular time schedule.

A fourth strength of task-centered group work with older persons is its emphasis on task accomplishment. Defining a particular task to accomplish gives older persons a sense of purpose that is sometimes lacking because of the reduction in roles that accompanies old age. In attempting to accomplish tasks, older persons often become involved with family, neighbors, or friends, thereby expanding their support networks. The completion of a task also reinforces older persons' coping abilities and confirms that they are "survivors" in an ever-changing world.

Adaptations When Treating
Older Persons

Despite its many strengths, several adaptations should be made in the task-centered model when using it to treat older persons. These adaptations are consistent with an interactional approach to group leadership (Toseland and Rivas, 1984). This approach to group leadership suggests that practitioners modify their leadership of a group based on the needs and characteristics of the group and its members. Adaptations of the task-centered model of group work with older persons include modifications in the model's structure, problem focus, time focus, and task focus.

Although the structure of task-centered group work helps older persons to stay focused and to gain a feeling of accomplishment, it has some limitations. Often, older persons' motivation to attend a group comes from their need to overcome their isolation as well as their need to solve a particular problem. They enjoy peer contact. Too much pressure to conform rigidly to the structure of task-centered treatment will not allow for a sufficient balance between the task and the socioemotional foci of the group (Toseland and Rivas, 1984; Toseland, Sherman, and Bliven, 1981). This, in turn, will reduce rather than enhance the attractiveness of the group for members, thereby reducing group cohesion.

The group work practitioner should help members to share concerns with their peers, to help each other with their concerns, and to engage in social interactions which are intrinsically satisfying. This has the effect of expanding members' friendship networks, which can be relied on for mutual aid during the group and after the group ends. An expansion of members' social networks can, in itself, become a group-as-a-whole purpose. Older persons sometimes perceive little need for additional purposes prior to beginning a group. As the group progresses and trust develops, members begin to share other issues which concern them. These frequently include conflicts with family members, coping with physical problems, loss of social roles, loss of loved ones, and the like.

In order to encourage the development of trust, cohesion, and mutual aid networks within groups composed of older persons, the task-centered model should be adapted to increase attention to members' socioemotional concerns. The practitioner should encourage members to express their concerns, their feelings about these concerns and the historical context in which their concerns have developed. Moreover, the practitioners should help members develop warm, supportive relationships with one another. In addition to a socioemotional focus within the actual group session, members might also be encouraged to stay after the session to socialize over coffee or other refreshments.

A second adaptation which is helpful in working with older persons concerns the task-centered model's problem focus. In helping older persons become more like their own self-image (Lieberman and Tobin, 1983), practitioners should encourage members to focus on maintaining existing functional skills rather than on remediating functional deficits. Older persons tend to resist a problem focus by responding "I've been doing it this way all my life." Therefore, it is often helpful to focus on maintaining coping skills, revitalizing friendship networks, and maintaining and enhancing currently existing functional abilities rather than to focus on remediating dysfunctions or changing coping patterns that have been established over a lifetime. While the end result may be the same—that is, the maintenance or enhancement of existing skills—reframing problems or concerns into positive opportunities to maintain or enhance existing coping capabilities helps to overcome older persons' resistance to identifying problems and establishing contracts to change behavior patterns.

A third adaptation of the model concerns its time-limited focus. While a time-limited focus has several benefits which are mentioned above, it has two limitations. Older persons do not respond well to time pressures. They compensate for sensory losses by slowing their pace. When they do not feel pressured by time in taking tests or completing tasks, older persons perform as well as younger people, but when they perceive a pressure to perform in a short period of time, they do not do as well (Botwinick, 1977). Likewise, practitioners should slow the pace of task-centered group work to compensate for members' sensory losses and to help them participate as fully as possible.

A second issue related to the time-limited focus concerns older persons' need for continued support. As older persons age, they continue to experience role losses, increased sensory deficits, and chronic health problems. For this reason, and because older persons need more time to formulate tasks and carry them out than younger people, it is sometimes helpful to recontract for additional task-centered group sessions. Recontracting also allows time for practitioners to help members maintain and generalize the gains that they have made during the initial contract period. During additional group meetings, members can focus on learning general problem-solving skills through role-playing and practice as described in other chapters. In order to accomplish these purposes, practitioners may also consider helping members form a self-help group without a professional leader so that they can continue to meet after the group ends.

A fourth adaptation of the task-centered model of group work with older persons should concern its task focus. While a task focus also has several beneficial aspects mentioned above, practitioners should be aware that older persons may have a more difficult time completing tasks than younger persons. Older persons may have difficulty remembering the task they agreed to accomplish. Memory aids such as writing the task on a piece of paper, repeating the tasks agreed to by each member at the end of the session, and having members exchange phone numbers and remind each other of their tasks can be helpful. Rose (1977) and Garvin (see Chapter 2 of this text) refer to this latter memory aid as a "buddy system." It is also suggested that the practitioner be quite clear about specifying who is responsible for what task. Because they have few demanding social roles, older persons often do not experience requests to perform tasks on a regular basis. Therefore, they may need extra attention and praise from the practitioner and other group members to help them complete a task.

Another reason why older people may have a more difficult time accomplishing tasks than younger people is that physiological changes may reduce the energy they have available to complete a task. Practitioners should make sure that the task is small enough that it can be completed successfully without too great an expenditure of energy. Dividing a large task into small steps can make it more manageable for the older person. For example, the task of visiting a neighbor could be divided into several smaller tasks including calling the neighbor, setting a specific time to visit, selecting what to wear, and making the visit. Functional deficits may also make it difficult for an older person to complete a task. For example, an older person living in a rural area who is unsteady on her feet may have a difficult time negotiating weather conditions in order to visit a friend who lives on a neighboring farm.

A third reason that older persons may have a more difficult time accomplishing tasks is that they have developed established habits and behavior patterns over a lifetime. These behavior patterns have helped them to survive, and are maintained by extremely complex reinforcement schedules. In order to change these ingrained behavior patterns, practitioners should be sure that older persons are highly motivated to make changes and that tasks are seen as congruent with the continuity of their established behavior patterns. Radical shifts in behavior patterns are unlikely unless the older person is someone who is accustomed to making such shifts throughout his or her life.

When considering the needs of individual group members, as well as the group as a whole, the practitioner should assess the unique needs of each older person in the group. Older persons are in the most highly individualized and differentiated developmental stage of their lives. While some gross developmental distinctions can be made between the young-old and the old-old (Neugarten, 1977), older people of the same chronological age are developmentally more different from each other than are, for example, two-year-olds. Thus, when considering adaptations of the task-centered model in working with older persons, their unique needs should be considered.

Case Example

The following case example is taken from a group for frail, socially isolated, older persons.[1] The case example illustrates some of the adaptations that were made in the task-centered treatment model and provides some brief excerpts of the group in action during the beginning, middle, and ending phases.

Planning the Group

The group was conducted in a family service agency which is located in a small city in a rural county. The idea for the group arose as practitioners in the agency began to realize that frail, homebound older persons in their caseloads needed additional services which practitioners did not have time to provide on an individual basis. The 15 older persons who belonged to the group resided in rural areas which surrounded the small city. Although 15 group members may seem to constitute a rather large group, previous experience has shown that because older persons have chronic health problems, fewer members—approximately 10 to 12—are able to attend any given session.

Because the majority of the group members were in their 70s and suffered from chronic health problems including hearing and visual impairments, driving to group meetings was difficult or impossible. Others did not know how to drive or could not afford the cost of a private car. For these reasons, members were transported to and from the group by volunteers, each of whom was responsible for picking up and dropping off several group members. In addition to making the group feasible, this method of transportation gave members an additional opportunity to socialize as they drove to and from the agency.

Members who were selected for the group were (1) confined to their own homes on a regular basis due to multiple physical constraints, (2) accustomed to only infrequent contacts with significant others, and (3) isolated from their peers for long periods of time. Other criteria for

[1]The group was led by an experienced MSW social worker, the junior author. The names of group members have been changed to protect their confidentiality. The excerpts of dialogue were constructed from memory and from written summary recordings of group sessions.

selection included (1) living within an accessible distance to the sponsoring agency, (2) demographic characteristics (old age, an equal number of males and females, etc.), (3) an ability to articulate experiences, including clarity of thought patterns and an absence of physical disorders that limit communication such as deafness, and (4) motivation to attend the group.

To compose the group, recruiting efforts were conducted by practitioners during their home contacts with clients. Practitioners described the agency atmosphere and pointed out positive aspects of attending the group. A written pamphlet about the group was also distributed to each potential member during home contacts. In addition to the written pamphlet, which acted as a memory aid, members were telephoned on the day of the meeting to remind them that someone would come to their home to transport them to the group.

After carefully reviewing the treatment plans and service contracts of the potential group members, the group leader and the practitioners from whose caseloads the potential group members were recruited agreed that the basic commonality among members was their felt difficulty in the area of social relations. Thus, the primary purpose of the group was defined as the members' need to expand their social relationships. Specifically, it was planned that group sessions would emphasize (1) practicing social skills, (2) discussing and overcoming problems in daily living which affected social relationships, and (3) exploring ways of developing new social relationships.

It was also decided that the group would meet for a total of six one-hour sessions. However, to encourage informal socialization and the growth of new relationships, an additional half-hour after the group meeting was reserved for having coffee and other refreshments before members were transported back to their homes. For some members, the group sessions provided the only human interaction that they experienced that day. This may have contributed to members' decisions to continue meeting informally, without the leader, after the task-centered group sessions had ended.

Beginning the Group

In preparing for the first meeting, the practitioner considered several special needs of the members based on their age. Since many members suffered from multiple chronic illnesses, the physical environment of the meeting room was modified to provide for their comfort and to assure their continued attendance. This meant, for example, straight-back chairs which provide support for the back and are easier to get out of, a warm temperature, and a small room to capture voices. It also meant a room with easy access for those with difficulties in walking and in ascending and descending stairs.

Problem specification and priority setting, which usually occurs in the first two sessions of a task-centered group, was delayed for some members. This occurred because the group had to remain open to allow for slight changes in composition as required by frequent illness, physician's appointments, and hospitalizations. Because several members had very infrequent social contact and socializing was so highly valued, special efforts also had to be made to curtail socializing and defer it to the informal social time after the group meeting in order to move ahead with problem specification and priority setting.

During the beginning phase of the group, exploration of members' difficulties in the area of social relationships was accomplished by helping them to talk about their daily living situations. By sharing some personal history through reminiscing, as well as by discussing their current situations, members began to assert their own identity, to feel comfortable with one another, and to develop trusting relationships. Our clinical experience suggests that task formulation takes longer to accomplish in groups for older persons as compared to groups for younger adults. Thus, we agree with Macy-Lewis and Garvin (Chapters 2 and 4) that six sessions may be too short a time to fully implement the task-centered approach with groups.

By the middle of the second session, members were ready to begin to formulate individual target problems in relation to the group's purpose. These included conflicts in relationships with adult children, friends, and with sons-in-law and daughters-in-law, and helping members with concerns about their own health or their spouses' health.

The following excerpt demonstrates the practitioner's attempts to help members plan details of task implementation by examining their current behavior patterns and the obstacles that might interfere with their attempts to complete a task. It also illustrates the process by which members begin to feel that they are a part of the group. For example, members share personal concerns, express the specialness of "group day," and two members (Alice and Sam) help each other remember to get ready to come. The practitioner encourages the formation of a group identity by addressing the entire group and by relating individuals' comments to each other.

PRACTITIONER: So you all seem to agree one of the major difficulties in getting out of the house to see other people is simply getting started in the morning?

ANNE: Oh, yes. I find by the time I get moving to get myself washed up and dressed, and do a few chores in the kitchen, half the day is gone. It takes me so long to do everything these days. Why, I used to be able to clean my house in nothing flat.

BETTY: Ain't it the truth. I am up so much earlier now since Fred passed on . . . but I just can't seem to push myself to move fast for anything. When I can't sleep anymore I get up and read or think about my children and how it was when Fred was with me. I get so lonely and sad, I don't feel like doing much of anything that day, so I just putter around the house with my cleaning. Before I know it, it's time for lunch and my soaps.

P: Perhaps you'd be more tempted to move in the morning if you had something planned to look foward to instead of the daily routine of cleaning. For instance, you all seem to have made it on time for our meeting last week and today.

BILL: Well, sure . . . it's someplace special to go and I like being here with everybody. I keep telling myself today is Wednesday and I have to be ready by 1:00 for my ride. If the dishes aren't done, I know they'll be there for me when I come home (group laughter).

P: That's a good positive outlook, Bill. You kind of adjust your day to come here for our session. Does anyone else have a way he or she gets prepared in the morning to come here?

ALICE: Yeah, I have. Sam reminds me that today is Wednesday so I can get my dress and his suit ready ahead of time. I am so forgetful about days of the week—this way I can get things laid out ahead of time.

P: You seem to be suggesting it is easier to get started on Wednesdays when you know you have someplace to go or something important to do. Also, you plan around activities by alloting yourself more time or rearranging your day. I wonder if you all could try to do the same thing on other days of the week where you took responsibility for planning something different, like taking a walk with a neighbor?

Middle Phase

The next excerpt comes from the middle phase of the group. It illustrates how one member, Betty, had difficulty completing a task due to age-related physiological changes. The practitioner intervenes to ensure that tasks include steps that are small enough to be accomplished successfully. The excerpt also illustrates how group members can be helpful by sharing their own concerns, by encouraging and reinforcing each other for efforts to accomplish tasks, and by developing an informal buddy system to help each other complete tasks. Although the practitioner focuses on individuals, she intervenes on behalf of the group as a whole by reinforcing members' efforts to help each other.

P: Last week we ended with everyone agreeing to get out of the house once during the week for some new activity. Would someone like to start and tell us about their experience?

SAM: I went over to my neighbor's house last Friday. I used to go over there all the time before my eyes started getting worse. Since the operation, I haven't been doing much of anything.

P: Did you enjoy your visit?

SAM: Oh sure, Charlie and I sat around, talked about old times and drank coffee for a couple of hours. We didn't go down to the cellar to woodwork like we used to, but it was good to see him.

BETTY: Isn't that discouraging though? I mean, I was planning on visiting with my neighbor where I used to sew all the time on projects. Then I thought about how I can't sew much anymore, and got real depressed. Never did pick up the phone to call her.

SAM: Well, yeah. I called Charlie about seeing him and come Friday morning, I didn't feel like going. My eyes have been giving me a little trouble lately . . . on top of that, my back was acting up.

P: What did you do to get going, Sam?

SAM: I didn't feel up to going but I thought about how we talked about feeling better after doing something. I knew I should try to go 'cause otherwise I'd sit around all day and become part of the rocker. Figured I should try at least while I can still move about and see to do some small things.

BETTY: But it's so discouraging not to be able to do what you'd like to do and used to do all the time. Now it's like a special event just to sew a small piece when I used to make things for my family all the time. I tell myself I'll do it tomorrow when I get down.

P: Only tomorrow never seems to come, Betty (group voices chiming in to note agreement). Maybe if you would take things one step at a time, as we discussed, you would feel better. Next time perhaps you could try just making a date to visit your neighbor.

MABEL: You can come over to see me, Betty. We live close by, I could show you my flowers that you were interested in . . .

P: Do you think you can make that a date, Betty?

BETTY: Why, I'd like to, if you don't mind how an old lady looks in the morning.

P: If Mabel is willing, maybe she can be your "buddy" and give you a call in the morning about an afternoon visit.

In this phase, the specific ways that older persons define themselves now emerge. Sam, for example, has a need to perceive himself as an artisan, which in this session was expressed in woodworking with Charlie. Socialization with Charlie where they could reminisce about achievements in this area becomes symbolically equivalent to the actual activity. Also, Betty, who defines herself as "making things for my family," can now recapture that experience when socializing with Mabel. In this way, older persons maintain their sense of self.

The next excerpt of dialogue from the fifth session illustrates the way the practitioner achieves a balance between the socioemotional and the task focus of the group. It also illustrates the development of group cohesion and trust as members share similar concerns and support a member's efforts to improve her relationship with her daughter-in-law.

ANNE: My daughter-in-law visits quite frequently.

BETTY: Well—I'm having some trouble with mine.

JOE: Children are a worry. Ed (Joe's son) finally got a good job. He's working for Mutual Life. I was really concerned because he wasn't working for three months. I—

P: Joe, it seems like your concerns about your children are similar to other members'.

JOE: Yeah, I think all of us that have children are concerned about them.

P: I was wondering what Betty meant when she said she was having trouble with her daughter-in-law.

ANNE: Yeah, what trouble, Betty?

BETTY: Well, my son says that I don't like Jane (his wife). But that's not so. It's just that I'm concerned how she treats him and the kids.

MABEL: Well, maybe you shouldn't get so involved. My son and daughter-in-law were having a tough time—arguing—and I used to try to smooth things out when I could see that they weren't getting along. But they told me to "butt out" —I did and they seemed to work it out. They're getting along much better now.

HELEN: Sometimes I think Frank (her son-in-law) stops Mary (her daughter) from inviting me over to their place, but I guess they're busy. They have a right to their own life, too, I guess.

P: Can you see any value in what Mabel and Helen have said, Betty?

BETTY: Well—yes—I guess so—because whenever I say anything to Teddy (her son) it seems to make things worse.

SAM: What do you say, Betty?

Group members go on to discuss how they communicate with their married children. Both Betty and Helen are helped to develop alternative ways to communicate with their children and both agree to complete tasks related to this concern. Both share the results of these tasks in the next session.

Ending Phase

This last, brief piece of dialogue illustrates the changes which occurred in members from the beginning to the ending phase of the group's development. Helen shares her successful task achievement without prodding from the practitioner. While taking initiative in the situation, it is obvious that she has given thought to what she chooses to disclose to her daughter. A review of achievements and a realistic acknowledgment of work to be done in the future is characteristic of the ending phase.

HELEN: I want to start out today with telling something good if everyone doesn't mind my going first (group gives unanimous approval). Well, I just wanted to say I had a good time at my daughter's this week. I tried what you suggested—about telling her how I felt about seeing her and the kids more often—it worked. She was very nice about having me over. It was a little quiet at first, but we got talking soon enough.

P: Did you talk to her about your surgery?

HELEN: No, no, I didn't . . . because we hadn't seen each other in so long I didn't want to push . . . but I will call her this week to let her know how I made out at the doctor's.

Although it is not apparent from the dialogue, Helen appeared to be better groomed than she had been the beginning of the group. She had her hair done and was wearing a new dress. She was also using more expressive facial gestures in speaking. In addition to smiling more often, she responded more readily to the group. This can be seen, in part, by her initial comment, i.e., seeking the group's approval to proceed. Although some members showed more improvement than others, the changes that occurred in Helen's demeanor from the beginning to the ending phase of the group are typical of the changes found among other members of the group.

During the last session members expressed their interest in continuing to meet. Unfortunately, the practitioner could not offer to recontract with the group for additional sessions because she had made prior commitments. However, as suggested earlier in this chapter, the practitioner was able to provide other means through which members remained in contact with one another. For example, the worker notified other staff members of the members' desire to continue meeting. Through her advocacy efforts, the agency made a commitment to utilize their transportation program to help members meet together in each other's homes. The buddy system established during the group facilitated the process of members getting together in each other's homes and keeping in contact with one another by telephone. Thus, the group resulted in an improved support network for members. The agency also provided opportunities for members to meet during outings such as a fall foliage trip, a picnic, and the like.

Summary

This chapter examines the use of the task-centered model in working with a group of frail, socially isolated older persons. Consistent with an interactional approach to leading different types of groups (see Toseland and Rivas, 1984, for more information about this approach), adaptations of the task-centered model were suggested for practitioners who are called upon to lead groups for older persons. Adaptations that are particularly useful when working with older persons in groups include increasing the focus on the socioemotional needs of group members, maintaining and, if possible, increasing current skills as well as maintaining rather than changing long-term coping patterns, slowing the pace of group activity rather than using time limits to focus on change, and adapting tasks to take into account long-term behaviors and physiological changes.

To illustrate these adaptations, some excerpts of dialogue are presented from the beginning, middle, and ending phases of a group conducted at a family service agency. The case example suggests that task-centered group work, with adaptations, is an effective treatment modality in helping older persons to improve interpersonal relationships with family and friends. It is also helpful in overcoming the social isolation and the decrease in supportive social network relationships which often occurs as a result of the role losses and chronic health problems that are frequently a part of the aging process.

Working with Families

6 Families and Family Treatment

Anne E. Fortune

The family is the most important social institution in human society. It is the major source of support and psychological, financial, and material assistance for the individual (Sanders and Seelbach, 1981; Veroff, Kulka, and Douvan, 1981). Among adults, being married is related to greater satisfaction, well-being, health, and mental health (Campbell, 1981; Ilfield, 1982; Verbrugge, 1979; Veroff, Douvan, and Kulka, 1981). For children, the family is critical in nurturance, development, and socialization (R. Anderson and Carter, 1978; Zimmerman, 1980). What affects one individual in a family affects all the other members, the family as a whole, and the family's ability to fulfill its basic functions (Terkelson, 1980). Consequently, the family is a major focus for social work practitioners. Whether clients are seen together as families or individually, the practitioner must keep in mind the family, its experience, and the interaction between family, individual, and treatment.

The idea of offering treatment to families is a recent one, and there is as yet little consensus about theory, treatment techniques, or even who should be involved in treatment (Gurman and Kniskern, 1978). However, in most approaches, the major difference between individual and family treatment is the view of the family as a functional unit, a system. Like other systems, the family is made up of subunits—individuals—but is more than the sum of those subunits; it transfers energy within itself and between itself and the environment; this energy is "the system's capacity to act, its power to maintain itself and effect change" (R. Anderson and Carter, 1978:14); it has external boundaries which may be more or less permeable; it has some form of organization, including internal boundaries delineating subsystems; and it attempts to maintain a steady state in which it is simultaneously changing and remaining the same (R. Anderson and Carter, 1978).

The emphasis on family as system has several consequences for the practitioner. First, it shifts thinking about causation from a linear cause-and-effect model to an interactive, feedback model in which every action and change reverberates throughout the system (Fisch, Weakland, and Segal, 1982). It focuses attention—and change effort—on the family and on transactions between members rather than on the individual (Sluzki, 1978). Second, the family as system moves through time with relatively predictable stages of development. The family's stage of development is an important consideration in assessment and treatment, often more important than individual members' stage of psychosocial development.

Since task-centered work with families borrows many of these systems concepts, this chapter reviews selected aspects of family treatment and family life cycle as background for the task-centered approach to treatment of families offered by Reid in the next chapter. Other, more specific concepts from various treatment theorists are discussed in later chapters, as relevant to the cases illustrated.

Family as Interactive System

The shift to an interactive feedback model of causation and change influences who is invited to participate in treatment, how problems are formulated, what those problems are, task-planning, and the tasks themselves.

If the family is the unit of attention, and problems lie in interaction rather than within individuals, then logically the entire system or its affected parts should be invited to participate in treatment. However, there is considerable controversy but little evidence about whether the entire family must in fact participate to benefit from treatment. On the one hand is evidence that marital and family treatment is more effective than no treatment (D. Beck, 1975; Gurman and Kniskern, 1978, 1981; Jacobson, 1978) and yields more durable outcome than individual treatment (Conway and Bucher, 1976; Israel and Saccone, 1979; Patterson and Fleischman, 1979). On the other hand, it is not clear that family treatment is more effective than individual treatment or other interventions such as hospitalization or medication (DeWitt, 1978; Masten, 1979; Wells, 1981). A practical solution is to offer marital or family treatment for relationship problems—marital, parent–child, or whole family relations (D. Beck, 1975; Kniskern and Gurman, 1980)—but to be cautious about total-family involvement with other types of problems until evidence is clearer. In task-centered practice, Reid recommends family involvement when the target problem involves family processes or when the family is an affective resource for problem resolution (Chapter 7, this volume). The members available and the resources they can bring to treatment vary over the family life cycle, as will be discussed.

In many instances, task-centered practice with families is a cyclical process of moving into and out of the family system at various points in treatment (Tolson, personal communication). For example, a child may be referred by a teacher for academic problems; problem specification includes the parents to determine the involvement of home factors in the child's poor performance; parents and the sibling group may work together to restructure time at home and improve quarrelsome relationships to expedite completion of all the children's homework. The practitioner may then work individually with the child to overcome difficulties in classroom peer relations which interfere with classwork and, at a later date, work again with the sibling subgroup when it becomes apparent that the child's interpersonal difficulties carry over to sibling relationships. Conversely, in treatment with the whole family, individual or subgroup interviews may be used differentially, to change or strengthen internal family boundaries (Minuchin, 1974) or to resolve issues limited to certain members (Reid, 1978; Chapter 7). For example, in the case of Martha (Rathbone-McCuan, Chapter 8), a potential change in the relationship between one daughter and her ex-husband threatened plans made by the mother–adult children group; an interview with the daughter alone was used to explore her ambivalence about and conflict between her former husband and her family of origin.

When only an individual or subgroup of family members is involved in treatment, the practitioner must consider possible reverberations in the rest of the family. For example, a mildly retarded youngster was involved in treatment with his single-parent mother. His brother, until then reasonably well-behaved, suddenly became a disciplinary problem at home. When he was invited to participate and treatment focused on interaction among the three, rather than between mother-and-first-child, the home situation improved dramatically, with the mother able to discipline both children appropriately.

The process of developing and implementing tasks must similarly take into account the family as system. Not surprisingly, marital and family treatment makes heavy use of tasks involving two or more family members simultaneously (Reid, Chapter 7). Such shared and reciprocal tasks, as well as independent individual tasks which require cooperation from another family member, are more likely to succeed when all involved are knowledgeable about their purposes and committed to carrying them out (Fortune, 1976). Obviously, the process of formulating tasks should include all participants. The interaction among family members can provide diagnostic information, may lead to identification of the interaction as a new relationship problem or obstacle to problem resolution, or as Reid details (Chapter 7) may result directly in contextual change such as new attitudes toward each other or new patterns of communication.

The Family Life Cycle

The family can also be viewed as a system developing over time, with stages characterized by typical compositions, transitions, developmental and adaptive tasks, and problems. Knowledge of these stages provides the practitioner with a framework of experiences common to families, and of likely participants, strengths, resources, and difficulties relevant to a particular stage.

The most widely used model of the family life cycle is Duvall's (1977), with stages based on the age of the oldest child and the points at which family members enter and leave the family system. Table 6.1 outlines these stages and their developmental tasks, with adaptations and elaborations suggested by Carter and McGoldrick (1980) and Rhodes (1977b). Also noted are typical difficulties a practitioner may encounter among families in each stage or transition between stages.

There are several limitations of a life-cycle approach that should be mentioned. First, life-cycle approaches have not been very useful in research and several authors question whether such models are appropriate (Giele, 1982; Nock, 1979; Spanier, Sauer, and Larzelere, 1979). Nevertheless, they do provide a useful conceptual framework for viewing the family as a unit moving through time.

Second, using age of oldest child to demarcate phases underestimates the complexity of a family with several children. A family may be dealing with several phases at once, depending on number and age of children. However, a model which takes into account all children is too complex for a useful conceptual tool.

Third, any discussion of stages, timing, and characteristics confounds two factors, the effects of aging and the effects of generational differences (Hess and Waring, 1978; Veroff, Kulka, and Douvan, 1981). One generation may experience the same event differently from another generation because of differences in ages at which it occurred. In some cases such as the postparental and postretirement stages, previous generations had little opportunity to experience the events.

Fourth, a danger in utilizing a life-stage approach to describe family experience is that it becomes viewed as "normative," or what everyone "should" experience in order to be normal. This view is *not* intended. The life-stage model is simply a way of characterizing commonalities of experience. In fact, the ideal of a nuclear, two-generation family has never characterized the majority of American families, and the proportion of families that follow the stages has varied at different points in American history (Uhlenberg, 1974). Currently, the proportions of individuals who remain single beyond normal marriage ages, couples who remain voluntarily childless, and families which divorce appear to be increasing (Macklin, 1980; Norton, 1983; Spanier and Glick, 1981; U.S. Census, 1976, 1977, 1982).

Despite limitations of a life-cycle model of family development, knowledge of the stage offers cues for assessment and treatment planning: who are family members to be involved in treatment or who may be affected by subsystem change; what are strategies used by other families to cope successfully with difficulties or transitions; what are developmental tasks the family will encounter; who and what resources may be available to the family, etc.

For example, at the Unattached Young Adult stage, the client is most likely to be seen as an individual, especially if target problems include establishing an adult identity separate from the family (Northen, 1982). Later, in the Childbearing stage, the husband and in-laws might be included to assist a woman with postpartum depression, since the couple is susceptible to marital-role and in-law strain during this period (L. Fischer, 1983; Golan, 1981). Once the children are near school age, the entire family may be seen, and the sibling subgroup may be especially important (Bank and Kahn, 1975, 1982).

As mentioned, at any stage, who is invited to participate in treatment depends on the problems and the resources to alleviate them. For example, the Knights (Mills, Chapter 9) were in the School-children stage, but the children were excluded because the problems focused on the parents' marital relationship. By contrast, Martha (Rathbone-McCuan, Chapter 8) was a widow, but her adult children were brought into treatment as crucial resources and participants. In some cases, circumstances dictate who may be seen; the Haley parents were seen without children because the preschool children had been removed by court order (Rzepnicki, Chapter 10); in Protective Services, individuals often become clients precisely because supportive family members are not available (Rooney and Wanless, Chapter 11).

In other instances, services may be offered to individuals rather than families because of the nature of the difficulties. Single parents, for example, frequently encounter loneliness and difficulty establishing an adequate adult social life (Hetherington, Cox, and Cox, 1976; Price-Bonham and Balswick, 1980). Treatment groups composed of single parents thus meet a common need for adult interaction as well as permitting work on individual and family-related problems (Macy-Lewis, Chap-

Table 6.1. The Family Life Cycle, Developmental Tasks, and Difficulties Commonly Encountered by Practitioners

Stage of Family Development	Developmental Tasks	Common Difficulties
Unattached Young Adult	Differentiate self from family of origin (Carter & McGoldrick, 1980) Develop intimate peer relations, work career, adult life-style (Carter & McGoldrick, 1980; D. Levinson et al., 1978)	Emotional differentiation (McGoldrick & Carter, 1982) Peer relations: isolation, loneliness (Cargan & Melko, 1982) Unemployment (Williams et al., 1981) Vocational choice (D. Levinson et al., 1978).
Transition to Marriage: orientation to marriage, courtship, engagement (Golan, 1981)		Isolation, lack of social skills to locate mates
Married Couples without Children	Establish mutually satisfying marriage (Duvall, 1977) Shift from idealized view of partner to intimacy (Rhodes, 1977b) Fit into kin network (Duvall, 1977; Golan, 1981)	Sexual difficulties Difficulty with intimacy, role negotiation, interpersonal patterns (McGoldrick & Carter, 1982) Practical family and home management problems (D. Beck & Jones, 1973) In-law problems (Golan, 1981) High divorce rate (U.S. Census, 1976)
Transition to Childbearing	Accept childbearing role (McGoldrick, 1980) Prepare psychologically for childbirth (Entwisle & Doering, 1981; May, 1982)	Unwanted pregnancy, with negative impact on parents and child (David & Baldwin, 1979; Russo, 1979) Psychological stress and anxiety (Golan, 1981; A. Rossi, 1968)

(continued)

122

Table 6.1. (continued)

Stage of Family Development	Developmental Tasks	Common Difficulties
Transition to Childbearing (continued)		Infertility (C. Shapiro, 1982) Potential genetic problems (Hamilton & Noble, 1983)
Childbearing Families (oldest child, birth to 30 months)	Adjust to and encourage development of child (Duvall, 1977) Establish home satisfying and nurturing to both parents and child (Duvall, 1977; Rhodes, 1977b) Shift in marital, kin, and peer relations (Barnhill, Rubenstein, & Rocklin, 1979; Carter & McGoldrick, 1980; Winborn, 1983)	Maternal postpartum depression and decrease in self-esteem (Entwisle & Doering, 1981; Notman & Nadelson, 1980) Poor adjustment to physical or role demands from infant (Golan, 1981) Lowest marital satisfaction (Spanier & Lewis, 1980) Strained in-law relations (L. Fischer, 1983) Financial difficulties (Golan, 1981) Reactions to non-normal birth (Entwisle & Doering, 1981; Kennell, Voos, & Klaus, 1976) Women's decision about whether to continue working
Families with Preschool Children (oldest child 2½–6 years)	Adapt to child's needs in growth-promoting ways (Duvall, 1977) (Parents) cope with energy depletion and lack of privacy (Duvall, 1977) Accept new members into system (Carter & McGoldrick, 1980)	Birth of subsequent child(ren); potential sibling rivalry (Schvaneveldt, & Ihinger, 1979; Tsukada, 1979) Day care, role overload if mother works (Ericksen, Yancy & Eriksen, 1979; Leuck, Orr & O'Connell, 1982)

(continued)

123

Table 6.1. (continued)

Stage of Family Development	Developmental Tasks	Common Difficulties
Families with Preschool Children (oldest child 2½–6 years) (continued)		Parenting stress and restriction (Campbell, 1981; Veroff, Douvan, & Kulka, 1981)
		Child-management difficulties (D. Beck & Jones, 1973)
		Financial, marital, practical problems as for earlier stages
Families with Schoolchildren (oldest child 6–13 years)	Share socialization responsibility with external institution (R. Anderson & Carter, 1978)	Difficulty releasing child emotionally (Scherz, 1971)
	Fit into community of school-age families in constructive ways (Duvall, 1977)	Difficulty adjusting to new influences in family from school, child's peers (Scherz, 1971); conflict with different culture (Sue, 1981)
	Encourage child's educational achievement (Duvall, 1977)	Child unprepared for school; peer interaction difficulties; school phobia
	Develop individualized roles not based on family responsibilities (Rhodes, 1977b)	Child's school difficulties (Howard & Anderson, 1978)
		Family violence, child abuse and neglect (identification increased with child in school) (Gelles, 1980; Walters & Walters, 1980)
		Men—marital problems at highest rate (Veroff, Kulka, & Douvan, 1981)
		Women—job and school decisions and

(continued)

124

Table 6.1. (continued)

Stage of Family Development	Developmental Tasks	Common Difficulties
Families with Schoolchildren (oldest child 6–13 years) (continued)		difficulties (Veroff, Kulka, & Douvan, 1981) Financial, parent-child, practical problems as for earlier stages
Families with Teenage Children (oldest child 13–20 years)	Balance freedom and responsibility as teenagers mature (Duvall, 1977) Increase flexibility of family boundaries as children move in and out (Carter & McGoldrick, 1980) Develop companionship and identity in and outside family (vs. parenting roles and isolation) (Rhodes, 1977b; L. Stone & Church, 1973)	Parent–adolescent conflict, especially over independence (D. Beck & Jones, 1973; Scanzoni & Szinovacz, 1980) Adolescent delinquency, status offenses, drug use, pregnancy, unemployment (Bachman, O'Malley, & Johnston, 1978; David & Baldwin, 1979; Teitelbaum & Gough, 1977; Williams et al., 1981) Financial, marital, school, practical problems as for earlier stages
Families Launching Young Adults (first child gone to last child's leaving home)	Release young adults but maintain supportive home base with adult-adult child relations (Carter & McGoldrick, 1980; Duvall, 1977; Rhodes, 1977b)	Difficulties in separation (Rhodes, 1977b; Wechter, 1983) Financial problems: college expenses, preparation for retirement (Lowenthal et al., 1975) Child(ren)—Start family life cycle as Unattached Young Adults or Married Couple without Children

(continued)

Table 6.1. (continued)

Stage of Family Development	Developmental Tasks	Common Difficulties
Middle-age Parents (last child leaves home to retirement)	Rebuild marital relationship (Duvall, 1977; Rhodes, 1977b) Maintain kin ties with older and younger generations (Duvall, 1977) Maintain identity/functioning in face of physiological decline (Carter & McGoldrick, 1980)	Difficulty around loss of parenting role or renegotiating spousal roles (McCubbin et al., 1980; McGoldrick & Carter, 1982) Individual transitions: menopause, midlife career "crises," confrontation with aging (Golan, 1981; D. Levinson et al., 1978; Nathanson & Lorenz, 1982) Inability to accept grandparent status; in-law conflicts (L. Fischer, 1983; McGoldrick & Carter, 1982) Difficulty providing emotional, financial, physical support to adult children and own aged parents (Lee, 1980; Miller, 1981; Shanas, 1980).
Transition to Aging Family—Retirement	Accept and adapt to retirement (Duvall, 1977; Golan, 1981)	Difficulties adjusting to marital role changes, loss of work-related social networks, leisure time (Lowenthal et al., 1975; McGoldrick & Carter, 1982; Scanzoni & Szinovacz, 1980) Financial problems: reduced or insufficient income (McCubbin et al., 1980) Health problems (often cause of early retirement) (Golan, 1981)

(continued)

126

Table 6.1. (continued)

Stage of Family Development	Developmental Tasks	Common Difficulties
The Aging Family (retirement to death of first spouse)	Adapt (further) to physiological decline (Carter & McGoldrick, 1980; Duvall, 1977)	Chronic age-related health and mental problems; drug and alcohol abuse (Blazer, 1980; Raskind & Storrie, 1980; Rathbone-McCuan & Hashimi, 1982)
	Accept "elder generation" role, including transfer of centrality to older children (Carter & McGoldrick, 1980; Rhodes, 1977b)	Deteriorated relations with children and physical and psychological strain on caretaker of debilitated spouse (E. Johnson & Bursk, 1977; Stoller & Earl, 1983)
	Close or adapt family home (Duvall, 1977)	Conflict related to generational power shifts (McGoldrick & Carter, 1982)
	Psychological preparation for death (Carter & McGoldrick, 1980)	Financial problems as for Retirement stage
Widow(er)hood (death of first spouse to death of second)	Cope with bereavement and living alone (Duvall, 1977; Golan, 1981)	Grief reactions (Golan, 1981; Hiltz, 1978)
		Adjustment to relocation (Lieberman & Tobin, 1983)
		Loneliness, social isolation, other role-dislocations (Atchley, 1975; Rathbone-McCuan & Hashimi, 1982)
		Health, financial, family-conflict problems, as for earlier aging stages but often exacerbated by widowhood

Stages adapted from Elizabeth A. Carter and Monica McGoldrick, "The Family Life Cycle and Family Therapy: An Overview," in *The Family Life Cycle: A Framework for Family Therapy*, edited by Elizabeth A. Carter and Monica McGoldrick (New York: Gardner, 1980); Evelyn Millis Duvall, *Marriage and Family Development*, 5th ed. (New York: Harper & Row, 1977); and Sonya L. Rhodes, "A Developmental Approach to the Life Cycle of the Family," *Social Casework* 58 (May 1977): 301–311. Some transitional stages are added and developmental tasks shifted to take into account recent demographic trends (Glick, 1977; Norton, 1983; Treas, 1977).

ter 4). Toseland and Coppola's group of rural elderly (Chapter 5) similarly assumed a common need to interact with age-peers. In both examples, groups of adults in similar circumstances provided resources not available within any single family.

The family life stage is also important in difficulties which may occur at any age or stage, for example, divorce, adaptation to remarriage, unemployment, or death of a spouse. For example, children's reactions to divorce vary by age and developmental level (Hetherington, 1979; Rohrlich et al., 1977; Wallerstein and Kelly, 1979, 1980). The life stage of the family thus influences what reactions the parents will have to cope with, as well as ease of their adaptation, for example, whether a single-parent mother will encounter child-care difficulties in order to work or have an adequate social life.

Similarly, family life stage can influence a remarried family, especially if two families from different stages are joined. The adults do not have an opportunity to establish spousal intimacy before dealing with children (Sager et al., 1983) nor do they share common experience and knowledge of children at various ages. Remarriage may also alter or make more difficult family developmental tasks, for example, joining families with late adolescents at the same time the families are in the process of releasing those children (Launching) or the complications to kin networks and intergenerational responsibilities when an older couple divorce and remarry (Middle-Age Parents).

Summary

In sum, a systems perspective on treatment of families adds a focus on interaction among family members and requires the practitioner to take into account all members of the system whether actively involved in treatment or not. In addition, the view of the family as passing through time offers a perspective on who are likely interactants, whether present or not, and on resources and difficulties typical of family developmental stages.

7 Work with Families

William J. Reid

During the course of its evolution, the task-centered model has been applied in various ways in work with families, mirroring the wide variety of forms of family practice in clinical social work as a whole. Many of these applications have been family treatment in the broad sense of work with one or more family members usually seen individually, but sometimes together, for problems of concern to the family unit (Ewalt, 1977; Reid, 1978; Reid and Epstein, 1972, 1977; Wodarski, Saffir, and Frazer, 1982). Several projects have consisted primarily of marital treatment using both individual and conjoint interviews with spouses (J. Butler, Bow, and Gibbons, 1978; Reid, 1977a; Tolson, 1977; Wise, 1977) and several undertakings, carried out in child welfare settings, have involved efforts to help parents reunite with children in foster or institutional placement or to prevent such placement (Bass, 1977; Rooney, 1981; Rzepnicki, 1982; Salmon, 1977). Reflecting these practice emphases, development of task-centered theory has emphasized marital and parent-child subsystems (Reid, 1978; Reid and Epstein, 1972) with only modest attention to larger family units (Reid, 1981).

This chapter presents developments in theory and methods that have generic application to family units of any size. It deals with family treatment in the sense of work on family problems through conjoint interviews with two or more family members. The developments are the outgrowth of recent work conducted as a part of the task-centered family treatment project at the School of Social Welfare, the State University of New York at Albany (Reid, in press).

Applicable Problems

Within the task-centered system, work with family members together is clearly preferred over one-to-one treatment when the targets of intervention are family problems. In this category fall difficulties in family relations, such as marital discord and conflict between parents and children, as well as troubles affecting the family as a whole, for example, an impending eviction. Seeing family members together for such problems facilitates assessment, problem formulation, task planning and review, and provides opportunity for in vivo work with families on problem solving, communication, and other types of tasks that can be done in the session.

The choice of intervention modality is not as clear-cut when target problems are centered in difficulties of individual members, such as depression, alcoholism, delinquency, or school underachievement. Traditionally, individual treatment has been applied to such problems, but family therapy is being used increasingly. In task-centered practice, conjoint treatment would be indicated when either one of two conditions obtain: when the problem appears to be related to family processes, as in the case of a wife who is depressed over her marriage, or when the family may provide an effective resource for resolving the problem regardless of its causes—for example, a child having trouble with his studies may be helped by the parents' assuming a more active role in tutoring, structuring time for homework, and providing rewards for improved academic performance. In general, if a client is a member of a family, and most are, almost any problem area needs to be examined with an eye to potential involvement of the family in treatment.

Treatment Strategy

The first order of business of task-centered family treatment is to help the family alleviate *target problems*—that is, problems that are expressly identified and agreed to by the family and the practitioner as the focus of work. Change in target problems represents a desirable goal in its own right and fulfills the service contract. At the same time, target problems are part of a larger *context* which must always be taken into account. The context of a problem can be seen generally as a configuration of factors in the family and its environment that may interact with the problem. Context includes immediate causes of the problem, obstacles to solving it, and resources that can be applied to work on it. These causes, obstacles, and resources in turn can reflect almost any aspect of family life, such as the values, expectations, and perceptions of family members; communication and problem-solving skills; patterns of family relationships; and environments of which the family and its members are a part.

An effort is made to help families alleviate the target problems in ways that will exert a positive influence on the context of the problem. Whereas significant contextual change is not a fixed objective in all cases, it is generally sought after as a means of facilitating solutions, of preventing recurrences and side effects, and of strengthening the family's problem-solving abilities. Contextual change is essentially defined and limited by the nature of the target problem. It is not just any change that would help the family. Practitioners move from the target outward by degrees, giving priority to contextual change most directly relevant to the problem at hand. Also it should be obvious that the boundaries between a target problem and its context are seldom clear-cut or fixed. Basically the distinction is between a particular issue defined and specified in a given way (the target problem) and a host of factors that bear upon the issue (the context). Contextual change does not necessarily mean structural realignments or other major modifications in family life. It may be as minor as a subtle shift in attitude on the part of one family member toward another.

Change in the target problem as well as contextual change is brought about primarily through application of different kinds of tasks to the *target* problem and to *obstacles* arising from work on the target problem. After the initial phase, in which target problems and goals are identified and the treatment contract is formed, the practitioner helps family members review accomplishments on problems and tasks, explore and reformulate problems, deal with obstacles impeding progress, work together on problem-solving tasks within the session (*session tasks*), and plan tasks to be carried out at home (*home tasks*) or in the family's environment (*environmental tasks*).

The treatment strategy is guided by principles which maximize the family's own problem-solving activities and potentials. It is assumed that in general families can be best helped if they are provided with an orderly, facilitative structure in which to work out immediate problems and to develop problem-solving skills, with the practitioner in the roles of guide and consultant. Although the family's limitations are realistically appraised, emphasis is placed on identification of strengths, competencies, and resources within the family. Accordingly, the family members are helped to devise their own solutions with the practitioner's assistance. Should these efforts be blocked by obstacles, increased attention is paid to contextual factors that may be responsible for the obstacles. Session, home, and environmental tasks addressed to these obstacles may be developed. The practitioner assumes more of a leadership role and pushes for such contextual change as is necessary in order to help the family work through obstacles preventing problem solution.

Within this structure, use is made of methods from other approaches. In developing session tasks, the practitioner may draw on communication and problem-solving training models (Baucom, 1982; Jacobson and Margolin, 1979; Robin, 1979; Stuart, 1971, 1980; R. L. Weiss, 1975) and for home tasks, on contracting approaches (R. L. Weiss, Birchler, and Vincent, 1974). In resolving obstacles, use may be made of session and home tasks following structural and strategic approaches (Aponte and Van Deusen, 1981; Haley, 1976, 1980; Madanes, 1981; Minuchin and Fishman, 1981; Stanton, 1981).

Assessment

The gathering and evaluation of assessment data about contextual factors is primarily determined by the target problems. From these focal concerns, the practitioner branches out into other areas of the family's functioning and situation. The intent is not, as in some models of practice, to gather and sift a large body of information about these areas to serve as a basis for determining what the client's difficulties are. Rather, the practitioner's purpose is to secure information that will provide guidance in work with problems whose essential outlines have already been determined, not on the basis of what is "wrong" from a theoretical perspective but on the basis of what is troubling the client.

The practitioner's assessment activities are responsive to difficulties encountered in resolving problems. If problems can be moved readily toward resolution, a minimal amount of assessment data may be obtained. When obstacles are encountered or when the complexities of the problem make it difficult to arrive at suitable tasks, more understanding is required. Assessment data are obtained and processed within whatever mix of theoretical frameworks seem to provide the most useful understanding of the problems, with priority given to formulations that have research support or that can be specified in measurable terms. Depending on the problem, the practitioner's attention may focus on the expectations, values, perceptions, and actions of particular family members, on specific interactive patterns or rules, on the family system as a whole, or on transactions between the family and its environments. Although a systems perspective provides a general orientation, this perspective does not preclude efforts to understand the individual. Formulations most heavily used include conceptions of problem dynamics developed for the task-centered model (Reid, 1978, 1981), communication theory (Watzlawick,

Beavin, and Jackson, 1967), and the assessment theories of selected approaches to family therapy, principally behavioral (Jacobson, 1981), structural (Aponte and Van Deusen, 1981), and strategic (Stanton, 1981).

Contextual Change

Although the model is directed at alleviating target problems, considerable attention is currently being paid to contextual change, particularly when target problems are narrowly defined or lack stability. A discussion of the ways in which positive contextual change can occur will add to the theory of the model as well as serve as a vehicle for illustrating its strategies and methods.

First, contextual change can occur as a direct consequence of alleviation of a target problem. In some cases, changes in other limited problems can produce ripple effects, setting in motion "beneficial" cycles of interaction. In other cases, work on the target problem itself can bring about change in attitudes, expectations, or interaction patterns that "go beyond" the problem, even if obstacles are not encountered. For example, the process of negotiating a specific disagreement may give participants new appreciation for each other's feelings about a number of considerations related to the disagreement or may result in some modification of how each relates to the others. In general, work on the session tasks, as well as successful attainment of tasks outside the session, can help family members improve communication, problem-solving, and coping abilities.

Second, efforts to change the target problem may be accompanied by concomitant attempts to modify factors closely related to the target problem. This strategy can be illustrated by different approaches that might be taken to help John and Betty work out a target problem involving care of their infant son, Tony. Betty, who has just resumed working part-time, is upset over John's apparent unwillingness to assume greater responsibility for care of Tony so she can increase the hours she spends working. Her husband, a draftsman, could do some of his work at home. In fact, he had agreed to get permission to do so before Tony was born but has been putting this off. John admits that he did promise to arrange to work at home but says that his work situation has become tense and he is reluctant to make any demands at this point. Remarks made by Betty and John in the ensuing discussion give the practitioner reason to believe that John was opposed to having a child at this time and viewed Tony somewhat as Betty's project; Betty in turn seemed to resent John's hands-off attitude and his lack of appreciation for her assuming most of the child-care responsibilities for Tony.

A practitioner might deal with the target problem in one of two ways. She could concentrate on resolving the immediate problem through session tasks in which the couple worked out a compromise about care of Tony. Issues concerning John's reluctance to have a child and Betty's feelings of not being appreciated would not be taken up. On the other hand, in addition to dealing with the target problem, the practitioner, perhaps through additional session tasks, might help the couple clarify these issues and attempt to achieve some resolution of them. In the first approach, the focus is limited to change in the target problem. In the second, an effort is made to alter the context of the problem.

It is seldom completely clear whether contextual factors should be dealt with or to what extent. In the example just given, it could be argued that resolution of the target problem might be sufficient. A change in the problem would presumably bring about some positive change in its context. The partners could be given the responsibility for dealing in their own way with remaining issues. In fact, it might be better to allow the issues to remain dormant for the time being—to give both Betty and John time to adjust to their new roles as parents. But justification for going further can also be found: any solution to the immediate problem might be short-lived or comparable problems might flare up unless these issues were satisfactorily dealt with. Moreover, the contextual change being attempted would have a generally beneficial effect on their relationship.

Third, contextual change may occur in the process of working through obstacles preventing resolution of target problems. For example, in one case, the target problem consisted of a conflict between a father and his daughter over her coming home excessively late, or on occasion staying out all night. Efforts to reach a compromise between father and daughter on this issue were undermined by a mother-daughter coalition against the father. The obstacle was defined as this triangular pattern. Working through this obstacle involved session tasks between father and daughter accompanied by a calculated effort to prevent mother from siding with daughter (or daughter turning to mother) and session tasks between the parents, who were asked to develop a plan for dealing with the problem. Home tasks called for the daughter to come home at a mutually accept-able time and for the father to give her driving lessons if she did; as her task, the mother was asked to demonstrate support for the contract between father and daughter. These tasks not only alleviated the target problem but brought about at least temporary modification of a "problem-breeding" coalition.

The primary approach to contextual change is, however, through work on the target problem. Although the task-centered approach makes use of structural change and methods (Aponte and Van Deusen, 1981), as in the example above, structural modification is not a prerequisite of problem change. Moreover, work on structural as well as other patterns is carried out in a more explicit and collaborative way than is typical of structural therapy. In the illustration given, the nature of the obstacle (the mother–daughter coalition) was made clear with the family and an effort was made to engage their active cooperation to work on it.

The final way in which contextual change can occur is through use of resources within the family as a means of resolving the target problem. Although most successful tasks in family treatment involve use of resources within the family (strengths, skills, coping abilities, and so on), reference here is to more explicit use of the family as a resource. Perhaps the clearest examples occur when the target problem involves difficulties that a member is experiencing outside the family. (For purposes of the present discussion I assume the member is a child; an example involving an elderly member is given in Chapter 8.) In some situations these difficulties can be best tackled through work on dysfunctional patterns within the family that may be causing the problem or that may constitute an obstacle to its resolution. In other situations, however, the connection between the child's difficulties and family functioning is not clear but still the practitioner can identify resources within the family that might be brought to bear on the problem. In applying these resources to the problem, benefits beyond problem alleviation can occur. For example, in another case, the target problem concerned behavior difficulties that David, age 15, was experiencing at school. He would "mouth off" to teachers who tried to reprimand him for minor infractions. The mouthing off had resulted in repeated suspensions. David had recently begun to live with his father, having left his mother with whom he was having serious conflicts (the parents had divorced some years before). His relationship with his father, which had not yet jelled, was beginning to develop tension around the school problem.

The practitioner used the father as a resource in work on the school problem through a series of session tasks. The tasks stressed role-plays which were used in part to avoid tempting the father to lecture to his son about the school difficulties. Instead, the father took the role of his son with the son in roles of a critical teacher or provocative peer. In these tasks, the father was able to model for his son means of handling the kinds of situations that were getting him into trouble and to do so in specific and convincing ways. What might be useful for the son was emphasized by the practitioner in the post-task discussion. (Other types of session tasks as well as home tasks were used to reinforce the theme of how the father might help the son.) The immediate objective was to alleviate the school problem; at the same time, father and son were being given the opportunity to develop their relationship around a meaningful issue while avoiding disruptive conflict.

Phases and Procedures

What follows is an outline of steps of the model currently used in the Task-Centered Family Treatment Project. Material available elsewhere (in this volume and in Reid, 1978, 1981) has been highly condensed in order to highlight newer developments.

A. Initial Phase

The initial phase is ideally accomplished in a single two-hour session, though it may involve two or more sessions. Whatever its span, the following steps are followed.

1. Problem Survey. The practitioner elicits statements from family members on what each sees as the problems to be worked on. She or he permits the family to present its problems in its own style. She allows give and take among family members but makes sure that each has a chance to voice his or her opinions about the problems for which help is sought. The practitioner's role at this point is primarily that of facilitator of the family members' presentations. Questions are few and aimed primarily at clarification of meaning and detail.

2. Initial Problem Exploration and Formulation. After each family member has been heard from, the practitioner explores more actively the areas of difficulties that have been presented. Explorations are guided by hypotheses about what family members view as problems rather than by notions of what the underlying issues "really" are. In other words, she attempts to help family members explain what is on their minds rather than to investigate her own ideas about what might be wrong. In this process, she may help clients put into words thoughts and observations that they have been reluctant to reveal in the initial problem survey or may raise questions about apparent areas of difficulty that have not been presented as problems.

As the exploration proceeds, she begins to organize points of concern into tentative conceptions of problems. The emphasis at this point is on *what* the trouble is as the family members see it and not on how things got that way, although the practitioner may need to be tolerant of the clients' needs to trace the origins of the problem as they see them. At this point, it is not necessary to require a large amount of detailed knowledge on the frequency of the problem or the intricacies of its operation. But enough detail is needed in order to describe it adequately for subsequent prioritization and to see whether it may be combined with other issues. Sweeping or vague statements of issues need to be specified. Family members agree that "we fight all the time." The practitioner wants to know about what and how. Who does what to whom, how, and under what circumstances is a question that is repeatedly asked in different ways at this stage of the process.

Sometimes a problem is expressed originally in terms of some very specific, often transient issue. When asked what she sees as problems in the family, Jody says only, "My mom won't let me go to Sandy's party on Thursday." Or sometimes it is stated as a series of specific behaviors: "Mike doesn't keep his room straight, won't take out garbage like he's supposed to, talks back when he is asked to do something." Although expressions at this level should be taken seriously and in fact provide essential details of potential target problems, they may be too limiting to provide adequate foci for work or may result in an unwieldy number of issues.

An attempt is made to explore more general problems that are reflected by these very concrete difficulties. The practitioner tries to help the family formulate problems that are specific enough so that it will be clear what will be worked on and when, but not so limited that their solution would not make an appreciable difference in the life of the family. Thus, in the first case above, the practitioner after some exploration might offer the thought that Jody and her mom seem to be at odds about Jody's choice of friends. In the second, the practitioner, again after some more exploration, might suggest that there seems to be a tug-of-war between Mike and his parents about what chores Mike is to do and when he is to do them.

As the foregoing examples suggest, "For whom is what a problem?" is another central question in this phase. The practitioner attempts to be clear about who is troubled—the acknowledger of the problem—and where the acknowledger "locates" the problem—that is, who or what is viewed as generating it. For example, is the problem located in another person in the family relationship (Doris is a screamer), or in the community (Pat's teacher is a cipher)? If one family member acknowledges a problem, how do others view it?

The practitioner attempts to identify shared acknowledgments of problems and where possible to recast problems expressed in individual terms as problems of interactions between family members or as problems of the family as a whole. These reworkings of the problem are checked out with the family.

Fred, do you share your wife's concern that the two of you don't do enough together?

Joyce, you think that Harry never wants to part with a dime—and Harry says you are an impulsive spender—so this seems to add up to a disagreement about how your money should be handled.

Each of you seems to think that someone else in the family causes
these arguments. That's natural, but at least you agree that continued arguing is a problem.

The major reason for securing shared acknowledgments and putting
problems in terms of interactions in family units is to begin to create a
climate of joint responsibility for the family's difficulties. Sometimes it
may not be possible to move very far in that direction in the initial
interview. Problems expressed by family members may not be closely
related and each may be expressed as faults in another's behavior. Under
such circumstances, the practitioner tries to help each family member
articulate some change he or she would like to see in the family so that
each has some investment in at least one problem. To be avoided are
problem formulations in which one family member is given or accepts
total responsibility for the family's troubles.

Finally, the practitioner may suggest problem formulations based on
difficulties that family members refer to or act out in the interview but
which are not verbalized as problems. These formulations, which may be
used to broaden the family's conception of its difficulties, are offered as
possibilities for the family to consider and react to. If there is recognition
that the difficulty the practitioner has formulated is in fact a concern, the
problem may be added to the list for the family to rank in the next step.

3. *Determining Target Problems and Goals.* The initial problem
exploration should usually produce several issues that have been clarified
in the preceding step. The practitioner states these roughly in the order of
their presumed importance to the family. The following guidelines are
used:

- The problems are stated in terms that are readily understandable
  to the family members.
- To the extent possible, problems should be expressed as difficulties
  of interactions or of family units.
- To the extent possible, each family member present should view
  himself or herself as gaining from the solution of at least one
  problem.
- The responsibility for problems identified should not be located
  in one family member.

The problems are then ranked by the family members in the order in
which they would like to see them solved.

The practitioner records and reviews the rank orderings and suggests
a way of proceeding based on the data the family members have supplied.
Generally the practitioner suggests which problem she thinks should be

dealt with first and indicates how other problems can be worked in. Normally the problem suggested for immediate work is the one selected as the most important by most family members present. If the family is split on its choice, then the practitioner usually selects the problem that seems most amenable to change on grounds that it is important to achieve some progress quickly. The second problem can be phased in almost immediately (the following week) and the two then can be worked on together.

Even if the family agrees on the "number one" problem, there may be grounds to suggest that it not be taken up at once—it may need further clarification, it may be laden with more conflict than can be handled, and so on. It may make more sense to begin with a more readily manageable problem of lower priority to start positive changes in motion and to set the stage for work on the more important issue. Reasons for these variations are shared with the family and its approval obtained.

Generally no more than three problems are chosen as targets at this point. It is pointed out, however, that the problem list can be modified as work proceeds. Problems can be revised, added, or dropped, and priorities can be rearranged.

Once agreement on problems has been reached, goals for each problem are clarified. Goals reflect what family members hope to achieve in effecting solutions for the problems. Often the practitioner can suggest goal statements based on prior discussion of the problem or the way the problem is formulated. For a problem of conflict between mother and daughter over the daughter's boyfriend, the goal might naturally be some reduction in conflict. It may be neither realistic nor necessary to call for elimination of conflict on this issue. Or if the problem of natural parents is the loss of their child to the child welfare system and they have made it clear that they wish to have their child back, then the goal is again rather apparent. However, if the problem were stated as "missing their child" and it was not clear what they wanted to do about it, there could then be several goal possibilities: reducing their feelings of longing, securing visiting arrangements, or a return of the child. When the goal is not apparent, the practitioner needs to explore possibilities with the family members, beginning with those who appear to have the greatest stake in the solution of the problem.

4. Orientation and Contract. Once agreement on target problems and goals has been reached, the practitioner explains the approach she plans to use. The explanation makes clear that service will concentrate on the target problems and their immediate causes, that the practitioner's major role will be to guide the clients' own problem-solving efforts, which will be organized in the form of tasks, and that service will consist of so many interviews—usually 8 to 12.

The orientation to the model can precede the initial problem survey, and should if clients have questions at the beginning about the service the practitioner plans to offer. However, delaying the orientation to this point enables the practitioner to be more specific about what is to be done.

Client approval of the service plan is obtained; in the process clients' questions are answered or a rationale for different parts of the service plan are given. Some explanation of the reason for the service limits should usually be offered. The best rationale that can be given clients is simply that short-term service, according to a considerable amount of research, is usually as effective as a longer period of service—that whatever can be gained from counseling is usually gained quickly. Still, clients can be advised that service limits can be reconsidered as the agreed-on termination point approaches and more service offered if it seems indicated in their particular case.

Basically, the family's acceptance of the service plan as offered, explained, and qualified by the practitioner constitutes the service agreement or contract. It should be explained that the agreements are open to revision. Not only service limits but problems and goals can be modified with the clients' consent. It should be understood and can also be explained that the initial contract is an expression of a process of proceeding by explicit agreement that is designed to give the family clear control over the objectives of treatment.

5. *Detailed Exploration of the First Target Problem.* The target problems established in step 3 are explored in greater detail. The amount of time to be devoted to this step and what exactly is to be covered will depend on what has been revealed about the problem in previous steps. The following data, if not already obtained, are secured for each problem: (a) when approximately the problem began and outstanding facts about its course to present; (b) its severity and frequency during a brief period —from one to two weeks prior to the interview; (c) what efforts have been made to solve it; (d) obstacles preventing solution of problem and other relevant contextual factors.

6. *Initial Session Task.* The practitioner structures a session task on which family members work together for about five minutes on the first problem to be dealt with. The task serves both an assessment and therapeutic function. It provides the practitioner with in vivo data on how family members interact; more specifically, it provides data on their problem-solving and communication skills. Additional facets of the problem may also be brought to light. As a therapeutic device, it provides family members with an opportunity to begin to develop a solution to one of their problems and to begin the process of developing more constructive ways of interacting. The task may involve all family members present

or some other combination, such as a dyad, depending on the problem and communication patterns exhibited thus far in the session.

7. *Post-Task Discussion and Planning Initial Home Task.* After the session task has been brought to a close, the practitioner responds to the family's effort. Participants in the session task are given credit for positive aspects of their interactions. What has transpired in the task may lead to additional clarification of the problem. For example, some pattern of communication may be noted and the practitioner may enquire as to whether the pattern is similar to how the family members communicate at home.

The practitioner then generally helps the family develop one or more home tasks that can be carried out by family members prior to the next session. Usually the session task will have set the stage for the development of home tasks. In some cases, family members will have arrived at some type of action plan addressed to some aspect of the problem. The practitioner may need only to make sure that the plan can be set out in the form of specific actions or tasks that family members understand and agree to carry out. In other instances some directions for task planning will have emerged and can be built upon. When the session task does not provide momentum, the practitioner may need to determine what family members think they can begin to do about the problem. Their ideas then become the stimuli for task development. If the family cannot provide ideas, the practitioner then suggests task possibilities or one or more tasks. Tasks are planned and, if necessary, rehearsed, incentives established, and other task implementation procedures used (see introductory chapter).

In general, tasks are designed to be simple enough so that likelihood of their attainment is high but still should make a significant "bite" in the problem. They should be clearly stated, call for specific, feasible actions, and should be expressly agreed to by family members who are to carry them out. The principle of balance in who carries out tasks is important. Generally each participant in a problem should take on some task responsibility.

In trying to achieve appropriate task balance, it is useful to classify tasks into three types: *shared, reciprocal,* and *individual. Shared* tasks call for family members to work closely together in a cooperative manner. A couple agree to complete a home improvement project together on the weekend. *Reciprocal* tasks call for different actions by family members on the basis of a *quid pro quo* exchange. Nancy agrees to be home by 10 P.M. If she is, mother agrees not to ask her with whom she has been out. *Individual* tasks are carried out independently of others' task efforts. A father agrees to talk to neighbors about their children picking on his son, while mother and son will do a shared task.

Home tasks may be augmented by environmental tasks undertaken either by the practitioner (practitioner tasks) or by family members. For example, the practitioner may agree to confer with school officials about reinstatement of a child who has been expelled or an unemployed parent may agree to contact an employment agency. Depending on the problem, only environmental tasks may be used.

B. Middle Phase

The middle phase of treatment, which ideally begins with the second interview, consists of a series of weekly or twice-weekly sessions. Each session in this phase follows a similar format as that described below.

1. Task and Problem Review. The interview opens with a review of tasks attempted since the previous session as well as of developments in the target problems. Generally the task review is attempted first, although it may get temporarily displaced by developments in the problems, particularly if major changes for the better or worse have occurred. Should that be the case, the task review can be deferred until developments in the problems have been considered.

The task review covers what the clients or the practitioner have actually done in relation to the tasks agreed upon. Successful efforts or "good tries" by clients are credited. Difficulties in task implementation are explored. The resulting data may be used to guide subsequent task development.

Review of changes in the target problems is actually an elaboration of the task review which normally includes information on developments in the problems. Changes in the frequency and severity of problem occurrence are obtained as well as additional detail on the characteristics and context of the problem.

What happens next in middle phase interviews depends on the outcome of the problem and task reviews and related contextual factors. Several options are presented below together with consideration for their differential and combined use.

2. Problem Focusing. In family treatment, problems are often cast at a fairly general level or, if specific to begin with, may expand or shift. Tendencies toward diffuseness and instability in problem formulation is more of an issue in family than in individual treatment for several reasons.

Family members may be hard put to articulate amorphous interpersonal issues and to maintain agreement about their nature or relative importance. The family's concerns may jump from one issue to another depending on the course of interactive or environmental events. Finally, given the complexities of family interaction and constraints on communication in group sessions, hidden or underlying problems may surface after the initial contract has been formed. When the problem focus becomes blurred or unsteady, the practitioner faces a dilemma. On the one hand she wants to avoid drifting aimlessly with the flow of the system. On the other there is little point in rigid adherence to obsolete problem formulations. Problem focusing may be called for. In this procedure the practitioner attempts to make explicit connections between the issue on the table and agreed-on target problems. If some reasonable link can be made, work may proceed, perhaps with a modified conception of the target problem. There may be need for further focusing, however, on what is to be dealt with in the session. If a link is not possible, the practitioner has three options: (1) to deal with the unrelated issues as a temporary diversion, which may be the only course of action if the issue is of crisis proportions (Rooney, 1981); (2) to take the position with the family that the issue, while of legitimate concern, is tangential to the original target problem(s) and would be better left for the family to deal with; or (3) to formulate the issue as a new target problem, possibly replacing an original problem that is no longer of major interest. Which of these options is best pursued is largely a judgment call, but whatever is done there should be clarity with the family about what is being worked on and agreement with the family about any significant changes in the formulation of the problem.

3. *Analysis of Obstacles.* During the course of the review of tasks and problems, obstacles to task achievement and problem change are frequently encountered. The essential difference between a target problem and an obstacle is that the former is a difficulty that the family and practitioner have contracted to change, and the latter is a difficulty standing in the way of progress toward resolution of the target problem. An obstacle may reside in the functioning of individual family members, in their interactions, or in external systems. Obstacles may range from minor matters to issues of greater magnitude than the target problem itself.

In analysis of obstacles the practitioner uses a variety of cognitive approaches to understanding and resolving barriers to forward movement. The process may overlap with the problem and task reviews, when obstacles may be identified and explored. Methods of cognitive restructuring may be used to help individual family members modify distorted perceptions or unrealistic expectations of one another (Reid, 1978). Dysfunctional patterns of individual behavior or family interactions may be pointed out. Obstacles involving the external environment, such as interactions between a child and school personnel or the workings of a recalcitrant welfare bureaucracy, may be clarified. An effort is made to avoid concentrating attention on the functioning of any one family member as well as explanations that would provoke defensive reactions. Explanations, when used, are couched in terms that show the constructive intentions of family members ("positive interpretations"). The focus is on interaction rather than on individual behavior. When obstacles involve family interaction, analysis works best when overt conflict in the session is not too high and when family members are able to profit from an understanding of what is going on among them.

4. *Session Tasks and Discussions.* Session tasks enable family members to work together on their problems as well as to improve problem-solving and communication skills. Tasks involve family members communicating directly with one another for a few minutes as in the initial session task, with the practitioner in roles of observer, facilitator, and coach. The tasks are designed by the practitioner to achieve limited objectives, which include negotiating a conflict, planning an activity, arriving at a decision, clarifying feelings and expectations, or practicing communication skills. Because experience with session tasks within the framework of the model has just begun to accumulate, indications or contraindications for their use are not yet clear. They present an obvious challenge to the practitioner when a family member, often an adolescent, is reluctant to participate or when conversations become quarrelsome. It should be noted that the notion of "session task" preserves an essential criterion of a client task as it is used in the model—that is, a task involves work that clients can do on their own. Any session task should be capable of being done by family members at home.

Before setting up the first of these session tasks, the practitioner explains their purpose—to help family members work out their own solutions and to improve their ability to communicate with one another—and goes over certain "ground rules" that will facilitate their work. For example, participants are advised to talk directly to one another, to concentrate on the problem at hand, to avoid abusive language, and to be as concrete as possible when discussing problems or solutions.

Each session task is followed by a short discussion which may involve all family members present. The practitioner generally starts off with comments or questions related to the implementation of the task. Comments might include what was accomplished, what is demonstrated, what obstacles seemed to occur. Efforts of the participants are praised whenever possible. Possibilities for home tasks may be identified. The post-task discussion may also provide the basis for structuring another session task.

The most important criterion in choice of session tasks is the problem or obstacle addressed. The practitioner normally proposes a particular kind of task for a given problem or obstacle. For example, if the target problem consisted of family members not spending enough time together, an appropriate session task involves their planning joint activities. It is assumed that work on such straightforward tasks will often be blocked by various obstacles, usually in the interaction between the participants. These obstacles can be addressed by additional session tasks. For example, a couple attempts to negotiate an issue between them but fails to do so. One reason seems to be that they are "talking past one another and not listening to what each is saying." This pattern is called to their attention but they continue to exhibit the same communication problem. The practitioner, observing that their emotional involvement in the issue may be preventing them from correcting the communication difficulty, devises a task in which they communicate about a less volatile issue, beginning each of the responses with a paraphrase of what the other has just said (Jacobson and Margolin, 1979). Alternatively, obstacles arising from session tasks, particularly if they reflect larger issues, may be dealt with through the methods discussed in the preceding section (Analysis of Obstacles).

5. *Planning Home and Environmental Tasks.* The latter portion of the session is devoted to planning of home and environmental tasks. Procedures for planning the initial task are followed, although the planning process may be begun earlier since there may be a larger number of possibilities to be considered. Session tasks may have suggested possibilities that can be pursued or may have produced plans that need only to be fine-tuned.

When session tasks are not used or do not provide a sufficient base, planning for tasks outside the session is derived from the problem and task reviews, problem exploration and focusing, and analysis of obstacles. Regardless of the source of task possibilities, the practitioner is guided by one central question: Who can do what about the problem between this session and the next? The remainder of the session will focus on considerations in planning home tasks, the most common and most important tasks done outside the session. Additional material on task planning may be found in Reid (1978, 1981) and in Fortune's introductory chapter to this volume.

A fundamental principle in helping clients plan home tasks is to concentrate on alleviating target problems through relatively simple, straightforward tasks. These tasks may be designed to effect contextual change in passing but the target problems should be the first priority. Structural dysfunctions, underlying pathologies, and so on are left alone unless they intrude as obstacles. To the extent that they do, practitioners can then shift toward tasks more directed at contextual change—tasks, including paradoxical varieties, that may be aimed at structural modifications. This progression from the simple to the not-so-simple has a good fit to the model used by social workers who deal with a wide range of family types, from normal to highly disturbed, across a wide variety of problems and settings, and who may not be expert in family therapy. Many families do not want a change in structure; many problems do not require it; and many practitioners lack the skill to effect it.

Certain functions, limitations, and planning requirements can be identified for each of the major types of home tasks—shared, reciprocal, and individual. Shared tasks provide a means for continuing at home problem-solving and communication tasks worked on in the session, for enabling family members to work together on practical projects, such as home improvements, and for affecting relationships between family members. In respect to the last function, family members can be brought closer together through activities that are mutually enjoyable, or alignments can be strengthened or weakened. For example, two sets of shared tasks, one set involving both parents in some activity, and the other set, the siblings in a separate activity, can be used to strengthen the boundary of the parental subsystem and weaken a coalition between a parent and a child.

Reciprocal tasks make use of the principle of reciprocity in arranging for exchanges between family members. Exchanges may involve comparable behaviors, as is usually the case among family members who occupy equal statuses, such as husband and wife. In another form, compliance to rules may be exchanged for rewards (or noncompliance for penalties)—the form reciprocal tasks usually take between unequals, such as parents and children.

Whatever their form, reciprocal tasks require that participants express a willingness to cooperate and regard the exchange as equitable. Although it is important to work out the details of the exchange in the session, a "collaborative set" (Jacobson and Margolin, 1979) is essential to ensure that participants are prepared to accept reasonable approximations or equivalents of expected behavior rather than letter-of-the-law performance and are willing to adjust expectations in the light of unanticipated circumstances. All of this suggests that work in the session toward clarifying and negotiating conflicts around particular issues precedes the setting up of reciprocal tasks to deal with the issues at home. If reciprocal tasks are "tacked on" at the end of session without sufficient preparatory work, they are likely to fail.

Individual tasks, which do not require collaborative activity or specific reciprocation, serve several important functions in the model. First, they provide opportunities for family members to volunteer independent problem-solving action for the common good. Much problem solving in everyday family life seems to occur this way. Family members may do what needs to be done to help solve a problem without expectations of immediate pay-back, though they may expect that others will eventually do their share. Second, individual tasks are useful in situations of conflict too intense to allow for collaboration or exchanges between family members. For example, a husband and wife may agree to take on tasks with provisions for self-administered rewards if completed, along lines of the "parallel" contract (R. L. Weiss, Birchler, and Vincent, 1974). An adolescent who is rejecting parental authority may be willing to pursue tasks in his or her self-interest that may also help alleviate a family problem. A third function for individual tasks arises when the lack of autonomy in a relationship is an obstacle to change. For example, a diabetic youngster who is being smothered by overprotective parents might undertake a series of tasks designed to enable him to be responsible for his own medication. Finally, independent tasks can be used to involve a family member left out of reciprocal or shared tasks undertaken by other family members.

Practitioners make use of formulations concerning task functions in suggesting task possiblities to clients, in responding to the client's ideas for tasks, and in the give-and-take of the planning process. These formulations as well as other knowledge inform the practitioner's contribution to collaborative work with the family; they do not provide a set of rules for "task assignments."

C. Final Session

The terminal interview should begin with a review of the family's progress during treatment. It helps the family examine what has been accomplished and sets the stage for subsequent consideration of what it may wish to work on after treatment has terminated. The review should begin with examinations of change in the target problems. For each problem, the practitioner should determine the extent and direction of change from the point of view of each family member present. Remaining issues relating to these problems as well as other problems of concern to family members should then be explored.

The family's plans for dealing with difficulties that they are currently facing should be considered, with emphasis on how the approaches used in the model can be applied to them. Plans for a follow-up session or needs for additional help and how it may be obtained can be discussed. The family's sense of having made some progress, which should be present in most cases, is highlighted and reinforced. More detail of the final session is included in Reid (1978, 1981) and in Fortune's introductory chapter to this volume.

Concluding Observations

The developments emphasized in this chapter can be seen as an experimental and theoretical effort that will evolve as work continues. They can also be viewed as adding to, rather than supplanting, existing task-centered family approaches, which give less explicit attention to contextual change and place relatively greater stress on the planning, implementation, and review of tasks done outside the session.

Further work on the present variant of task-centered family treatment will be guided by certain goals. A sharper definition of contextual change will need to be developed and better ways of measuring it devised. We shall try to enlarge and systematize our array of session tasks and improve procedures and criteria for their use. Finally, we shall attempt to identify effective sequences of session, home, and environmental tasks for given types of problems and obstacles.

Intergenerational Family Practice with Older Families

8

Eloise Rathbone-McCuan

Introduction

This chapter provides a brief overview of the task-centered approach in situations where the elderly and their family members are experiencing problems in daily living. In working with the elderly, inclusion of the family is recommended for ameliorating problems that have impact on the family unit while also maintaining a sense of personal security, dignity, and worth for the older person (Kent and Matson, 1972). The role of the practitioner is primarily to act as a catalyst to maintain or activate the supportive functions of the extended family (Bloom and Monro, 1972). In the midst of crises, practitioners can rally the older family into a working unit (Kuypers and Trute, 1978) and help them move beyond crises into increased functionality. The task-centered model provides guidelines and techniques which are readily adaptable to such work with older families.

Despite all the literature on the aged and the family published throughout the past two decades (Streib and Beck, 1980; Troll, 1971), there has been a lack of field research that investigates treatment approaches with the older family. The available outcome data do not answer the question of which treatment approaches are most effective with this type of family. The task-centered model is like other approaches in the lack of extensive testing with older families and individuals (Reid, 1975, 1978; Reid et al., 1980). However, the task-centered approach has been utilized as the clinical method in the training of gerontologists who specialize in mental health practice with older women (Rathbone-McCuan, 1982) and as a methods base to provide supportive services to elderly with health and mental health problems (Fortune and Rathbone-

McCuan, 1981). These efforts have emphasized primarily elderly persons receiving individual services.

This chapter extends the model by exploring why the elderly and their families may benefit from a short-term family-oriented problem-solving approach in both crisis and noncrisis situations. Several approaches are analyzed for their relevance to helping intergenerational family members cope with stressors associated with the aging process. A case is discussed indicating how to apply the task-centered method with an elderly woman and her middle-aged daughters. Problem resolutions are very likely to occur if therapy increases awareness and mutual support of individual needs within the daily life of each member. Short-term action-producing therapy can improve the unit's functionality if this is a family goal. Specific suggestions are made about how to modify the task-centered approach to maximize its potential with older families.

Issues Relevant to the Older Family

A multigenerational and extended family context is useful in discussing treatment of the elderly. The family of the aged can be defined as that group of individuals to whom older people are related by blood or marriage; thus, the family goes beyond immediate members to include persons somewhat distantly related by blood or marriage (Shanas, 1979).

One of the possible reasons for the lack of development of family counseling approaches with older families is a widespread belief that there is alienation between the elderly and younger generations. This misperception has been challenged by leading gerontologists such as Shanas (1979, 1980) and Brody (1966, 1977, 1981). The majority of older persons are part of a family or kinship structure. Siblings and children are important family members who maintain communication, provide supportive care, and are engaged in helping the aged. Helping need not necessarily be given by the young to the old in a one-way pattern. Rather, there is a mutuality in the family support pattern (Riley and Foner, 1968) that occurs within and between generations and among blood- and marriage-connected individuals. Older people have something to give within the family and in their friendship networks that can reduce isolation and promote emotional well-being for the family (Dowd, 1981). Although perceptions of the older person as chronically ill or impaired are negative stereotypes, increasing dependency on family support is a natural part of the aging process for many older people. Families do provide the majority of care and assistance to the aged (Uhlenberg, 1974), often at costs to themselves and the larger family unit.

Between 1900 and 1977, the percentage of the population age 65 and older more than doubled from 4.1 percent or 3.1 million to 10.9 percent or

23.5 million people. Older people may comprise 12 to 13 percent of the total population by the year 2000. Simply stated, as America is aging so is the family; more attention must be given to this issue at the national social policy level and among the social, health, and mental health professions (Brody, 1981). For practitioners, this suggests that elderly and families with elderly members will be an increasing target group for social work intervention.

The family frequently experiences stressors in relation to elderly parents or other relatives. R. Hill (1949) defines stressors as those life events or occurrences of sufficient magnitude to bring about change in the family system. The range of events is broad and involves issues of personal and environmental resource availability, power and control, losses, changes, restrictions in functioning, finances, illness, and death. Streib and Beck (1980) suggest that specific stresses encountered in older families are related to the nurturance, economic, residential, and legal/cultural functions family units fulfill. Older individuals and their younger relatives react and cope with these stressors. How the family system as a whole responds will influence the aged individual, and what the elder does about stress feeds back into the family unit's coping. Stressors and stress within the older family can create isolation among family members in their intrafamily as well as extrafamily context. Isolation of individual family members and the disconnectedness of families from the resources in their external environment place families at risk (Rathbone-McCuan and Hashimi, 1982).

Intervention Perspectives with Older Families

In general, older families require interventive assistance because of daily living problems manifest in relation to basic functions. Inadequate emotional support, overwhelming caregiving activities, the absence of economic resources or poor management and distribution, difficulties ensuring adequate living arrangements, and questions of competency and incompetency are a few examples of the types of problems that families experience and bring for intervention when they seek help.

The process of obtaining professional help is difficult for some families, but no single barrier is impossible to resolve. Accessibility to counseling can be increased for the family if traditional geriatric services introduce some supportive counseling programs for families. These programs can be added to home health services, adult day centers, or outpatient clinics. Older families can also be referred to mental health clinics or to private practitioners. An increasing number of geriatric practitioners are beginning to develop skills to work with older families as part of the elder's informal support network and to introduce respite care into the home care plan for community-based aged clients. However, this greater availability does not preclude the need for new more efficient counseling approaches. The need for these is increasing. Adaptations of systems theory as a framework for analyzing the problems of older families can be essential to improving practitioners' skill and effectiveness. Familiarity with short-term counseling approaches can also increase the competencies of the counselor.

The family systems framework is a basic foundation for much of the family counseling now being offered by mental health practitioners. Evolution of family system theory has progressed steadily in the past 20 years (Kerr, 1981). Precisely how the assumptions of that framework apply to older families is undeveloped. The author suggests that priority should be given to this development. First, the boundaries of a family must be expanded to accommodate the elderly individual or the oldest generation's place in the family system. The eldest members are part of the family and are as interrelated as younger members even if all generations are not living in the same household. Second, the interactive influences of subsystems within the family do include behaviors of elderly parents and relatives. These aged persons, regardless of physical and mental ability, are part of the family group and their problems cannot be understood in isolation from other subsystem influence. Third, the functionality or dysfunctionality of oldest members is included as part of the overall patterns within the family. The structure and functioning of the family system will have impact in a cause-and-consequence pattern on the aged. Fourth, the generational communication channels extend beyond the younger members to include communication among older members and between the youngest and oldest members. Interactions between the elderly members and other family members will have influence on the behaviors of all members.

Further understanding of the family systems theory as appropriate for older families can be gained through an analysis of certain theoretical concepts. Examining concepts must be built into theoretical development. Bowen, a well-known family therapy theorist, has attempted to sort out which of his eight theoretical concepts have special relevance in later life and impact on dynamics of older families (Bowen, 1977).

Differentiation of Self and Emotional Cutoff are the two concepts that have been explored most intensely by those practicing within a Bowen perspective. Differentiation of Self is a conceptual scale that provides an orientation about the degree and pattern of individuation of each member from the larger system with a mix or balance between independence and togetherness being viewed as optimal. Individuals in the middle generation have needs to develop and maintain some autonomy from both the older and younger generations. Personal goals and responsibilities for meeting individual needs must be balanced with needs of children and aged parents. If some balance is maintained, a differentiation of self within family relations is possible. Emotional Cutoff refers to the way people handle fusion with families of origin, especially in relation to connections or disconnections with parents (Kerr, 1981). Emotional attachments to older members are likely to change over time. Middle-aged children can be successful in completing some emotional cutoff from older parents without a complete disconnection. Complete breaking of the bonds is a probable source of anxiety and guilt for adult children.

The conceptual principles developed by Boszormenyi-Nagy and Spark (1973) are also useful in evaluating the dependence–interdependence–independence struggles among generations of family members. These dynamics may extend into the children's adulthood and become a focal issue among middle-aged children and their aging parents. Specific concepts that are evolved from systems theory guide an evaluation of the type and degree of connection appropriate to specific situations and offer clues about the desired direction of stress-reducing change. However, these efforts at relating the psychodynamic-based family systems theories to the aging family are of limited value. They do not produce information useful to the design of specific intervention strategies.

Practitioners working with the elderly are often placed in a position of having to intervene under less than optimal circumstances. Not only are there gaps in the theory of family intervention, but the problems which bring the older family into treatment often have an immediate urgency to them and problem-solving must be initiated rapidly. The assessment and diagnostic activities of the practitioner continue to be essential, but the time available for diagnosis may be greatly reduced compared to families where the aged member's situation is not a focal concern.

The task-centered model, with its problem specification, time limitations for treatment, contracts for therapeutic activities, active client input in problem definition and needs identification, and clarity of task definition, is a promising approach for immediate short-term intervention with older families. It has already been field-tested with cases of elder abuse and victimization (Rathbone-McCuan, Travis, and Voyles, 1983). It can also be easily integrated with the selected concepts of systems theory already mentioned to provide a family-systems approach. The next section describes a case that illustrates such an integrated approach.

Balancing Needs among Oldest and Middle-aged Generations

This section presents a case illustration where the task-centered approach was applied with an older family. The case was selected to illustrate some of the common relationship issues among middle-aged daughters and their mothers. The case was not considered crisis intervention at the point of initial contact, but during treatment there was a near crisis which required a shift in problem priorities, after which the focus of activity returned to the original tasks.

Martha, a 68-year old white woman, was self-referred to the Older Adult Counseling Program at a multiservice senior center. She had been widowed several years and was paying large house payments and struggling to live on a fixed income. She was in good health and irregularly active at the senior center. She had two living daughters: Alice was 37 years old, married, with two children in grade school and a husband recovering from a heart attack. Barbara was 35 and had recently been divorced after a brief and conflictual marriage. Martha expressed her anxiety about managing her finances, fearing she was headed for an economic crisis, but was very angry at her daughters for trying to run her life.

Martha's statement of her problems indicated her blaming her daughters for behaving in ways that she did not want them to; she did not perceive the situation in either a transactional or relational context, but purely as an unwanted excess of their behavior.

At the end of the first meeting, the practitioner asked Martha to invite Alice and Barbara to come to the next session. They came, expressing pressure to find the time. The practitioner explained that Martha's situation seemed to involve her daughters and that she wanted to work with the family if they were agreeable, since she preferred to involve families whenever possible. Both daughters recognized their mother's anxiety, but were ambivalent about their participation. The practitioner requested that they come for another session before deciding not to participate.

In the second joint session the practitioner engaged the three in problem specification by encouraging them to express their feelings and stressing the legitimacy of those feelings. Eventually they were able to articulate a number of problems:

> Martha's problem statement: I don't want to lose my house, it is the
>   only thing I have which gives me financial security. Barbara
>   could come and live with me because she is divorced and has no
>   children, but she isn't concerned about me, just herself.
> Alice's problem statement: I cannot stand being pulled by my
>   mother's needs and my husband and kids. Everybody demands
>   of me, but nobody seems to take any responsibilities to help me.
> Barbara's problem statement: Mother has always dominated my life,
>   but this time I won't let her. I am planning to go to the West
>   Coast because I may have a good job there and I need to get on
>   with building a new life.

The practitioner summarized the problems, attempting to underline the transactional factors involved: Martha felt that Alice had greater loyalties toward her husband and family and that Barbara just simply did not care at all what was happening. Alice felt her mother was playing up her dependency and trying to manipulate everyone and that her sister was not giving any of the support she'd promised. Barbara blamed her mother for worrying her father to his grave and her sister for being unable to accept help. Each agreed with the practitioner's summary, but expressed anger at each other. The practitioner offered support by saying that each was being open and sharing feelings and perceptions that were painful to express.

The emotional isolation each family member was feeling from the others was evident in their statements, but there were also emotional pulls toward more closeness, as suggested by their willingness to express direct anger. The dynamics of self-differentiation among the three seemed to be creating conflictual behaviors and feelings. Unresolved emotional loyalties to self, others, and each other were also present.

At the third session the attributed problems previously given by each person were framed into target problems. One common target problem for the family was identified as lack of supportive behaviors to help the family through transition. An individual target problem was also identified for each in relating to the particular transition event each faced so that the value of mutual support was underscored. The individual goals were:

Martha: Get a roommate to reduce house payment burdens.
Alice: Reduce anxiety over Martha's demands.
Barbara: Prepare to relocate in California.

The mother and daughters had many unmet needs which were being presented to the practitioner. Some of these needs could be addressed through a change of behavior and communication, but also there was the immediate need to resolve basic problems or prepare for change. The practitioner found it useful to have them keep brief notes about the ways they needed help or support from each other and why that support was hard to either give or receive. When each person shared some of the content of her journal, it was easier for all to see that common feelings of nonsupport for each other could be more clearly and consensually formulated.

At the beginning of the fourth week a verbal contract was developed that encompassed the common target problem and the three individual target problems. Nine sessions with the possibility of several sessions within one week were included in the contract because Martha had to develop another source of funds immediately to cover her housing costs.

Alice wanted to work out an immediate way to provide more time to help her husband in his recovery and Barbara wanted to make preparation to go to California.

During the fourth and fifth sessions, held during the same week, emphasis was on planning tasks. Initially, all three women talked about individual tasks and did not propose any interactional, reciprocal, or shared tasks. The practitioner raised the question of why they were not considering more cooperation to get important things accomplished and pointed out that the family task was to be more supportive to each other. There was some resistance to the idea of shared tasks based on a lack of either trust or belief that some good for the individual could emerge from pooling efforts, but one shared and two reciprocal tasks were formulated. The middle stage of the intervention was devoted to the accomplishment of the following tasks:

Individual	Shared	Reciprocal
Alice was going to get more information from the physician about the in-home rehabilitation program for her husband and try to implement his suggestions.	Martha and both daughters would do a detailed assessment of the economics of their family.	Martha would be available to help Alice with children and Alice would pay her for her services.
Barbara would contact a former roommate now living in California to see if she could help begin finding housing for the move.		Martha agreed to have Barbara help her appraise her antiques and Barbara would help her dispose of them at a good price.
Martha was to look for a roommate and investigate the possibility of a second house mortgage.		

The implementation of these tasks progressed at different rates. Martha did not take much initiative to find a roommate and rationalized this by the amount of time she was spending with Alice's children. The three of them were able to complete an economic assessment of the resources, largely because Barbara pushed to use an accountant. Alice became angry at her mother's domination of her children and one session was held with Alice and Martha to develop clear ground rules over Martha's authority with the children. Several weeks before Barbara was to go to California for a job interview, her former husband initiated contact with her to explore the possibility of a reunion. Barbara requested an individual session with the practitioner in which she revealed her need to run to California as an escape from her positive feelings toward her former husband.

The formation of a possible relational triangle existed as Barbara and her former spouse contemplated the renewal of their interaction. Barbara had been uncomfortable with her mother and had been unsuccessful in eliminating the discomfort. One alternative, however counterproductive to the goals of the family intervention, might have been to draw the ex-spouse into an insider position. This could have resulted in a relationship fusion that would put the mother into a further dislocated position.

The practitioner suggested that the ex-husband and Barbara might seek some couple's counseling if she really wished to avoid her move until she had resolved the relationship issues. A near crisis occurred when Alice's husband had a major setback in his rehabilitation. At that point, without input from the counselor, Barbara and Martha rallied to support Alice by assuming numerous household and family responsibilities.

The eighth session was devoted to a review of what had been accomplished toward increased family supportiveness. The three shared their feelings about themselves as a family and felt that they could now feel more confident in their ability to support each other. Individual tasks were reviewed in the ninth session which completed the contract period. Martha had been able to locate a roommate, but was now considering selling her house and moving into senior citizen housing in a neighborhood closer to Alice so she could continue some supportive child-care functions. Barbara was in the final stages of her move to California. Alice was feeling very upset by the slow recovery process of her husband, but there was no further medical treatment that could be offered. There was some discussion about barriers the family might face if Martha became ill and Barbara was in California. All three were confident that they could resolve such a future problem and agreed that the family should keep in close touch and work together in any difficulties. The practitioner felt comfortable with the status of the family's functioning at that point so termination was completed.

Adaptation of Task-Centered Practice for Older Families

This case illustration involved two generations of women working toward bringing together their individual resources to strengthen a family system. To a limited extent, the original contact made by Martha represented the urgency of an aging mother not to drift into further isolation from her daughters. As she was becoming more fearful of her probable increased dependency, she was unconsciously testing Alice and Barbara. The benefits to this family were considerable; the approach provided an opportunity for Martha to take responsibility for herself and to give support. In cases where the older person is more impaired than Martha, it may be harder to involve the older generation. However, the task-centered approach provides sufficient flexibility in the design of tasks so that if the functional capacity of an older member is reduced, the difficulty and types of tasks can be modified to meet the level of functioning.

Families with multiple generations have a longer and more entrenched family dynamic history compared to younger two-generation family groups. If there is an accumulation of noncooperative behavior and conflicts, it may take longer than was required in this case to develop a family-focused target problem. The prompt introduction of clinical intervention is critical and even brief delays can be serious for all family members. The geographical dispersion of family members may make it impossible for all members to participate directly in each session; sometimes these individuals can be brought into the context with shared and reciprocal tasks. Finding ways of involving family members who are not frequently part of the immediate environment does require direct exploration of options before a task is finalized. At-distance family members do have some important limits that must be recognized in order to have realistic roles for them to play. Another issue is the extent to which family members who have not communicated with each for long periods of time may need the opportunity to update each other, especially if the kin is more distant. This can be handled by introducing the option of more sessions at the beginning of counseling.

The inclusion of systems theory helps the practitioner understand the patterns of family interaction. The establishment of tasks must fit within the family structure; otherwise tasks are hard to complete. Tasks can have some impact on changing structure, but must also rely on interactional patterns acceptable within the family. The practitioner cannot demand or expect immediate acceptance of unfamiliar patterns of family interaction; threatening new demands are likely to produce resistance throughout the family. The practitioner's understanding of problems of resistance is definitely increased by application of systems theory.

Some general recommendations to consider when working with the older family are as follows:

1. Participation of the elderly person must be safeguarded as there is a tendency in many families not to recognize the older member as able to be an equal participant—families may not want to include the older person in task accomplishment activities.

2. The likelihood of a severe illness occurring within the time frame of treatment suggests the need for practitioners to be competent to move into a crisis counseling context while continuing to adhere to the task-centered model.

3. The practitioner may need to be prepared to assume responsibility for more tasks than normal, especially when there are referrals for other service or the need to serve as family advocate.

4. The family treatment may need to be linked more closely with other supportive services utilized by some member of the family.

Conclusion

A major strength of the task-centered approach for working with older families may be that it fosters an opportunity for participation in actions relevant to issues of dependence-independence-interdependence. In family systems theory, this complex family dynamic has been considered with the child as the reference point, but it is a dynamic that is very much present in older families. Blenkner (1965) described the process of filial maturity, or appropriate acceptance of parental dependency, and others have suggested that it is an issue of boundaries and functions. However conceptualized, the search to find and maintain the independence-dependence balance is very central to the older family.

Families dealing with older members who are experiencing decreased functioning or environmental restrictions beyond the elderly person's control may find the elder struggling against the family's offer of help or resources. On the one hand, the significant others who wish to help may blame the older person for being resistant to help. On the other, the elderly person may interpret verbal and nonverbal behaviors as a threat to limited independence. These tensions can result from an infinite array of experiences. The more obvious ones include events such as institutionalization or relocation of the elder when the choice to do so is not under the full control of the older member. Lesser events such as changes in the care of grandchildren or divorce can also trigger anxiety and conflicts with intergenerational relations over independence.

The author has found that the fear of dependency is prevalent among older people and among many middle-aged persons. When the family begins to assume more direct hands-on caregiving or less intimate support functions for elders, it usually involves doing a task, taking an action. The range of interventive possibilities using the task-centered approach with older families facing the general dependency problem is probably very diverse. For the most part, work with older families takes place in a somewhat different therapeutic context than more traditional family therapy. Older families usually obtain treatment in the process of getting some tangible service. Their search for a resource(s) is an action of high enough priority to set help-seeking behaviors in motion. The counseling they receive should not disrupt this help seeking. It should facilitate the family system's access and utilization of resources. A significant amount of constructive change can occur within the system by using the service utilization event as a time for improving relational potential. The task-centered approach can be adapted to aiding the family to deal with tangible behavioral change as well as to facilitate insight and growth through task performance and goal accomplishment vital to the well-being of the older family.

9 Conjoint Treatment within the Task-Centered Model

Paul R. Mills, Jr.

Issues in Contextual Change

The escalating divorce rate and the pervasiveness of marital conflict have brought many couples to social workers for marital treatment. One approach to marital treatment is that provided through the task-centered model (Reid, 1977a, 1978, Chapter 7, above). This chapter discusses some issues in applying the model to marital treatment in general and illustrates these issues through the discussion of conjoint treatment with one couple.

Reid (1978, 1981, Chapter 7), Reid and Epstein (1972, 1977), Wise (1977), and Tolson (1976, 1977) have all discussed the extension and adaptation of the task-centered model to marital treatment. The core concepts those writers and this author found need most examination if the model is to be extended to marital treatment are task definition, task work, and task evaluation. The other core concept of time limits does not require additional conceptual work in applying the model to marital treatment. The need for further development of the concepts related to "task" derives from the interrelationship of tasks irrespective of the problem categories used to classify marital problems. Most couples define their problems within the category of interpersonal conflict, although marital problems have been classified under other categories such as problems of dissatisfaction in social relations, difficulties in role performance, inadequate resources, and decision problems. However, the distinction between interpersonal conflict and the other problem categories may be somewhat arbitrary, as in most cases the means or the effect of decisions and task work must take into consideration the marital partner and the relationship.

This dyadic context forms the major difference between individual and marital treatment and is the backdrop for the discussion of issues concerning task-centered marital treatment.

Extension of the model from work with individuals to work with marital couples may proceed in several ways. First, the model can be expanded as a simple extension of work with individuals, with each marital partner working on tasks in a marital context. Second, the level at which task work is done can be shifted to the metarule level, with a systems rather than individual focus. Each of these approaches will be discussed in detail.

By following the direction of the model's development with individual clients, the extension into couples treatment parallels the extension of the model to group treatment, where the focus is on the individual member's task work within the context of a group. In marital treatment, each partner's task is combined within the context of the couple (and family if appropriate). Since the individual level on which task work is performed has not changed in such an extension, the adaptations to marital treatment are readily apparent. Reid (1978), and Reid and Epstein (1977) propose that such an extension is appropriate if the behavioral task emphasis takes place within the norms of marital reciprocity and mutual devotion to each other. This set of norms helps preserve the character of the marital relationship as a group which has a life that extends beyond the treatment context. These norms may be understood by the practitioner as a metarule for working with marital couples. However, the addition of metarule analysis within the task-centered model may change the level of analysis and task definition, as will be discussed later in the chapter.

Framing the treatment as an extension of individualized task work within the context of a marital treatment focuses the treatment on the level of the couple's rules. Reid states (1978:191) ". . . 'rule' refers to regularities in interaction, either actual or potential. . . . For couples in marital conflict, descriptive rules generally describe the problem aspects of their relationships [actual], whereas prescriptive rules usually express the kind of relationship that one or both would like to have [preferred]." The degree to which descriptive rules are dysfunctional or the degree of felt dissonance between what is actual and preferred marital interaction form the marital problems from which tasks are formulated, worked on, and evaluated.

Such rule definition and task work become complicated, however, if the couple does not define its interactional problems in terms of mutually-agreed-upon rule problems. Often the stimuli for treatment occurs when one partner defines the other as owning the problem, while overlooking his or her own reaction or investment in the problem. Marital treatment can then degenerate to a triangular situation where the practitioner and one mate may try to assist the other partner in completing tasks beneficial to the first spouse. For example, defining the need to break off an extramarital affair as a task for one spouse may take into consideration only one partner's definition of a descriptive or prescriptive rule. One solution to this problem is to select tasks for which there is true reciprocity, as for a problem in which both partners participate equally in its origin and solution. For example, both may plan for a vacation which would be satisfactory to each of them. A second solution is to find individual tasks which, when put on that couple's "marital scale," balance each other out so each contributes equally. The tasks may be different, but both partners judge them to be of equal value for their marriage. An example here is that they may decide that one will be responsible for cleaning the outside of a house and the other the inside.

The first solution to imbalance, true reciprocity, has received more extensive development in the task-centered model than the second option. Building upon the approaches suggested by Rappaport and Harrell (1972), Azrin, Naster, and Jones (1973), and Tolson (1976), Reid (1978) suggests that the couple record events in detail so that the sequence of interactions in a problem area can be apparent to the couple. In this way, a specific problem is translated into a descriptive or prescriptive rule. Tasks are then derived which operationalize the changes the couple desire. Such tasks may be used to stop following a marital rule such as the previous way they disciplined the children (descriptive rule), or the tasks may be used to work on a prescriptive rule, such as finding a way to improve the romantic aspects of the marriage. By using a linear analysis of a sequence of events, task definition becomes designing actions which the client can take to alter the early steps in the marital sequence. This prevents the couple from repeating a dysfunctional cycle or introduces new alternative patterns which help them achieve their desired outcome. The practitioner in such treatment acts as an observer, assists the couple to become more aware of the steps in the sequence, and contracts with them to alter the sequence.

Examples of such an application are found in Tolson's work with a couple's communication problems (1976, 1977). She found that the way the couple interrupted each other, rather than listening and taking turns, prevented them from giving or receiving new information. By breaking the cycle of their noncommunication and making their communication more effective, Tolson and the couple hoped to deal effectively with other referent marital problems. Work on communication exercises and selection of well-defined tasks preserved the centrality of the task-centered model's reliance on client work and utilized their motivation to enhance task completion. A second example was in the treatment of the Knights, discussed later. Both partners wanted to recapture their early romantic feelings and so the first task was to reflect on what they previously found to be romantic. They returned to the next appointment reporting that they had enjoyed fishing together but had not done so for years. The task then was to plan and go on a fishing trip by themselves. Later they reported going on a day's fishing trip during which they caught few fish, but enjoyed being alone with each other to talk about their relationship.

The second option for developing balanced task work uses tasks in a different way. Rather than selecting tasks which the couple do together or simultaneously, and from which they both benefit (shared tasks), the tasks selected are different for each partner. As one partner performs a task, he or she is rewarded by the task work of the partner (reciprocal tasks). This approach recognizes that each partner is an individual within a relationship. If both partners complete the individualized tasks, the combination should lead to a more satisfying marital relationship and both should report an increase in marital satisfaction. Wise used this type of task in the White case (1977:86–87). Mrs. White improved her organization and implementation of housekeeping tasks in exchange for an increase in the frequency and length of time Mr. White spent with her in enjoyable activities. Tolson (1976) also used a similar approach in asking the wife to be more sexually assertive and the husband to be more supportive and less critical of the wife.

The use of reciprocal tasks in the treatment of marital conflict may be difficult to achieve when the practitioner is also trying to utilize the metarule of marital reciprocity. Wise (1977) reported that a lack of reciprocity or balance in couples' exchange of task work may have led some couples to fall short of completing individual task work. Part of the difficulty in balancing reciprocal tasks may be in selecting tasks which are too global, which allow one partner to work on tasks at a symptomatic level while the other is engaged in tasks more central to the marital problem, or which are specific for one partner and abstract for the other. Another issue is that of assessing the commitment to task work and to maintaining the marriage in general. If one partner is less committed than the other, it is difficult to formulate appropriate reciprocal tasks or to maintain both in treatment. Knox (1971), R. L. Weiss, Birchler, and Vincent (1974), and Stuart (1968) give useful means for developing different but mutually satisfying tasks while preserving the norm of reciprocity. Each of these authors recommends a procedure of giving a spouse credits or tokens for daily task completion. The tokens or credits are then used by that spouse to obtain a desired product or activity. For example, a husband may pay his wife for improved meal preparation and the wife may use the money to purchase new clothing.

With either the interaction-sequence or reciprocal-task approach to task planning, the emphasis is on extending the task-centered model's approach with individuals to marital treatment. Task work preserves many of the model's foundation concepts by utilizing the clients' own definition of problems and building on the clients' motivation to implement the steps in the treatment sequence. For example, the removal of barriers to task work or the implementation of guided practice is similar to the examples reported in work with individual clients. Work on contextual change (Reid, Chapter 7) is explicitly acknowledged and is at a specific, concrete level of individual behavior (or feelings) or at the level of descriptive and prescriptive rules.

The second major approach for extending the task-centered model in marital treatment is to conduct task work at the level of the couple's metarules (Reid, 1978, 1981). This moves the task work from the more concrete level of acknowledgeable descriptive and prescriptive marital rules to the more abstract level of metarule and a systems approach to marital treatment. Reid (1978, 1981) suggests that such a shift may be necessary for couples who are attempting to alter their relationship, rather than changing specific problems. Such a shift may also be necessary when obstacles lie in the couple's relationship and contextual change is therefore necessary to resolve target problems.

The shift to an analysis of the couple's metarules follows the work of Watzlawick, Beavin, and Jackson (1967) and Haley (1963, 1976), who state that communication has at least two components, a content component and a relational component. The content level is found in the couple's descriptive and prescriptive rules, while the relational level is evident in the metarule analysis, where the relationship is defined.

Utilizing a metarule analysis as a basis for treatment may do more than merely extend the task-centered model; it may significantly alter the model. First, these two approaches differ in their epistemology. The individual task-centered model rests on many of the assumptions found in other behaviorally oriented treatments, while metarule analysis uses the concepts found in systems theory (Colapinto, 1979). The meaning of concepts must be changed if the focus is not on the individual partners but on the system of the marital relationship itself. For example, linear analysis of cause and effect must be replaced with an analysis based on patterns or systems with interacting feedback.

A second problem is the degree to which treatment based on metarules can engage the client's awareness and conscious work on tasks. The task-centered model relies on the client's investment to complete tasks which the partners can accomplish themselves. Shifting to a metarule level may require that the clients think about their relationship in a different way. The relationship is then the focus, not the completion of tasks. Moving to the metarule level of abstraction may also open the door for the practitioner to work on her or his agenda, which may be outside of the couple's awareness, violating the key concept of using client awareness.

A third problem with use of metarules occurs if the couple works at the descriptive or prescriptive rule level, while the practitioner works at a metarule level which does not utilize the client's own problem-solving skills. The clients and practitioner may have a different orientation to the impact of task work on the marital relationship. At the metarule level of analysis the content may be reframed or the relative importance of content used to change the context of that content. This changes the relationship itself, not just its content. Changing the marital relationship then may so change the marriage that the old content of problems no longer fits the marriage, and a new set of problems may emerge. At other times such shifts help to resolve old marital problems in the way the birth of the first child changes the marital relationship. However, that change may create new descriptive and prescriptive rules or problems with those rules.

Bernal and Baker (1979) suggest that these levels of analysis may not be separated but rather nested within each other. This means that even though the couple may be working at a descriptive or prescriptive level, they may also be altering their relationship at the metarule level. Likewise, it may be that the practitioner working at the metarule level may also use descriptive or prescriptive rule work. The distinction is in the purpose or intent: change in the relationship or change in a marital rule.

A fourth problem is the allocation of power through designation of task work. Systems theorists such as Haley (1963, 1976) and Hoffman (1981) plan strategies directed at blocking or segregating the couple from other family members so that former ways of interacting can no longer be used and the relationship must change. These strategies require the practitioner to be directive and superior. Additionally, the use of paradoxical injunction is often aimed explicitly at enforcing the practitioner's control over the marital interactions. Such a shift to the practitioner in the power base of treatment seems alien to the basic tenets of the task-centered model.

One solution to the problem of combining the two levels of rules in the treatment of a marital couple is to select elements which preserve the basic components of the task-centered approach. This may be accomplished by allowing the practitioner to understand the marital couple at the level of the metarule but to assist the couple to select tasks which are in the awareness and motivational context of the couple, so that both the metarule and descriptive or prescriptive rules are worked on simultaneously. Bernal and Baker (1979) suggest that analysis at the metarule level also includes the earlier levels of concrete task work, so the practitioner may be working on both levels at once. Such a combination of task work led to the successful treatment of the Knights, whose case will be used to illustrate this extension of the task-centered model in the treatment of marital conflict.

The Knights[1]

The Knights are a white working-class couple who live in a community of 250,000. Mr. Knight, 33, earned a G.E.D. and works the night shift in a factory. Mrs. Knight, 32, a high school graduate, works days as an aide in a school. This is their only marriage and it has lasted 14 years. They have two children, a son, age 10 and a daughter, age 5. Each partner stated that their marriage began as a means of leaving their families as much as it was to be with each other. Almost from the beginning of the marriage, Mr. Knight used drugs including alcohol to excess. On many occasions, with the combination of a chemical substance and a natural quick temper, he became verbally abusive and several times physically abused his wife. He also destroyed furniture during his angry outbursts. Mrs. Knight's way of coping with the marriage was to become depressed, respond with verbal anger, withdrawal, and at times return to her family of origin.

The couple requested treatment at the point where they had decided they wanted to improve their marriage, but did not know how to do so. Six months before beginning treatment, Mr. Knight had experienced a religious conversion which led him to give up his reliance on drugs and to decide to improve himself and his marriage. He began to attend technical classes and attempted to find ways to improve his relationship with his wife. Mrs. Knight also wanted to improve the marriage, but found her lingering anger and lack of skills in relating to her husband a barrier in deepening the marital relationship. A contract for brief treatment of 12 sessions over 4 months was agreed upon during the intake interview. All interviews were conjoint as the assessment indicated that the couple shared equally in family power, commitment to treatment, and commitment to the marriage (Reid, 1981, Chapter 7, above).

Two intake interviews were used to explore their relationship and to locate problems. Baseline data were collected to measure problem areas. The Stuarts' (1973) *Marital Pre-Counseling Inventory* was used in conjunction with the intake interview data to arrive at three problem areas. These were: (1) Anger—Mr. Knight's loss of control and guilt over his past angry outbursts and Mrs. Knight's inability to express her anger directly

[1]The treatment of the Knights was conducted by Alice A. Jackson, a D.S.W. candidate at the University of Alabama.

toward her husband and her pattern of withdrawing from the relationship was selected by the couple as their major problem. (2) Lack of mutually rewarding activities—the Knights' current work schedules and life-style left them with a paucity of enjoyable experiences. They wanted to find ways of rekindling their earlier enjoyment together as a couple. (3) Inadequate sexual relations—both expressed the desire for more frequent and satisfying sexual relations. During the treatment the couple reported that their sexual relations had improved and they substituted as a third problem the difficulties they were experiencing in disciplining their children.

The initial task for the first problem, anger, was to spend 30 minutes a day in conversation about the events of the day. They were to express their emotions and report on their day in a relaxed sitting position. Should either report becoming angry, they were to turn away and resume work only after the anger dissipated. This task was followed up by teaching them the fair fighting rules developed by Bach and Wyden (1981). As the Knights reported a marked change in frequency, intensity, and duration of angry feelings toward each other, the task work on the second problem took place. The task now was for them to continue to practice the newly learned skill of speaking with each other without being angry, while planning at least one "date" each week. This they practiced for two weeks with success and enjoyment. Partly because of the change in their behavior and attitude, they found that their sexual relations were more satisfying. They then asked for help with another problem, disciplining their children. Again the task was to use their previous experience of talking with each other for 30 minutes, but this time to focus on reaching agreement on what to do with the children and to plan a family activity each week. This new third problem moved the couple beyond their own transactions to incorporate the problems they reported in being parents. The children were never included in the treatment.

All three problem areas were related as each displayed the problems of similar metarules. The events at the time of Mr. Knight's conversion had apparently rendered the earlier metarule ineffective. Before these changes the couple had each acted as if they were not responsible for their behavior, with Mrs. Knight operating as if reacting to his angry outbursts and Mr. Knight under the influence of a drug. Both avoided taking responsibility for themselves and their marriage, expecting the other to meet their unspoken needs. They had incorporated that metarule into their life-style with their work schedules and interests keeping them apart. The event of the conversion was interpreted by both partners as meaning they were now to be responsible for their behavior and improve their marriage. However, they did not know how to effect a change in their metarule, nor how to deal with their marital problems. The difficulties in anger and disciplining the children were descriptive rules, while the desire for companionship in activities and sexual relations was a prescriptive rule. Both of the Knights readily acknowledged these as rules and worked to change them.

The treatment itself took place at the two levels of abstraction discussed earlier. On one level, tasks aimed at changing content and alleviating target problems were developed at the level of the couple's awareness, and they assisted in the selection of them. However, the tasks also intended to help them redefine their relationship so that a new metarule could develop and become strengthened. In the task of using the fair fighting techniques, the practitioner not only helped them to be more effective in resolving conflict, but paradoxically gave them permission to do what they previously could not do, act in an angry way while continuing to be responsible for self and to show concern for the partner. Such a task blocked their angry outbursts while allowing them time to find new rules regarding means of eliciting each other's needs and ways to resolve their differences. Unable to excuse themselves from being responsible or to withdraw, the couple found that talking and compromising was a good solution. Similarly, the permission implicit in the task to go out on a "date" allowed them to feel comfortable with each other and to enjoy the other's companionship. This may have been why they spontaneously resolved some of their sexual problems. The new metarule was to talk openly about difficult issues with a spouse and to do so until some compromise was reached. The shift to working at the metarule level effected a change in the metarule while giving them skills to work on concrete problems.

Another example of contextual change relates to a descriptive rule which was not a primary target for change. Mr. Knight tried to monopolize the early interviews by talking about how guilty he felt for the past, even while acknowledging that he could neither change the past nor describe how guilt would lead to task completion. As he found the use of guilt as an excuse for not working on current tasks was unacceptable, he spoke less of it and turned his attention to task work. By selectively ignoring his discussion of the guilt, the practitioner changed both the descriptive rule and the metarule which permitted him to lay blame on factors outside of his control.

A different aspect of the Knights' treatment was the incorporation of crisis theory into the task-centered model. During the treatment the Knights experienced two crises. The first, which occurred during the work on the target problem of anger, concerned the anniversary of the miscarriage of Mrs. Knight's first pregnancy. In previous years they had marked the anniversary by employing an earlier metarule, with Mrs. Knight becoming depressed and withdrawing from the family. Mr. Knight typically abused a drug, became angry, and either broke objects or verbally lashed out at his wife. Mrs. Knight then returned to her family of origin and Mr. Knight would carry the fight to that home, with the parents intervening. He would apologize, become guilt-ridden and beg forgiveness. Mrs. Knight would then take him back and the marriage would resume.

Neither felt they had resolved the grief over the unborn child's death as they had never talked with each other about it. This time, outside the treatment sessions, they found themselves blocked from repeating the pattern and instead used the time in their conversation periods to talk about the event. Both were surprised that the other had similar reactions to the death, and they decided that they had resolved the problem. This also reinforced the newly developing metarule of discussing emotions openly.

The second crisis resulted from the discovery of a lump in Mrs. Knight's breast. She began a series of diagnostic tests, and the couple had to cope with the threat of cancer and surgery. This occurred at the time the couple was working on the problem of disciplining their children, and the crisis gave urgency to the need to cope with the children. Because of the crisis, the treatment was extended two weeks. Ultimately, surgery was not necessary, but the preparation for the children's care proved to the couple that they could work together on meeting the needs of their children.

The evaluation of the treatment using Hudson and Glisson (1976) and Spanier (1976) scales indicated an increase in marital satisfaction. In an interview with the Knights one year after closing, they both reported that their marital relationship had changed as they are now able more openly to address problems and to resolve conflicts without withdrawing or continuing an argument without ever resolving an issue. Mr. Knight has not resumed his use of drugs, has continued in school, and moved to the day shift so he has evenings with his wife. The Knights also planned for and had the child they wanted to fill their desired family size. Mrs. Knight was particularly grateful for her husband's increased participation in child care.

The task-centered model and crisis treatment share many concepts. Both use time limits and client motivation for work on tasks (Golan, 1979; Reid and Epstein, 1972). In the Knights' treatment the two crises also allowed the couple to further solidify the changes in their metarules while working on the crisis tasks. Furthermore, it allowed the practitioner to evaluate a blending of the two treatment models and to assess progress. That the couple was able to resolve a longstanding conflict and to "rewrite history" was an indication that the treatment had succeeded. The couple also had an opportunity to apply task work to the content of a crisis and to practice the task work through generalizing it to other referent problems. In each crisis, they were able to plan together, rather than withdrawing and acting irresponsibly.

Summary

The treatment of the Knights demonstrates the utility of the task-centered model for treatment in a marital relationship. It also demonstrates the incorporation into the task-centered model of concepts and techniques from other treatment approaches, crisis intervention, and family systems treatment. Rules and metarules can be combined in treatment of couples if the practitioner is conscious of both levels and is careful not to violate basic assumptions of the task-centered model. In any adaptation of the task-centered model, the impact of the adaptations on the basic tenets of the task-centered model must be evaluated in order to preserve the model's integrity.

Task-Centered Intervention in Foster Care Services: Working with Families Who Have Children in Placement

10

Tina L. Rzepnicki

Child welfare is one field of practice in which task-centered procedures are especially applicable. Recent federal legislation, such as the Adoption Assistance and Child Welfare Act of 1980 (P.L. 96-272) requires agencies to document efforts to prevent foster placement and, when out-of-home care is necessary, to provide evidence of efforts to return the child home. Also, juvenile and family court procedures are becoming more formalized. Practitioners are increasingly expected to base testimony on facts rather than on impressionistic information (Bell and Mlyniec, 1974; Institute for Judicial Administration, 1977). Parents are being asked questions related to their involvement in the case planning process, to their agreement with service plan goals and objectives, and what efforts the agency has made to provide the services outlined (National Council of Juvenile and Family Court Judges, 1981).

A number of elements make the task-centered model particularly appropriate for use in foster care services. Identification of problems according to the client's view and reliance on explicit client agreement for all steps in problem solving may make the offer of services more appealing to clients served in the public sector. An emphasis on the specification of problems and goals is an important feature that permits measurement of case progress. Very often court recommendations and agency expectations are vague. The specificity of the task-centered approach enables the worker to provide evidence of change that is likely to be helpful in court and administrative review of cases. Finally, the use of an intervention contract requires that a case plan be formulated. Clear documentation of problems, goals, client and practitioner responsibilities for problem solving, and time limits have been shown to be effective in reuniting children who have been in foster care with their families (Emlen et al., 1978; Stein, Gambrill, and Wiltse, 1978).

Several modifications to the task-centered model are suggested by the research findings of Rooney (1978) and other investigators in child welfare settings (Emlen et al., 1978; Stein, Gambrill, and Wiltse, 1978), and based on practice theory (Epstein, 1980; Reid, 1978). These modifications are described in this chapter. In addition, a case illustration is provided, and implications for practice in child welfare are discussed.[1]

Adaptation to Foster Care Services

Target Problems

Because of the complexities of child welfare cases and the number of participants involved (i.e., natural parents, foster parents, foster child), several sets of problems may be identified. Some of the problems may be shared by several participants, and some may not be shared. It is important that all of the individuals be given the opportunity to identify potential problems for intervention. Since concern is for the child's welfare, target problems are limited to those conditions which if not resolved are harmful or likely to be harmful to the child. When a child is already in foster care and where reunification of the natural family seems feasible, barriers preventing family maintenance or the child's return home should be targeted for intervention. These barriers may be determined by obtaining information from the natural family, agency, and court personnel. If the parent is undecided in the selection of a case goal (family reunification or adoption, for instance), indecision can be identified as an initial target problem.

Court and agency mandates are described to the client and consequences of nonintervention explained. These problems may or may not be harmonious with the client's view of his or her problem situation, but there is often some overlap. Frank presentation of mandates may enhance client cooperation and motivation. For each identified problem, objectives are formulated. These problem-solving objectives define the end product of intervention efforts, such as safe conditions in the home or minimally acceptable parenting skills. Objectives are stated in specific and behavioral terms so that the client knows what must be accomplished for services to be terminated successfully. Examples of problem-solving objectives are: "Ms. York will demonstrate that she can bathe and diaper an infant" or "Mr. and Mrs. Jackson will obtain dental care for their son, Robert."

[1]This chapter is based in part on the author's doctoral dissertation (Rzepnicki, 1982).

Permanency Plan

In foster care, the overriding goal of intervention is the implementation of a permanency plan. This plan describes a permanent living arrangement that will offer continuity of care for the child. Whenever possible, maintenance of the family unit is preferred. If out-of-the-home placement is necessary, an alternative goal is selected (in the following order of preference): family reunification, adoption, guardianship, emancipation, or planned long-term foster care. The discharge plan can be modified if it becomes clear that the preferred goal will not be achieved. For example, if sustained efforts to return a child home fail because minimal standards of parenting cannot be met, the practitioner and parents may decide that the child should be released for adoption or, if old enough, emancipated.

Social Context

A thorough evaluation of personal and social variables associated with the target problems can help identify environmental deficiencies that may interfere with problem resolution, as well as personal strengths and environmental supports that may be used for problem resolution. Environmental pressures are great on the clients typically served by public child welfare agencies. Based on data from studies in five states, Vasaly (1976: 21) developed a profile of natural parents:

> As a group they tend to be maritally unstable. Most report having several children; few of the children live with the parents. The parents are generally poorly educated. Many are unemployed and those that are employed are apt to be employed at unskilled or semi-skilled work. Most are below poverty level income, and many are receiving public assistance.

Findings from a number of studies suggest that environmental factors are major barriers preventing return home for the foster child (Fanshel and Shinn, 1978; Giovannoni and Billingsley, 1970; Jenkins and Norman, 1975; Olsen, 1970; Torczyner and Pare, 1979). Furthermore, emphasis on the social context of problems may result in less of a focus on pathology as a causative factor in foster placement. Therefore, in this approach, more attention is given to environmental pressures and other modifiable conditions that can be intervened upon and lead to reunification of the family.

Joint Case Planning

Clients involved in the foster care system typically have ties with other agencies, such as the department of mental health and juvenile court. Thus, change in the custody status of a child affects a large number of individuals and agencies. Coordination of efforts becomes crucial in providing the client with efficient and effective service, especially when the agencies have overlapping interests. According to Gambrill and Wiltse (1974), integration of services occurs infrequently. It is extremely important to involve all relevant collaterals in case planning and keep them aware of case progress. Professional collaterals are included on the basis of their authority and interest in the family or child. The degree to which they are involved will probably also depend on the time they have available. Personal collaterals (i.e., family members) may also participate. Serving as supports to the family, they can become task facilitators.

Clarification of Responsibilities

Accurate information should be provided to all the participants regarding what is expected of them by the agency, court, foster and/or natural parents, and each other. Legal sanctions, agency roles, and regulations should be communicated clearly and freely. This information is rarely provided to families served by the child welfare system. For instance, Knitzer, Allen, and McGowan (1978), reporting the results of their survey of 140 counties across the nation, found that when children are placed in substitute care, parents are typically not told of their ongoing responsibilities vis-à-vis their children nor are they expected to participate in decision making. Furthermore, many agencies have no specific policies regarding parental visiting. In the Knitzer, Allen, and McGowan study, 50 percent of the agencies had no such written policy. When policies did exist, they were often disregarded in practice. If agency policies or expectations of the parent are not communicated, there is little reason to believe that efforts will be made to actively involve parents in services.

Time Limits

Although time limits when working with these families are sometimes longer than in normal task-centered practice, the child may still be in foster placement at the end of the contract. If discharge must await the next court hearing, the case should be put on monitoring status. Another contract can be initiated at a later time by the direct service worker or by one of the participants. A series of contracts can also be established, each following the usual task-centered guidelines. This helps the practitioner focus intervention and evaluate progress.

Resource Provision

The agency may routinely provide certain resources to enhance the quality of the child's life (i.e., clothing or medical care). Regular guidelines of task-centered practice can generally be followed. Case management problems caused by several task-centered sequences running concurrently can be minimized by keeping the terms of individual contracts clear and distinct (Epstein, 1980).

Case Example: The Haley Family

In order to illustrate how the above modifications play out in practice, the remainder of the chapter is devoted to the description of a case example. The task-centered practitioner for this case was a first-year master's degree student who had no previous practice experience. The student had, however, completed ten weeks of instruction in this particular approach to intervention and was placed in an urban area office of a state child welfare agency for her field work.

Mr. and Mrs. Haley were the natural parents of Jeffrey, age 5, and Sharon, age 3, both of whom had been in foster care for 2 years. Neither parent was employed; the family income came from a combination of public aid and social security disability benefits (received as a result of Mr. Haley's history of epileptic seizures and emotional problems).

The children were removed from their home because of "failure to thrive," according to the agency record. The parents' perception was very different from what is implied in the clinical definition of "failure to thrive." Their understanding was that temporary removal was necessary due to Mrs. Haley's brief illness and the children consequently not being fed properly, although Mr. Haley did the best he could. In fact, once the problem situation was explored and target problems were specified, it became clear that a lack of knowledge of adequate nutrition and food preparation were antecedents to improper feeding of the children.

During the two years in placement, the children had been in two other foster homes. Visitation with their parents had always occurred sporadically, and always in the local office of the state's department of children and family services.

Assessment of the parent's ability to provide child care revealed deficits in the physical care of the child. Standards for *minimally* acceptable parenting skills were defined by the practitioner to include supervision, nutrition, clothing, hygiene, home safety, and medical and dental care. The criteria, derived largely from government publications, were used as guidelines in the specification of conditions to be changed for the Haley family.

The parents jointly agreed to the selection of four target problems for intervention. These were a combination of client-identified and mandated problem areas, considered to be of critical importance to the agency and court. Problem-solving objectives were stated in addition to a case goal. Specific objectives indicated the desired degree of problem reduction or an identifiable end point of the problem-solving efforts. Achievement of the individual objectives was expected to result in the accomplishment of the permanency plan, which was to return Jeffrey and Sharon to their biological parents.

The following target problems and problem-solving objectives were identified for the Haleys:

1. Mr. and Mrs. Haley have no evidence for the judge that they possess child-care abilities. (Mandated by court.)
   Objective: To obtain evidence for the judge that Mr. and Mrs. Haley are capable of caring for their children.
2. Mr. Haley has no evidence that he has taken steps to stop drinking. (Mandated by agency.)
   Objective: To obtain evidence that Mr. Haley has taken steps to stop drinking.
3. The Haley children have not had home visits.
   Objective: The children to have weekly home visits.
4. The Haleys have no phone.
   Objective: To obtain a phone.

The first two problems were mandates. Of the other two problems, one was considered to be a condition that was potentially harmful to the children. (No phone in apartment or building meant that emergency help might not be easily obtained in case of accident or fire.) The other problem (no home visits) was selected based on the importance of parent–child visits to family reunification (Fanshel and Shinn, 1978; Festinger, 1975; Maas and Engler, 1959).

A unique feature of the Haley's first two target problems and problem-solving objectives was the evidentiary requirement of court. The target problems were stated in a way that did not require the Haleys to fully accept the problems of lack of child-care abilities and Mr. Haley's alleged drinking. What was necessary was their acknowledgment that the court required some evidence that efforts had been made to resolve these problems that had been identified by the authorities. The child-care problem was, in fact, fully acknowledged by Mr. and Mrs. Haley. Mr. Haley's drinking problem was not acknowledged. He agreed, however, to obtain evidence to satisfy the court that he was complying with the mandate. There was no consensus that drinking was, in fact, ever a problem, although a practitioner at one time had recorded in the agency case record that she suspected Mr. Haley to be an alcoholic. As illustrated in this case, such an approach to defining problems is of value when there is not convincing evidence that a particular problem exists, yet powerful mandate is involved.

Specifications of the first target problem were revealed during the in-depth assessment. First, the parents lacked knowledge regarding proper nutrition and food preparation for very young children. The focus for conditions to be changed was thus both the development of knowledge and skills and documentation for the court. Second, in the Haley apartment were several safety hazards that could pose a danger to small children and infants. A "Home Safety Checklist" (Rzepnicki, 1982) was used to identify the following conditions: (1) uncovered electric outlets; (2) no telephone with the number of a physician, rescue squad, or poison control easily accessible; (3) no gate or fence for the stairway. Once these conditions were specified, the family immediately covered unused outlets and obtained a barricade for the open stairway, in order to make their home safer for visits by their two very young children. The only condition that was identified as a separate target problem was the lack of a phone. The phone was obtained within a few sessions with the help of the state agency worker.

The mandates were dealt with in a unique manner that may have resulted in a stronger commitment by the Haleys to pursue problem resolution. Instead of merely pointing out the consequences of nonaction, the practitioner made an attempt to negotiate and redefine the mandates in terms acceptable to the clients, the state agency worker, and the court. In doing this, the agency/court mandates actually became target problems compatible with the client's view of their difficulties.

Procedures for Evaluating Intervention

A single-subject design was employed to evaluate intervention effectiveness using data collected weekly during the client interview. The status of treated and untreated problems was reviewed and task accomplishment was recorded during each session, as is routinely done in task-centered practice.

The criteria for successful outcome was resolution of target problems, regardless of whether or not the overriding case goal, a permanency plan, was achieved. The student practitioner lacked authority to make major case decisions and her involvement with the family was temporary. It was unreasonable, therefore, to expect the permanency plan to be achieved by the termination of her services. Attention focused instead on the intermediate problem-solving objectives which had been identified as necessary steps in achieving a permanency plan.

A graph was constructed for each problem specification of each target problem. The steps taken to attain the objectives were recorded on the graphs at each interview. Steps were defined as problem-solving actions taken by the practitioner or client between sessions. During the intervention phase, these actions were formalized and discussed as tasks, using the task planning and implementation activities. Client data were verified by at least one other source (e.g., official records, personal or professional collaterals).

Cumulative recording was used to depict problem change. The practitioner believed that cumulative graphs provided a more accurate picture of problem change than did counting only the steps completed since the last interview, since achieving the problem-solving objectives required a series of steps which built on each other. Being able to see the graph climb steadily upward toward problem resolution was also a motivator for the Haleys.

Each graph began with the first day the practitioner and client met and continued through termination. The baseline period of no intervention included the initial problem identification phase, which was usually several sessions. Once problems were defined, retrospective baseline data were obtained for previous weeks. The baseline then continued for varying lengths of time until task planning and implementation activities were begun on the individual specifications, one after another. The beginning of the problem-solving phase for each problem specification is identified with a dotted vertical line in Figure 10.1.

Results: Comparison Across Problems

The first target problem, that Mr. and Mrs. Haley had no evidence of child-care abilities, included five specific conditions to be changed. Figure 10.1 depicts the progress on three specifications of this problem: obtaining knowledge of proper nutrition and food preparation, and then obtaining documentation of child-care ability from various sources.

Knowledge of nutrition and food preparation was identified by the clients and the agency as a major priority. As such, it was one of the first problems intervened upon. The practitioner gave Mrs. Haley in-session instruction about nutritional requirements for children of various ages, about meal planning and preparation, and advice about shopping. Client tasks such as reading pamphlets about nutrition and writing sample menus were developed to help Mrs. Haley learn more about these areas and to practice newly acquired skills between sessions. Her knowledge level was determined at the beginning of each session by asking her what she knew about these topics. By day 64, her knowledge level evened out at eight pieces of information compared to two pieces of information during the baseline period.

On day 72, task planning and implementation was begun to obtain a letter from Mrs. Haley's psychiatrist evaluating her ability to provide adequate child care for the children. Efforts to secure a letter from her family counselor were begun later (day 78), which allowed for a staggered

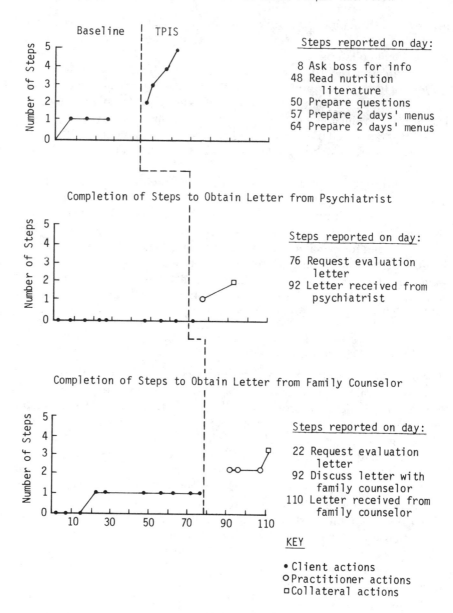

FIGURE 10.1 Multiple Baseline across Problem Specifications for Haley Target Problem 1

baseline. The letters were to be used as evidence for the court of the Haleys' adequacy as child caretakers. As Figure 10.1 indicates, there was little change in these problem specifications during baseline periods. However, once task planning and implementation activities were begun, progress was made toward achieving each problem-solving objective. Eventually, written evaluations were obtained from all the professional collaterals who had been working with Mrs. Haley.

Graphs (not presented) were also used to evaluate the effectiveness of intervention on target problem 2, that Mr. Haley has no evidence that he has taken steps to stop drinking, and target problem 3, that the Haley children have not had home visits.

In neither problem area were any steps taken toward attaining the problem-solving objectives (to obtain evidence that Mr. Haley has taken steps to stop drinking and for the children to have weekly home visits) prior to the problem-solving phase. Once the task planning and implementation activities began (day 43), there were several weeks of preparatory activity and then the objectives were accomplished quickly. For example, before Mr. Haley attended his first Alcoholics Anonymous meeting, three tasks were carried out to enhance the probability that he would get to the meetings. Mr. Haley phoned the organization to learn about its philosophy and operation. The task-centered practitioner found out the location of the meetings and arranged for the state agency worker to accompany Mr. Haley to the first one. Unfortunately, Mr. Haley missed the AA meeting when the state worker did not keep the appointment. In the following session, the student practitioner arranged to accompany Mr. Haley, and the success of this joint task was reported on day 76. Mr. Haley had attended two more meetings of Alcoholics Anonymous before the task-centered sessions ended.

Home visits with the children also began several weeks after tasks toward that objective were first implemented. The practitioner spoke once with the foster mother on the phone, then met with the Haleys and the foster parents together to prepare both families for the home visits. The first visit took place on day 64. During the next two weeks the student practitioner was out of town and no visits occurred, as transportation promised by the state worker was not provided. The home visits resumed when the student practitioner returned and continued fairly regularly until termination of the task-centered contract.

Observations of change across problems provide evidence that not only were all of the Haleys' problem-solving objectives met, but that the task planning and implementation activities were probably responsible for the progress made. In the multiple baseline design used with problem 1, little or no improvement was noted during the varying baseline periods. Once intervention began, progress was noted on the particular condition to be changed but there was no concurrent improvement in untreated problem areas. The successful results with problems 2 and 3 also provide additional evidence that task planning and implementation activities were influential in achieving the objectives.

Follow-up

Approximately three months after termination of task-centered services with the student practitioner, follow-up interviews were conducted with Mrs. Haley (who at this point was separated from her husband) and the state agency worker to review additional progress made toward return home of the children from foster care. At that time it was clear that Mrs. Haley had little information regarding her current status with the state child welfare agency. Because of the state worker's increased inaccessibility, visits with her children in foster care stopped after her task-centered contract ended. A scheduled court hearing received a continuance. Mrs. Haley was not aware of the hearing nor the postponement. Furthermore, her worker indicated that there had been a change in the projected date for the return home of her children from foster care. It was determined that because of the separation, the couple needed to receive marital counseling and the new plan was for the children to be discharged from foster care in another two years. Mrs. Haley had no knowledge of these changes at the time of the follow-up. Nevertheless, she indicated that she had been very satisfied with the task-centered services provided to her and found these services more helpful than previous experiences in counseling.

Conclusion

This particular adaptation of the basic task-centered model contains two major departures. The first is that the identification of the target problems is constrained to client target problems expected to be barriers to achieving permanency for the child. This kind of constraint on admissible target problems contains the probability that practice will be much more focused than has normally been the case in child welfare.

The other major adaptation is related to the legal ramifications of child welfare cases and to the varying investments of the child welfare bureaucracies in pursuing ideological and social control aims. The model adaptation takes account of the macrosystems influences that are present in any kind of child welfare case because these cases almost always involve public attitudes, professional ideologies, and scrutiny of a variety of public agencies from a social control angle. The task-centered approach, or any other model of practice, does not address agency policy issues. The model presented here, however, does address some of the problems over which the individual practitioner has a degree of control: inattention to the natural parents and the importance of continuing contact between parent and child, inappropriate problem and goal identification, the application of the practitioner's own values for making some intervention decisions, lack of case planning and systematic record keeping, poor problem-solving skills, and a lack of understanding and support for families suffering from severe environmental stress.

Emphasis is given to working with the natural parents toward maintaining the child in the home, family reunification, or the achievement of an alternative permanency plan. This case goal is the focus of all casework activity. Problems identified for intervention are those seen as impediments to accomplishing the permanency goal selected for each child. Whenever possible, the problems are defined as the client perceives them. When authorities identify the problems for intervention, an effort is made by the practitioner to negotiate a common definition satisfactory to all parties involved.

Intervention in this approach is conducted in the service of decision making for the child (i.e., determining where the child should live) rather than as treatment and cure of psychopathology. To reduce the application of individual or middle-class values in selecting criteria for change, the practitioner is encouraged to focus on minimal standards of parenting, below which a child is at risk of harm. Social science knowledge and practice knowledge are limited in the guidance that can be offered to public agency practitioners in making the decision to intervene into family life, as well as making intervention decisions after that. The task-centered model provides a commonsense approach to problem solving that recognizes these limitations and recognizes the benefits of encouraging autonomous client behavior.

Families who are served by public child welfare agencies are likely to be suffering from severe environmental stress. The practitioner for this case assessed the clients' social context to the extent that it was likely to impede progress toward target problem resolution or interfere with ongoing parent–child contact and contact with the agency. Available resources were provided as necessary. The clients were supported in their change efforts by the task-centered practitioner and important collaterals such as family members and the state agency personnel whenever possible.

Case planning, the monitoring of change, and structured record keeping are case management procedures that have frequently been neglected in foster care services. These procedures encourage the provision of efficient and effective services; they also enhance practitioner accountability to the agency and client. The practitioner in this study formulated a written intervention plan with the clients and relevant collaterals, reviewed problem status and task accomplishment at each session, and documented the results of problem-solving actions in a descriptive manner. Such skills are especially important in child welfare services where practitioner turnover is high, court involvement is frequent, and the call for justification of services is increasing.

The task-centered model provides a framework that encourages expedient problem solving and goal attainment. Furthermore, it offers clear and easily taught guidelines to case planning and problem solving. Together with training in caseload management, training in this practice model could result in practitioners being better equipped to meet the challenge of practice in child welfare services.

Using the Model for Administration and Management

11 A Model for Caseload Management Based on Task-Centered Practice

Ronald H. Rooney
Marsha Wanless

The practitioner serving a large caseload with accompanying paperwork pressures and frequent client crisis is fighting burnout. The literature on burnout suggests means to preserve practitioner sanity through jogging, meditating, or taking "mental health" days (Daley, 1979). However, the literature rarely addresses another issue in burnout: clients served by overworked practitioners may also be "burned" by inadequate service.

Delivering quality service and preserving one's own equilibrium should not be incompatible goals. This chapter describes a case management model based on the task-centered approach which attempts to meet both goals. The model was constructed and tested using a developmental research paradigm. Developmental research consists of four phases— retrieval of information, conversion and design, development, and diffusion (Rothman, 1980)—and is particularly appropriate when innovations in practice technology are needed to resolve practice problems (Thomas, 1978b). The model presented here is the product of development and testing of a practice technology intended to maintain quality service and yet reduce practitioner burnout.

Case management has been defined as a way of attaining clients' individual goals and objectives using other people's services (*Practice Digest*, March 1982). It includes coordination of service, brokerage, and advocacy. The decision about which professional is responsible for which service is a key issue. However, many case managers also provide direct service. This chapter will focus primarily on the direct service function. Caseload management will be defined here as a decision-making process used to proactively plan selective intervention and service throughout a caseload. The chapter offers guidelines to help the practitioner decide how often clients should be seen, balancing more intensive with less frequent contact.

Recognizing a Need

The setting in which the caseload management model was developed was the Adult Voluntary Service Unit of Dane County Social Service in Madison, Wisconsin. The Adult Unit serves elderly, disabled, and handicapped clients who request agency service and is typical of the heavy caseload demands of public agency practice.

The social work staff of the Adult Unit were surveyed in January 1979 about their work-related stress. The caseload of the unit as a whole had increased 25 percent in the 12 months prior to the survey. Practitioners served an average of 41 clients each and 38 percent of those cases were open at least 2 years.

The practitioners, perhaps influenced by the increasing caseloads, reported high stress and little time to plan interviews or organize their work. They noted, however, that their stress was related to the number of clients in crisis at one time rather than to the caseload size alone. They were not confident about the quality of their work, which one described as "putting Band-aids on open sores." Some practitioners reported that clients who did not demand to be seen could go unserved for long periods. Others "stacked" seven or eight interviews a day in order to see all clients. Rapidly completed, sketchy paperwork rarely reflected actual service provided.

Staff hesitated to offer to do things for their clients because they could not promise that they would follow through. Many lamented that they were not able to help their clients enough. Some practitioners tried to cope with the pressure by taking work home with them and skipping lunches to see clients; some even dreamed about their clients. Other practitioners felt troubled by an emotional hardening; they did not care as much now about what happened to their clients. One commented that she checked the obituaries daily as a death would at least mean one fewer case.

The survey responses parallel symptoms of incipient burnout reported by several authors (Daley, 1979; Pines and Kafry, 1978). The practitioners appeared to believe that an "ideal" worker would be able to handle the pressures and help all clients. In contrast, they found themselves struggling to survive on the job, reacting to crises rather than feeling in control of their work. An innovation in service delivery might be seen as an added burden. Consequently, an effective case management model would have to both reduce practitioner personal stress and benefit clients.

Developing a Caseload
Management Model

A review of the empirical and practice literature in the areas of practitioner stress or burnout, effects of caseload size on job satisfaction and direct outcome, and factors in effective casework service suggested:

1. Practitioners who had feasible expectations for their own role performance and who set realistic goals for their work with clients should feel less work-related stress (Harrison, 1980).
2. Efforts designed to improve service delivery may reduce practitioner stress while achieving greater client outcomes (Minahan, 1980).
3. Practitioner activity focused on decision making may influence client outcomes more than caseload size (D. Shapiro, 1976; Stein, Gambrill, and Wiltse, 1978).
4. Use of time-limited, intensive services, structure, contracting, emphasis on problem solving, and behavioral approaches have been associated with better casework outcomes (J. Fischer, 1978; Mullen and Dumpson, 1972; Reid, 1978; Reid and Hanrahan, 1982; Schinke, 1981; E. Schwartz and Sample, 1972; D. Wallace, 1967; Wood, 1978).

In addition to the guidelines based on empirical sources, value premises influenced development of the caseload management model. These values were as follows:

1. Clients should be helped to resolve problems of greatest concern to them. Practitioners should not require work on problems which the client is not concerned about unless such work is mandated by law or the client is in imminent danger of harming himself or others (Reid and Epstein, 1972).
2. Public social workers can be most useful to clients as facilitators of problem solving. However, the practitioner should not prescribe work on problems or enhancing independence if these are not the client's goals. The practitioner may, however, attempt to make a persuasive argument about the merits of a problem-solving approach. In the end, however, the practitioner is guided by the client's selection of goals (Epstein, 1980; Reid, 1978).
3. Clients who prefer to have a supportive rather than a problem-solving relationship with a practitioner should be aided in getting support (Nelsen, 1980). The practitioner, however, may arrange to have ongoing support provided by others in the community.

With this literature and these values as background, the practitioner responses and the current management methods were reexamined. Why weren't the current methods working? Analysis suggested that caseloads were managed reactively in response to crises rather than proactively with all cases. Practitioners were hesitant to develop specific goals and a schedule of contacts because they were not sure that the goals could be met nor that they would be able to meet with clients as often as planned. With caseloads of 40 and above, the practitioners' ideal of weekly contact with all clients was impossible. Consequently, practitioners responded to clients in crisis and maintained sporadic contact with other clients. This pattern appeared to encourage crises through neglect of routine matters and reinforcement of crises as a time when clients could see a practitioner.

As a first step toward proactive rather than reactive caseload management, the authors attempted to distinguish those practice decisions over which the practitioner had some control from those which were by nature reactive. Among the elderly, handicapped, and disabled clients served, frequent crises were inevitable; practitioners would always need to be able to respond quickly. However, practitioners could encourage more proactive contact with all clients by (1) focusing on case movement with a goal of greater self-sufficiency for all clients; (2) developing contracts with specified, feasible client-determined problems and goals; and (3) making explicit the services which the practitioner could offer or coordinate and managing the frequency of planned contact. Commitment to use of contracts would be done with the clear understanding that they are not "written in stone"; as needs and problems changed, services and frequency of contact would also change.

The Case Management Model

The model of case management developed conceptualized cases as entering and moving through the public service system, with the type of service offered and frequency of contact varying by plan at different times, in response to individual need. (See Figure 11.1.)

Case Movement

Practitioners and clients who see each other over a period of years can lose a sense of what they are working on and why. The practitioner, in this model, plans proactively with all clients with optimism that each can be helped to become more independent, if not to terminate agency involvement altogether. The practitioner regularly reviews agreed-upon goals with each client and charts case movement from opening through phases of more to less intensive service. While most cases do not move smoothly

PRELIMINARY CASELOAD MANAGEMENT MODEL

CASE MOVEMENT	CASE OPENING	SERVICE DELIVERY			CASE CLOSING
SERVICE METHOD	ASSESSMENT AND CONTRACTING	CRISIS INTERVENTION	TASK-CENTERED CASEWORK	SUPPORTIVE CASEWORK	TERMINATION
FREQUENCY OF CONTACT	1-3 SESSIONS OVER 1 MONTH	TWICE WEEKLY OR MORE	TWICE WEEKLY — BIWEEKLY — MONTHLY	BIWEEKLY — MONTHLY	2 - 4 SESSIONS OVER 2 MONTHS

FIGURE 11.1 Preliminary Caseload Management Model

191

through the progression depicted in Figure 11.1, locating a case on the chart helps the practitioner plan what service and contact is necessary at a given time.

Service Method

Service method refers to the type of service offered during a particular phase. Assessment and planning at case opening and termination procedures at case closing were standard for all cases. During the service delivery phase, cases received one (or more) of three service methods: crisis intervention, task-centered casework, or supportive casework, with options for scheduling frequency of contact for each method.

Assessment and Contracting. Assessment and contracting with new cases was estimated to take one to three sessions or up to a month. The practitioner expressed her opinion to all clients that they could be helped to be more independent. The practitioner and client then explored potential problems following a task-centered approach. Once problems and goals were identified, they decided together the service method to be used and a schedule of contact based on those problems and goals.

Crisis Intervention. Some clients entered the Adult Unit in a crisis state, when their "homeostatic mechanisms have broken down, tension has topped and disequilibrium has set in" (Golan, 1978). The practitioner then quickly determined the nature of the crisis and developed a plan of action with the client to resolve it. In some cases such as psychiatric decompensation, the practitioner was directive in mobilizing the client to take action to prevent harm. Crisis work then continued intensively (at least twice a week) until the crisis state abated and a different service method with less frequent contact could be used.

Other clients experienced a crisis state at some point after entering the unit. In such cases, the current service method was abandoned in favor of crisis intervention until the crisis was resolved.

Task-Centered Casework. Task-centered service was offered to any client who was not in a crisis state but who identified problems which he or she wanted to reduce and who was willing to carry out tasks to resolve the problems. The task-centered model's emphasis on reducing client-defined target problems in time-limited periods through mutually developed client and practitioner tasks made it particularly relevant to the goals of the caseload management approach. First, clients could be helped to resolve problems of concern to them. Second, client independence could be enhanced through modeling and teaching an approach to problem solving which could be used in areas other than those worked on in treatment. Third, the specification of problems and setting of feasible goals could aid the practitioner and client to assess progress, determine the need for further services, and reduce practitioner stress. Finally, there was a developing task-centered literature reporting effective outcomes with the elderly and chronically mentally ill clientele to be served (Cormican, 1977; Fortune and Rathbone-McCuan, 1981; Newcome, 1979).

When the task-centered approach was used, the frequency of scheduled contact included twice weekly, weekly, biweekly, and monthly contacts. The initial decision on frequency was based on the urgency of problems identified and the practitioner's available time. Some problems, such as an imminent eviction, called for intensive (at least twice weekly) contact to prevent eviction or find new housing. Weekly sessions were used if the problem was urgent, tasks could be completed over a week's time, and the practitioner's caseload permitted it. Weekly contacts lasted for 4 to 12 weeks. Biweekly contacts were used when problems were less urgent, tasks would take longer than a week to complete, or the practitioner's caseload pressure prevented more frequent contact. For example, many problems such as getting a ramp built to enable an ambulatory client greater access to her apartment involved tasks which would take longer than a week to complete. Usually, 6 to 12 biweekly sessions were scheduled over a 3 to 6 month period. With the twice weekly, weekly, and biweekly schedules, clients might shift to a different frequency of contact as problems became more intense or abated.

Monthly monitoring contacts were used with clients who had completed a contract but who were not ready to terminate. Monitoring, defined as checking or observing for purposes of keeping track of client progress or regulating control, should be done only for specific stated purposes and preferably on a voluntary basis (Epstein, 1980). Time limits for monitoring were set to avoid unnecessary client dependence. Monitoring was used to assure linkage to resources, to maintain progress toward goals, and to reinforce client competence in functioning without more intensive service intervention. Clients who feared they would be helpless without practitioner contact received infrequent supportive contacts to affirm their competence in maintaining an adequate level of functioning. Structured monitoring also prepared the way for termination and freed the practitioner for more intensive work with other cases.

Supportive Casework.   Some clients were neither in crisis nor had specific problems to resolve, but wished instead regular visits from a friendly, supportive person. Such clients were offered supportive casework, the service method already used at the Adult Unit for clients not in crisis. Like crisis intervention and task-centered service, supportive contact was explicitly agreed upon with the client. The practitioner was then responsible for ensuring that the desired support was provided. The practitioner might, however, help the client find other community supports such as friends, families, and groups rather than provide it herself. Supportive contact by the practitioner personally was thus offered to clients who would be in danger to themselves without ongoing professional support or who were so isolated that other sources of support could not be found.

Supportive contact was offered in biweekly or monthly contacts. Where the practitioner felt others might be located to provide the needed support, a contract for continued support until those others were found was planned.

Case Closing

Termination was considered at the conclusion of all contracts in any of the above service methods. In general, societal values and continued needs for access to services and resources have impeded closing of cases among elderly, disabled, and handicapped clients such as those served in the Adult Voluntary Service Unit. While Title XX goals specify prevention of undue dependence, the life problems of these clients create ambivalence among service providers about the pursuit of greater independence (Abramson, 1981). However, public social service workers may not need or be able to meet all such needs. Consequently, the desirability of termination was considered at the end of each contract. Choices available to client and practitioner included continuation of service delivery using the same or another service method as well as case closure.

When clients were ready to terminate, a process similar to that described by Epstein (1980) was used. In a final interview, client's goals and achievements were reviewed, and the steps carried out to identify and prioritize problems and goals were stressed. When clients had completed tasks, the steps involved in planning those tasks, assessing obstacles, and revising tasks were also reviewed. Potential future needs for services and resources were identified and plans made for the client to secure them. In general, the client's actual ability to function independently was emphasized, although the practitioners made sure the client knew how to initiate service again when necessary.

Implementation and
Evaluation of the Model

The junior author implemented and evaluated the case management model with her caseload at the Adult Unit over a ten-month period beginning in January 1980. For practical reasons, the entire management model could not be implemented all at once but was phased in according to priorities. The first priority was to effectively serve those clients who needed intensive crisis intervention. The second priority was to approach long-term clients now seen supportively for whom termination might be possible. These clients were given the choice of terminating contact now or setting a time-limited contract to explore other means of getting support. Third, new clients were offered task-centered or supportive contact contracts. Frequency of contact was determined partly by the number of clients in crisis and those in monitoring status or approaching closure and thus needing less frequent contact. Finally, for remaining ongoing cases, contracts were reaffirmed and clarified. A case management recording form was developed to monitor client movement across case phases, service methods, and frequency of contact.

Evaluation of the clinical trial of the management model was guided by six questions: Did the caseload management model contribute to greater self-sufficiency for clients and greater caseload turnover for the practitioner? Would clients whose cases were closed after time-limited intervention return for further service? How many clients would choose to be served with the task-centered approach? How would clients who selected supportive casework fare? Would the caseload management model reduce the incidence of client crisis? Finally, did the caseload management model reduce practitioner stress?

Case Movement

Data on the number of case openings and closings of all Adult Service Workers were collected for the period, January–October 1980. All practitioners opened an average of 26 cases and closed an average of 25 cases. Over the same period, Wanless, using the case management model, opened 45 cases and closed 40, one-and-a-half times the average of fellow practitioners. She was able to serve more clients over this period because the average length of time a client remained on her caseload dropped from a mean of 20 months before model implementation to 3.8 months afterwards. The increased turnover was accomplished while a caseload of about 30 clients per month was maintained.

Case Reopening

Only two of the clients whose cases were closed required reopening (about 5 percent). Three other clients whose cases were closed requested information on resources, which was provided over the telephone. Thus, concern that closing cases would mean reopening them when a crisis occurred was not substantiated.

Use of the Task-Centered Approach

Thirty-five of the 63 clients served chose task-centered contact. Nineteen of these clients completed contracts and terminated agency involvement. Ten did so directly following weekly or biweekly task-centered contracts averaging about four months in length. Six more clients received about three months of monitoring after a weekly or biweekly task-centered contract and then terminated. Six clients were in a crisis state at some point during the ten months (three with multiple crises), yet four of these reached case termination.

The proportion of the caseload served with task-centered methods increased over the ten months from 20 percent to 66 percent. The increase in task-centered cases was consistent with the gradual implementation of the management model. In addition, when early weekly or biweekly contacts moved to monthly monitoring contacts, more task-centered cases could be handled. An average of about 14 clients per month were served with the task-centered approach, most in biweekly contacts.

Use of Supportive Casework

Twenty-eight clients were served with supportive casework. Three-quarters of these reached termination within the ten months. Eleven clients were seen in monthly contacts and four in biweekly contact for an average of three months and then closed. Six clients experienced crisis status yet reached case closure. Hence, clients in supportive casework were seen more briefly and reached case closure more quickly than clients in task-centered service. Task-centered cases, however, included more intensive involvement and more work on problem solving.

Use of Crisis Intervention

The use of the management model and the task-centered approach did not reduce the number of client crises: the number of clients in a crisis state necessitating intensive contact remained stable at an average of two per month. As the level of crisis intervention was stable and predictable, crises did not impede time-limited, goal-oriented work toward greater independence and case closure with other clients on the caseload.

Practitioner Stress

The effect of the caseload management model on perceived practitioner stress was not assessed systematically. Wanless noted that her source of job-related satisfaction changed from long-term supportive relationships with clients to satisfaction that many clients had become more self-sufficient and no longer needed her services. Systematic planning of service methods and frequency of contact helped her feel more in control of her work. On the negative side, greater client turnover meant more paperwork in opening and closing cases.

Case Examples

The following examples give a flavor of clients' experiences with the caseload management and task-centered approaches.

Laura S.

Laura S., 31, was a single, developmentally disabled woman, living alone in the community. Laura had been in contact off and on with social workers for several years. She would ask for a practitioner to visit and then complain about how other services did not give her the help she requested. However, she was usually unable to focus on the same problem for more than a week at a time or organize herself to use services offered.

When Laura again applied to the Adult Unit, the new practitioner approached her about clearly defining some problems to work actively on over a brief time period. Laura identified two problems: (1) She ran out of money at the end of every month, and (2) the Vocational Rehabilitation Bureau (VRB) did not give her the services she requested. A 3-month contract specifying 12 weekly meetings was agreed upon. Weekly contact was selected because the problems identified appeared to be modifiable through tasks formulated on a week-by-week basis, the client favored this frequency, and the practitioner's current caseload permitted weekly sessions for this client. Laura S. appeared surprised by the practitioner's presentation of a time-limited approach and by her confidence that changes could occur with these problems.

A goal for the first target problem was to establish a budget that would help Laura avoid running out of money every month. Early tasks included keeping track of her expenses for several weeks, then arranging these in a weekly budget. As impulse buying was an obstacle to budgeting, Laura learned to take only a few dollars with her when she knew she might be going by a "garage sale." Laura was able to develop and maintain her budget over the three months of her contract.

The problem with the VRB was further specified to "Laura cannot get financial support to take the courses she wants." Laura wished financial support to take art courses, but the VRB counselor thought that Laura needed the support of a Sheltered Workshop. The Adult Unit practitioner generally agreed with the VRB counselor's reasoning, but followed the task-centered model in not forcing this view on Laura and suggesting to VRB that such a referral was unlikely to succeed without Laura's support. When VRB refused to support the art courses, Laura decided that with her improving skills in budgeting, she could pay for the course herself. Laura enrolled in the course and stopped contact with VRB.

Laura was seen weekly for eight sessions, then shifted to biweekly sessions for the last six weeks. Laura felt that the problems she wanted to resolve had been dealt with and there was no further need for service. Her desire for emotional support was discussed and affirmed. However, ways of getting support from others in her environment, such as a boyfriend and a woman friend, were planned. Laura's case was closed after three months of service. Unlike other earlier contacts with the agency, in this case Laura has not returned for further service in the year since her case was closed.

Jack L.

Jack L., 36, was chronically mentally ill since age 17 with a diagnosis of manic-depression. Jack had remained in frequent contact with social workers for 20 years because of periodic decompensation, not prevented by somatic treatment or counseling. Over the 10 months of the project, Jack passed through intensive contact, weekly, biweekly, and monthly phases several times. When Jack's symptoms recurred, he would spend all his money, become fearful and physically aggressive, and threaten suicide. Inevitably, Jack would be rehospitalized. Release from the hospital meant crisis intervention for a few weeks to aid him in stabilizing his living situation.

When his symptoms were in remission, Jack readily acknowledged and was willing to work on several target problems through the task-centered approach: Jack didn't like his job, didn't have enough money, and wasn't happy with his living situation. Tasks included exploring a transfer of jobs within the same job setting, developing a budget, and exploring the feasibility of moving. Jack's progress on his target problems was interrupted by acute episodes in February and April. He was seen for crisis intervention just prior to hospitalization and for a few weeks after his return to the community. The task-centered approach was used between hospitalization periods on a biweekly schedule to reestablish living and working arrangements. This frequency was utilized because Jack preferred it and the tasks developed often required two weeks for completion.

Jack's case was not closed. Lack of sustained progress and poor generalization of learning to new situations is typical of many chronically ill persons (Newcome, 1979). Over the course of their contact, however, Jack learned to recognize the onset of his symptoms and to contact the practitioner when they occurred. When he began to sweat profusely, tremble uncontrollably, hear voices, and have difficulty sleeping, decompensation was imminent. He also learned to recognize that the decompensation was an expectable part of his illness, and would be lived through. Knowing Jack's patterns also allowed the practitioner to plan her caseload time commitments better to anticipate need for intensive contact.

Discussion

The caseload management model allowed the practitioner to serve a larger number of clients, helping many to greater self-sufficiency and case closure. Client contact was brief and progressed to termination for the majority of clients served in both task-centered and supportive casework. The task-centered cases—about half the caseload—were usually longer and involved more intensive, problem-solving contact than supportive cases. Clients who completed service contracts and were terminated rarely required further service in the near future. Implementation of the management model changed the type of practitioner job satisfaction, but neither increased nor decreased job stress. Thus the management model appeared to increase the number of clients served without major detrimental impact. More field testing of the model is needed to determine whether the effects reported in this study generalize beyond the single practitioner who implemented the model in a public adult social services agency.

The contribution of the task-centered approach to the case turnover cannot be determined since the study was a preliminary field trial. Adaptations of the caseload management model with other intervention approaches would be useful to determine how the service interventions contribute to the overall success of the model. Further work is also required to determine adaptations for different agency settings and client groups. For example, contact with involuntary clients is often determined by court order and limits practitioner discretion in closing cases. Large numbers of clients with lengthy mandatory contact may preclude use of the caseload management model altogether, although its components—clear goals and distinctions among types of service methods—might still be useful.

Caseload turnover, the major positive effect of the model, must not become a goal in itself. Clients may be turned over quickly and not return for further service because they are not satisfied with the services received. Follow-up is essential to determine whether progress is maintained and how clients evaluate service.

Continued development of models for caseload management is one of the most crucial tasks facing those concerned with improving service delivery. Beginning evidence suggests that caseload management can not only benefit the client but also aid the practitioner in modifying some burnout pressures through feeling less powerless and less at the mercy of a demanding, unpredictable caseload. Efficient use of caseload management models on a unit or agency basis could result in increased efficiency and effectiveness of service delivery. This increased productivity might then result in expending fewer tax dollars or reallocating funding to more pressing service needs.

12 Problem-Oriented Management: An Administrative Practice Model

Bageshwari Parihar

Dealing with external and internal sources of problems in an organization is of crucial importance in the management of the organization. The internal structure of an organization predetermines work processes, but the structural elements often appear to be the areas where problems occur in day-to-day working. For example, some of the possible problem areas, as enumerated by Parsons (1957) and Vinter (1963), include the following domains: policies and procedures; staff-client relationships; acquisition and supervision of personnel and controlling professional behavior; complexity of change-oriented techniques versus standardization of procedures; and emphasis on professionalization and predominance of the medical profession, which brings about an unstable balance between the two different types of authority (the organizational administrator and the professional specialist). These potential problem areas suggest that ongoing systems generate ongoing problems that gravitate around goals, roles, and functions of organizations and their actors (Parihar, 1982). The effective resolution of such organizational problems is basically an administrator's responsibility.

This chapter presents a problem-oriented management model which offers an articulated and systematic approach to solving such problems confronted by treatment organization administrators. The model is an extension of task-centered practice principles (Reid and Epstein, 1972) to agency administration. As such, it is highly structured, goal specific, and time limited. It aims to improve the management practices and hence the effectiveness of treatment organizations.

Following model-building research paradigms (Reid, 1979; Rothman, 1980; Thomas, 1978a), the management model was tested in seven treatment organizations.[1] This chapter is based on the Administrator's Guide developed to assist administrators in that field trial. Illustrations of the management approach are drawn from problems and solutions encountered in a treatment organization.

The basic steps in the management model are (1) problem identification, (2) problem analysis and specification, (3) goal development, (4) task planning and implementation, (5) task review, and (6) institutionalization. The first five steps parallel the task-centered practice approach while the final step, institutionalization, is added as a substitute for termination because of the complex nature of ongoing organizational processes.

Problem-Oriented Management Model

As indicated earlier, organizational problems, regardless of their source of origin or identification, are the responsibility of the administrator. The administrator can influence problems because of his or her position in the structure of an organization and his or her authority to exercise general direction over policies concerning the organization's operations. It is the administrator who mobilizes different actors and resources for problem solving and attempts to enhance the efficiency and effectiveness of the organization. In the management model, the problems addressed are those of organization functioning which an administrator can resolve independently or through collaboration with other actors.

Problem Identification

The first step of the management model is concerned with acknowledging and establishing the presence of the problem and defining its precise nature. The problem may be internal or external, and may be perceived by the administration or by any one or more of the actors, including staff, clients, and other concerned sources such as family members, significant others, or prior service providers. The problems may be brought up collectively or individually in or outside of staff meetings or may be elicited by the administrator if he or she suspects a strain in organizational functioning. The "perceiver" or "informer" tries to define the problem and the consequences if the problem were left unattended. By himself or with informer input, the administrator attempts to define the problem in precise terms so that its genesis, circumstances, and actors involved can be clearly understood.

---

[1]The full study is reported in Bageshwari Parihar, "Management of Treatment Organizations" (Ph.D. dissertation, University of Illinois-Chicago Circle, 1982). Also see Bageshwari Parihar, *Task-Centered Management in Human Services*, Springfield, Illinois: Charles C Thomas, 1984.

The first example pertains to a problem raised by nursing staff at a hospital-based alcoholism treatment program. Nursing staff and resident physicians were having difficulty interpreting admission criteria. They claimed to be getting conflicting messages from supervisors, who criticized them one moment for being too strict and punitive in denying admission and the next moment for being too lenient and lax in admitting other patients. Asked to define the problem, staff identified certain admission criteria which were too vague and thus subject to different interpretation by different people. Two points were considered especially confusing: one that emphasized that medical condition must be the primary reason for admission, and the other that stated that uncontrolled and intractable drinking was a valid reason for hospitalization.

In the second example, administration at the same alcoholism treatment center realized that the center's utilization of services and percentage of occupancy had been decreasing over time. The Board of Directors also raised this problem. Continuing low census in the center was causing underutilization of available services and financial difficulty. In other words, the problem was one of resource (patient) procurement and counteracting environmental factors.

Problem Analysis and Specification

The second stage, problem analysis and specification, requires a clear understanding of the nature of the target problem and specificity of conditions to be changed. Of crucial importance here is exploring the implications and consequences of proposed changes. Contextual data and other relevant information are obtained and analyzed. For routine and repeating types of problems, prior experiences are also usually helpful. For nonroutine problems, thorough exploration and analysis are necessary. Analysis may lead to agreement among actors on the problem; however, if there is disagreement, the administrator defines target problems and target conditions utilizing the input of others. The administrator's willingness to accept and work on a problem is crucial.

The management model considers the administrator responsible for decision making, including not only problem definition and development of action plans for resolution, but also "problem dropping" if a problem is no longer relevant. However, decision making is not necessarily centralized or autocratic. The administrator also has the responsibility to see that the process is moving in a systematic manner, which usually involves actor agreement. Therefore, the model includes agreement-reaching strategies to foster consensus:

1. Agreement through improved understanding by:
   a. Information sharing and explanation.

      b.   Negotiation and compromise.
      c.   Relating to overall goals of the agency.
      d.   Identifying a common cause.
      e.   Confrontation.
  2. Agreement through administration directive.
  3. Agreement through any other situationally relevant method.

Since agreement is a significant feature of the model and strongly influences subsequent steps, it is important to determine if and how consensus was achieved. Only on rare occasions, if the nature of the problem requires strict confidentiality, will the administrator withhold all or most information from other actors in the situation.

In the first example, unclear admissions criteria, problem analysis involved calling a special staff meeting to discuss the problem and to determine conditions to be changed. In addition to the vagueness of admission criteria, the following were raised as contributing to the problem: (1) nursing staff's lack of experience and training in alcoholism, leading to a lack of understanding of the disease concept of alcoholism, lack of appreciation of factors surrounding recidivism, and consequently difficulty in evaluating repeat admissions; and (2) orientational and attitudinal dissonance toward alcoholism on the part of a few nursing staff. The nursing staff had difficulty accepting the last point; however, with the administrator's intervention, agreement was reached on other points. In light of earlier experiences, a suggestion for in-service training was made and agreed to. In addition, the administrator suggested holding a meeting to explain admission criteria.

In the second example, underutilization, the problem included external elements. Information about other treatment programs made clear that a sizable number of hospitals had developed comprehensive treatment programs offering a variety of services and treatment modalities as an answer to fragmented care. Since the center offered only detoxification services, its program was admittedly inadequate and fragmented compared to other programs. The comprehensive approach and accelerated public relations activities of other facilities created a situation of environmental turbulence and strain for this program, and thus the program lagged behind in recruiting patients. The Board of Directors agreed with this analysis of the situation and, in order to survive, opted to expand its program and authorized the administrator to do so. In terms of staff involvement in problem analysis, a few staff who had knowledge about other programs assisted in pooling the information and the staff in general analyzed the data. The administrator initiated the process and sought Board decision after preliminary agreement on the problem. Thus, the process involved three steps: pertinent data on the problem; consensus on the problem; and agreement and approval by the policy-making Board.

Goal Development

The third stage, determination of goals to be achieved in relation to each target condition, is essential in setting a direction for the problem-solving effort and in evaluating accomplishment. The process of goal development is the same as that of problem specification and agreement. A clear understanding of the implications of the goals in light of perceived or anticipated obstacles is emphasized. Agreement on goals may be reached by consensus through discussion and information sharing or by administrative decision. Goals should be specific, meaningful, attainable, and measurable. The more realistic and focused the goals, the more chances of concerted effort toward their accomplishment. While finalizing the goals, a tentative date for their achievement may be indicated; this may later emerge as a target date for task review.

In relation to the first example, the overall goal was to reduce inconsistency in admission of patients. The following intermediate goals were unanimously agreed upon: (1) to clarify admission criteria, (2) to provide an in-service training program for the staff including nursing personnel, and (3) to encourage staff to attend outside training programs, seminars, workshops, etc. The implied assumption was that training and education would change the orientation and attitude of nursing staff and would enhance the staff's appreciation of alcoholism and those afflicted by it. A review session to assess goal accomplishment was scheduled for after the in-service training program.

In the second example, survival of the organization was the overall goal. More precise intermediate goals included (1) internal reorganization and expansion of program base; (2) development of new tasks, role structure, treatment modalities, rules, and procedures; (3) publicizing of the newly developed program content; and (4) reaching out to the community to avoid being "detached" or "disconnected." Since resolution of the problem was believed to require long-term and experimental intervention, a preliminary review of the tasks and strategies would be done in six months, after which tentative review dates would be decided on.

Task Planning and Implementation

Following agreement on a target problem, target conditions, and goals, task planning is conducted to decide a course of action, details of implementation, and assignment of responsibilities. Two types of tasks have been identified: staff tasks and administrator's tasks.

Staff tasks refer to the role played by the organizational actors. The extent and mode of staff involvement is determined by the nature of the target problem and of alternative courses of action and their rationale. Possible obstacles and resources are considered, and out of this emerges a specific course of action for staff (task) and details of implementation.

Administrator's tasks involve the following organizational roles: deciding or agreeing to tasks and intervention strategies; helping break down tasks into more specific task units; and facilitating implementation through assignment of tasks and responsibilities. The administrator may also perform independent tasks when needed to facilitate the process. Staff input and collaboration is often helpful in making the problem more focused and tasks more manageable. Thus, the process can be a collaborative team effort. However, the administrator has responsibility and he must be able to agree to the problem, approve of the tasks, and undertake to implement the tasks to alleviate the problem.

An important perspective to maintain during task planning is that changes in the status of a problem can be accomplished through several ways. It can be achieved either by working on the target problem itself or by altering contextual factors that surround the problem (Reid, Chapter 7), or by attending to some elements of both the problem and the context. "Target problem" refers to the specified issue to be worked on, and "context" refers to the host of factors (causes, obstacles, and resources) that impinge upon the problem. The decision regarding which route to adopt is usually subject to the nature of the problem. In the first example cited in this chapter, tasks addressed both the specified issue of lack of clarity of admission criteria as well as the contextual factor of lack of training of staff in alcoholism. In the second example, tasks pertained to contextual factors in order to counteract environmental uncertainty to assure availability of patients. The goal in both cases is the successful resolution of the target problem.

What the issue of problem and context implies, however, is that problem resolution is capable of achieving contextual change regardless of which route one follows. Working on a problem may alter factors attending it; similarly working through a contextual factor (e.g., an obstacle) may facilitate problem-solving effort by addressing the impediments that played a part in the problem. A certain amount of contextual change is likely to occur either way. Furthermore, the resolution of a problem that impaired organizational functioning may have significant impact on other issues and may, in fact, engender positive consequences for the system. Thus, resolution of target problems can bring about contextual change.

In the first example, task planning and implementation addressed two target conditions: clarifying admission criteria, and developing a staff development program. The administrator assumed the task to call a meeting to discuss admission criteria, in consultation with the medical director and staff psychiatrist. The staff offered two suggestions for staff development: to arrange an in-service training program with guest speakers, and to allow staff participation in outside programs. The administrator asked the staff to develop a list of topics of interest to them and then encouraged the experienced therapy and nursing staff to volunteer to make presentations on the topics. Because this was a situation involving poor staff performance, it was necessary that training start immediately; arranging for guest speakers would have been time consuming. Hence, administrative intervention amounted to breaking the task down to a size that could be initially managed by internal resources. A series of 12 weekly in-service sessions was scheduled and the coordinator of the inpatient program was assigned responsibility to implement the series.

In regard to attendance in outside programs, the administrator agreed with the idea, but indicated that blanket approval was not possible and each request would be reviewed individually. In addition to these, the administrator's independent tasks included discussion with the nursing in-service training director to include topics on alcoholism in her staff development program, and discussion with the director of medical continuing education to arrange programs on alcoholism.

In the second example, the tasks were primarily administrative. In order to facilitate internal reorganization and expansion, the administrator prepared a blueprint outlining new rules, professional roles and task assignments, operating procedures, treatment programs and modalities, and a structure of programmatic staff hierarchy. At this planning and organization stage, staff involvement was marginal: their input was not formally sought, but was informally heeded by the administrator. After the Board's approval, the staff was formally apprised of the plan and their participation was solicited for the implementation stage. It may be noted that existing staff generally favored expansion and enthusiastically participated in the process.

As soon as internal reorganization was completed, the program publicized its approach in the community as "forward looking" with new ideas and techniques. Key people from different segments of society such as business, industry, schools, and churches were co-opted as members of a community advisory committee. The administrator's independent tasks at this point included visits to various agencies, speaking engagements, membership on committees, TV and radio appearances, community education programs, etc.

Task Review

Tasks have been conceptualized as a means to attain goals (Reid and Epstein, 1972). As such, review of tasks is essential to evaluate the level of accomplishment.

A tentative date for task review may be set in earlier phases such as goal development or task planning stages. However, the nature of the problem and the type of intervention influences when tasks are to be reviewed. For routine and repetitive problems, a weekly review during staff meetings may be advisable, or a specific target review date may be set. For problems needing long-term intervention, a periodic review at longer intervals may be more suitable.

The purpose of task review is to ascertain whether a given task has achieved its intended goal or at least contributed to progress toward the goal. Several questions guide task review: if the task has been completed, has the goal been achieved? If not, what are the obstacles? Was the time allotted to the task sufficient? If insufficient, should the time be extended further? If sufficient and yet the goal remains unattained, does the task need replanning? Through answering these questions, the extent of accomplishment or nonaccomplishment becomes clear. Also, any shift in the nature of the problem itself is revealed. Thus, the review indicates whether a task is to be extended, modified, terminated, or replanned and also whether the problem itself should be dropped in view of changed circumstances. In short, task review is used to appraise the present effort and guide future action.

In the first example, at the end of a staff meeting to clarify the admission criteria, staff input was sought to evaluate the outcome. While general satisfaction was expressed, staff pointed out a need to hold such meetings periodically for the benefit of new staff and for the reorientation of senior staff. Moreover, it was evident that the daytime meetings were inconvenient for the night staff, who could not attend or had to make additional trips to the facility. Staff consensus was to hold two similar meetings on the same day, one for the night shift and another for the day and evening shifts. The in-service training schedule was readjusted and a marked increase in attendance at the training sessions resulted.

After the completion of the 12-week training program, its outcome was discussed in a staff meeting. The feedback was positive to the extent that the overwhelming majority of staff recommended holding such sessions regularly on a monthly basis, and additional staff members volunteered to lead future training sessions. The review thus revealed not only the degree of task accomplishment but also the need to continue the program and the resources to make it possible.

In the second example, a preliminary review was done after 6 months, as decided, and another after 12 months. Staff provided input about internal structure and operating procedures, and the administrator reviewed the external elements. Except for some revisions in admission criteria and policies related to daily routines, the structure was considered functional at least for the beginning. However, after a year a structural change was introduced when the need for a new component, aftercare, became apparent. In addition, increased involvement of staff in providing a variety of services, more thorough but time-consuming documentation in patient charts, and increasing patient census made it difficult for existing staff to operate the program without additional personnel. The enhanced census enabled the administrator to gradually add staff to meet the problems identified during task review.

As noted earlier, the administrator's tasks included reaching out and projecting a "new" image through public relations activities and co-opting key persons through a community advisory committee. These tasks had helped in making people aware of the facility's new programs, in gaining the community's input, and in establishing contacts which often led to formal and informal agreements with business, industry, and social agencies.

Institutionalization

The final stage, institutionalization, involves resolution of the problem and institutionalization of the intervention technique. If the review indicates task accomplishment, the strategy used to handle the problem is established as one of the codified or uncodified policies of the organization.

It may be noted that the process reaches the institutionalization stage only after the tasks have been accomplished. If the review shows non-accomplishment, the management process will return to an earlier stage and start again. For instance, if time allocated to task completion needs to be extended, the duration of the implementation phase will be prolonged for a designated period of time. If the task needs to be modified, however, the administrator will go back to the task planning and implementation stage and restart from there. If dissonance in the goal is discovered, the process will restart from the goal development stage.

In the first example, as mentioned, task review resulted in awareness of the inconvenience of day meetings for night shift staff, which led to the modification of the schedule of the in-service training program at the implementation stage. The major outcome, however, was that upon successful accomplishment of both tasks (meeting to clarify criteria and in-service training program), the meetings became regular features at the facility.

The second example illustrated that the organization's effective survival involves not only internal functioning, but also environmental manipulation and adaptation. Internal restructuring in response to external constraints and exploiting external elements enhanced the organization's effectiveness. The strategies used proved fruitful and some strategies such as reaching out and extablishing outside contacts and working closely with the community advisory committees became a necessary and integral part of the administrator's role.

Features of the Model

Several features of the problem-oriented management model for treatment organizations deserve further comment. First, the development of the model was informed by an established practice method, the task-centered approach. The rationale for using a treatment model as an underlying basis is the premise that management process is "inherently a human process—people relating to people" (Gibson, Ivancevich, & Donnelly, 1976:50) and that one of the important managerial roles involves human skills—the ability to work with and through people, understand human behavior, and mobilize human resources to attain goals (Hersey and Blanchard, 1977). These skills appear to fall well within the domain of practice methods.

Furthermore, role mobility in treatment organizations is usually from clinical to administrative positions. The transition reflects significant role discontinuity among clinicians when they assume administrative roles (Patti et al., 1979). A management system informed by a practice method which not only offers distinct methods of problem solving but also promises "connection with the profession as a whole" (Reid, 1978:108) may reduce role dissonance among treatment organization administrators whose prior responsibilities have been in clinical treatment. The problem-oriented practice model developed by Reid and Epstein (1972) seems to fulfill this promise.

In addition, basing the management model on a practice model seeks to link two elements of the social work profession: treatment and administration. Such a linkage can illustrate how and with what adaptations the intervention strategies of one system can be used in another area. If such an articulation can be brought about, it may augment interconnectedness and relevant coherence between the different elements of the profession. In the field trial of the model, its clinical base was found to be particularly significant as the respondents, former clinicians, felt a sense of familiarity with the model and at the same time developed an appreciation for administrative processes.

Second, the model recognizes that alleviation of organizational problems is basically the administrator's responsibility. However, problems are not his or her personal problems; rather, they are role- and job-related problems which he or she has the responsibility and authority to resolve but which invariably involve other organizational actors. Thus, the model conceives the administrator as a practitioner rather than a client. However, in terms of whom the problems belong to, there is no clear-cut conceptual differentiation between the practitioner and the client in this management model. This marks an adaptation of the practice model for an organizational context.

Third, the model encourages a democratic style of administration. Although the administrator has responsibility for resolving problems, depending upon who brings them up and who is involved, the problems can be further classified as staff problems, client problems, etc. Thus, organizational problem solving involves not only an administrator but also other actors with primary or secondary responsibility. Such a situation calls for a collaborative effort in which concerned actors may participate. To facilitate collaboration, the model includes strategies to help reach agreement. Although the determination of responsibility and the extent of involvement of actors is subject to the nature of the problem, this conceptualization of primary and secondary responsibility and collaborative problem solving with designated roles and assignments can be viewed as a further adaptation of the practice model.

Fourth, specificity of problems and tasks is a crucial aspect of the model. Specificity through breaking down problems into smaller units and through developing tasks that are meaningful yet attainable assists in making the unit of attention focused and measurable. This is important to provide a firmer scientific base to the model (Reid, 1977b).

Fifth, the model integrates concepts from two schools of organizational theory: the scientific and the human relations schools of management. The goal-specific and time-limited aspects of the model are derived from the elements of the scientific school (Fayol, 1949; Mooney, 1947; F. Taylor, 1911; Weber, 1947) and the elements of democratic mode of administration and collaborative team approach are derived from the humanistic school (Likert, 1961; Maslow, 1954; McGregor, 1960; Simon, 1961). Thus, the model incorporates strengths of both approaches and offers an integrated method of problem solving.

Sixth, the model views organizations as adaptive, equilibrium-seeking, problem-solving systems that exist in and interact with an environment and are thus responsive to both internal and environmental demands. The processes of reciprocity, adaptation, and problem solving are critical determinants of organizational effectiveness (Bennis, 1966; Schein, 1965). The emphasis on process is of particular interest here as the management model approaches problem solving as an evolving process in keeping with the dynamic nature of the problems and precipitating factors. The process thus assumes importance as a primary focus of analysis.

Seventh, the use of time limits for the review of intervention strategies is an important feature of the model. It may be argued that it is not possible to set a time limit with all kinds of problems and especially those which need long-term intervention. However, a tentative date may be set for a preliminary review of tasks, as in the second example. The review may affirm the viability of the tasks or may indicate modifications and changes necessary to gain better results. This strategy enables one to measure the progress toward the alleviation of the problem and to revise the plan and institute corrective actions in light of new information. Thus, review of tasks at a designated time is important to provide corrective feedback as well as evaluation data.

At the same time, the problem-oriented management model's use of time limits departs from the task-centered practice model in two respects. First, time limits may be a great deal longer than the three months recommended by Reid and Epstein (1972). The complexity of organizational structure and the need to influence both internal and external factors often require a longer period of time. Second, the time limits may not be set until the Goal Development or Task Planning stages, rather than at the Problem Specification stage as recommended by Reid and Epstein (1972). The actors to be involved and the courses of action to pursue are often not clear enough to set time limits before these later stages. The example of program underutilization illustrates both points: the major restructuring of the program required 6 to 12 months, and even that time parameter was not evident until the course of action had been selected and planned. Despite these differences, however, the use of time limits to focus and structure problem-solving effort remains the same as in the practice model.

Last, institutionalization, although somewhat similar to generalization, is a concept unique to this model. Unlike termination with clients in clinical situations, in the management model successful intervention strategies become part of the organization's armamentarium as written or unwritten standing policies. The strategies then act as a point of reference for future use. Thus, the model recognizes proven strategies and provides for their reemployment under similar situations.

In summary, the problem-oriented management model provides a comprehensive approach to organizational problem solving. It is highly structured, time-limited, and goal-directed, and it emphasizes staff involvement, agreement, and communication in decision making and problem resolution. It is an administrative model which encourages participation and consensus and thus avoids what Simon calls, "the separation of decision from action" (1961:157). More specifically, the model offers:

1. A way of identifying and analyzing problems and their implications.
2. A way of defining problems and specifying goals to be achieved.
3. A way of developing action plans and implementing agreed-upon tasks.
4. A system of checks and balances through the use of time limits to review the extent of accomplishment and to institute corrective actions in the event of deviations.
5. A system of institutionalization of proven strategies for future use, and
6. A way of determining the nature and extent of staff participation in the process.

Teaching and Measuring Task-Centered Skills:
13 The Skill Assessment Teaching Model

Eleanor Reardon Tolson

Since its inception, proponents of the task-centered model have emphasized an empirical orientation, both in developing and refining the model and in the practitioner's approach to intervention and its outcome (Fortune, introductory chapter, this volume; Reid, 1977b). This chapter describes a less-emphasized aspect of the empirical orientation, the attempts to measure practice skills necessary to implement the task-centered model and to teach the task-centered model more efficiently by isolating and emphasizing those skills.[1]

The Skill Assessment Teaching Model focuses on the specific practitioner skills needed to implement the task-centered approach. The major characteristics of the Teaching Model are specificity, repetition, and feedback. The skills are identified and their use in cases measured from Case Recording Guides structured to highlight the steps of task-centered practice, rather than from process recordings or other sequential case narratives. Supervisors rate performance of these skills using either the Revised Profile of Practice Skills or the Skill Assessment Scale, with feedback to learners focused on use and improvement of the specific skills. The ratings for each skill are tallied at the end of each learning period on the Student Evaluation form. These three instruments—Case Recording Guides, Student Evaluation, and the Revised Profile of Practice Skills or the Skill Assessment Scale—provide the content and structure for the learning process.

Before turning to the content of the instruments, a word about their evolution is in order. The work to be described took place from 1973 to

[1]I am grateful to Laura Epstein for her ground-breaking efforts and to David Ayars for his contribution to the development of the Skill Assessment Scale. Mr. Ayars deserves particular credit for developing the termination skills.

1980 at the University of Chicago, School of Social Service Administration, where approximately 25 first-year students were enrolled each year in practice classes which emphasized task-centered casework. By 1973, Epstein had developed the first generation of instruments, the Case Recording Guides, the Student Evaluation, and the original Profile of Practice Skills, which contained one statement of definitions of a variety of skills (Epstein, 1980). After working with this package for a year or two, the author made two important revisions. First, the format for rating skills was incorporated into the Recording Guides, on the right-hand side of each page, so that supervisors could identify, rate, and provide immediate feedback about skills at the point at which they should have occurred, without lengthy and redundant notes to students. Including the ratings on the Recording Guide also sharpened the students' awareness of the relationship between what they did with the client and the skills they were expected to demonstrate.

The second important change consisted of defining two levels of performance for most skills. Previously, skills were rated as performed or not performed, without consideration of varying levels of proficiency. The Revised Profile of Practice Skills in addition rated performance as basic or advanced. However, recognition that the skills could be rated qualitatively led the way to a third rating form, the Skill Assessment Scale. The instrument, developed with the assistance of David Ayars, enumerates activities to be performed in the demonstration of a skill. Skill performance is then rated according to the number of activities that the student has performed. The second and third generations of the teaching model, involving the Revised Profile and the Skill Assessment Scale, are the focus of this chapter.

The process by which the instruments to measure and evaluate practitioner skill were developed is a combination of the logic-deductive and the constant comparative methods of research (Glaser and Straus, 1967). Beginning with a formal paradigm, task-centered practice, a number of practice skills were deduced. These skills were examined in work with clients; over 700 clients were seen by student practitioners between 1973 and 1980 with a minimum of four case recordings per client. As a result of this examination, some skills were dropped and others were added based on supervisors' comments about superior and inferior performance. More important, however, was that the opportunity to compare results of skill activities with large numbers of clients permitted *ad hoc* examination of what might be effective. For example, when work with children floundered, supervisors frequently suggested that the practitioners redefine the purpose of their work using concrete examples. Over time, the same suggestion emerged repeatedly and was found effective; thus, it appeared that an important skill (client role induction) and an important activity in the performance of that skill (concrete examples with children) had been identified.

The goal thus far has been to identify all skills and activities that seem to be associated with effective practice. The next step is to test the skills experimentally to see which ones are most related to positive outcomes. Such identification of valid skills (those associated with outcomes) is probably the next major step forward in psychotherapy research and one which has not yet been tackled (Matarazzo, 1978). Although the large sample size necessary and the cost of such a study have been prohibitive, Rooney (1983) is using the Skill Assessment Scale to measure middle-phase skills and to determine the extent to which reliable measurements can be achieved.

The Instruments

The materials to implement the Skill Assessment Teaching Model include three types of instruments. The Case Recording Guides and the summary Student Evaluation Form are similar but there are two approaches to measuring student skills, the Revised Profile and the Skill Assessment Scale.

The Case Recording Guides

The Case Recording Guides provide the structure for student descriptions of each interview and the evidence for skill ratings. They require the student to conceptualize how her client interactions relate to task-centered practice by responding to specific questions rather than by writing a narrative description of the process of the interview. There are three different case recording guides. The first covers the initial phase of work, which may last up to four interviews. The second is for the middle phase of intervention and is completed several times, depending on the number of interviews in the middle phase. The third guide is for the final, termination interview.

Initial Recording Guide. The information sought on the initial phase Recording Guide includes the following: demographic data on client's family; initial problems as stated by client, practitioner, and referral source; client characteristics; living or social situation; introduction to treatment; target problems; problem specifications; determination of priorities; assessment; treatment contract (including time limits); work with family; work with others; and resource provision.

This information is similar to that sought when teaching any treatment approach, with the exception of problem specification. In task-centered practice, problems should be measurable; hence, very specific information is necessary. This has proven to be a difficult skill for students to grasp, and thus the Recording Guide section on problem specification is especially important. The most revealing information about the student's understanding of the initial phase of the task-centered model comes from contrasting the student's response to the question, "What is the main difficulty in the client's opinion?" to her response to a later question, "What is the target problem statement?" If the responses are different, as they frequently are with beginning students, it is clear that the student has missed the basic tenet of task-centered practice to focus on problems identified by the client.

Middle Sessions Recording Guide. The Recording Guide for middle-phase interviews seeks the following information: review of task progress; review of problem status; changes in treatment contract; task planning and implementation (described for each task); use of time limits; activities with others; and resource provision. If work in the initial phase is sound, the middle phase is not complex. For example, if the problem specification is well developed on the Initial Recording Guide, evaluating problem change by comparing current to previous status is relatively straightforward. Students resubmit all earlier recording guides on a case with new ones; availability of the Initial Recording Guide is particularly important in order to identify difficulties such as "drift" away from target problems, inappropriate task plans, or deterioration in problem status. Occasionally, student work is subtly but substantially off the mark. For example, a student working with a learning disabled client with the target problem of not attempting to spell words on spelling tests set up rewards based on the number of words that were spelled *correctly* rather than the number attempted. Treatment was not successful until the incentive system was altered to base rewards on the number of words attempted, after which the client earned dozens of gold stars and improved the percentage of correctly spelled words.

The majority of student difficulties in implementing the task-centered model during the middle phase can be identified through the Skill Assessment Scale. However, one student difficulty that can be missed entails dealing with new concerns as the client presents them. While this skill is included in the Skill Assessment Scale in an item on changes in the target problem, students sometimes do not recognize a new concern nor provide sufficient information for the supervisor to identify that the client is expressing a new concern. There are insufficient data, not because of intentional omissions or distortions by the student, but as a result of pressures on the student to develop measurable problems and specifications and to ameliorate the problems within a limited amount of time. Students who have had difficulty with problem specification are often reluctant to retarget a new problem. Beginning students have a tendency to rush down an identified path once problems are targeted rather than to repeat the activities of the initial phase—exploring, targeting, and specifying problems—even when it appears that problems were incorrectly targeted or have changed. Currently, the supervisor's best clue to the existence of unidentified client concerns is consistent client nonperformance of tasks which appear appropriate and well-developed. If the supervisor suspects a lack of congruence between the practitioner and the client about the target problem, the supervisor can help the student clarify the client's concerns by asking the student to identify topics the *client* initiated, or topics accompanied by the greatest affect. Here, as elsewhere, the supervisor needs to be alert for the possibility that pressures inherent in the task-centered model may produce mechanistic practice on the part of the student.

Final Recording Guide. The Final Recording Guide seeks information about the final task and problem reviews; the client's accomplishments; any remaining areas of difficulty and plans for them; review of problem-solving skills; and a discussion of termination. It also asks students to identify their best and worst work with the client. The responses to this last item are often illuminating for the supervisor. Students frequently underestimate their accomplishments with both the extent of problem amelioration and the quality of their own efforts. They sometimes identify their very best efforts as their worst, usually because of a discrepancy between expectations of novices and realities perceived by supervisors who have survived trial by fire. For example, one student succeeded in involving extremely reluctant parents in several treatment sessions with excellent results (the target problem was resolved); she identified work with the family as her worst work because she could not secure the parents' participation in *all* treatment sessions.

The tendency of students to underrate their success combined with the pressures to effect change in a limited period of time occasionally produces a phenomenon that supervisors must be wary of: scolding the client at termination for lack of accomplishment. This tendency is reduced somewhat by including activities like "praises the client" and "emphasizes accomplishments" within the definitions of termination skills. However, it is wise to discuss the issue long before students reach termination.

The Revised Profile of Practice Skills and the Skill Assessment Scale

The Revised Profile of Practice Skills (Epstein, Tolson, and Reid, 1978) and the Skill Assessment Scale have the same objective: the identification and measurement of practice skills. The skills defined in the Skill Assessment Scale (SAS) are listed in Table 13.1.

Table 13.1. Skill Assessment Scale

Initial Phase Skills	Middle Phase Skills	Termination Skills
Explains role and purpose	Utilizes time limits	Assesses change
Obtains necessary facts	Alters time limits	Plans for work to be
Targets problems	appropriately	continued
Determines problem	Revises assessment as	Reviews problem-
priorities	necessary	solving skills
Explores target problems	Reviews problem status	Emphasizes positive
Develops problem specifi-	Formulates tasks	aspects of inter-
cation	Plans details of tasks	vention
Develops goals	Establishes rationale	Discusses feelings
Sets time limits	and incentives for	about termination
Contracts with client	tasks	
Makes an assessment	Simulates tasks	
Demonstrates empathy[a]	Anticipates obstacles to	
Secures resources[a]	task performance	
Consults and involves	Summarizes tasks	
family as appropriate[a]	Reviews task progress	
Consults and involves	Revises unsuccessful	
significant others as	tasks	
appropriate[a]	Addresses nonper-	
	formance of tasks	
	Addresses nontargeted	
	problems raised by	
	client	

[a]These items are rated during all phases of treatment.

While the skills identified on both rating instruments, the Revised Profile and the SAS, are basically the same, they are defined in quite different ways. In general, the SAS definitions are considerably more detailed and complex than the Revised Profile definitions.

In the Revised Profile, most skills are defined at a beginning and an advanced level. Each skill is rated as performed at the advanced level (* on Figure 13.1), at the beginning level [Y (yes)], not performed and should have been [N (no)], or not performed and not necessary [U (unobserved)]. In the following example, the beginning-level skill is printed in lowercase letters, the advanced in capitals (Epstein, Tolson, and Reid, 1978):

Skill: Establishes SUFFICIENT rationale and incentives.
Definition: Discusses with the client the potential gains to be had from performing the task. IDENTIFIES AND/OR PROVIDES THE CLIENT WITH RATIONALES AND REWARDS THAT MOTIVATE THE CLIENT TO PERFORM THE TASK.

In the SAS, each skill is defined by a set of activities whose presence or absence is evaluated. The student's rating for each skill is the sum of activities involved in the skill which are present in the Recording Guide. The same skill is used to illustrate the SAS definitions:

Skill: Establishes rationale and incentives for task performance.
Activities:
1. Elicits from the client (cues the client if necessary) the rationale for performing the task; some reasons or ways that performance of this task can contribute to target problem reduction.
2. Elicits from the client and suggests as many different reasons as possible that task performance may contribute to problem reduction.
3. Discusses with the client whether concrete rewards are necessary for successful task performance.
4. Permits the client to choose the reward(s) to be provided for successful task performance when indicated by No. 3.
5. Establishes systematic use of rewards for successful task performance when indicated by No. 3.

In order to obtain a summary rating for each skill, the proportion of activities performed to activities expected to be performed is identified. Thus, if 5 activities are expected but only one is demonstrated, the proportion is 1/5. The proportion is then compared to a predetermined scale, which ranges from 0 to 5 (U is included for situations in which the skill was appropriately not used). For example, the scoring system for the skill illustrated above, "establishes rationale and incentives," is:

U
$0 = 0/5$
$1 = 1/5$
$2 = 2/5$
$3 = 3/5$
$4 = 4/5$
$5 = 5/5$

The numbers on the left represent the scale, which is consistent for all skills. The number on the right identifies the proportion of activities that must be performed to achieve a particular rating on the scale. If 1 of 5 activities had been demonstrated, skill performance would receive a rating of 1.

The number of SAS activities is not consistent across skills. For example, the skill "develops goals statement" has only 3 activities whereas the skill "obtains necessary facts" has 17 activities. In those cases, the five-point evaluative scale is retained and the proportion of activities present is prorated (see Figure 13.2). If some activities are more important than others, they can be weighted so that more activities must be performed to achieve a higher skill rating.

An example of the difference between the Revised Profile and the SAS is from a student who describes her work in "establishing rationales and incentives" as: "I reminded Ms. Sutton that to continue performing tasks could lead to finding an independent living situation." On the Revised Profile, this skill would be rated "Y" (the skill occurs at a beginning level). The student has discussed the potential gains for doing tasks in a general way. She has not done so for each task, however, nor has she provided additional, specific rationales or incentives. Thus, the work is not considered advanced. On the more complex Skill Assessment Scale, the student earns a rating of "1." While she suggested or elicited a rationale (Activity 1), only one rationale was mentioned (Activity 2). Furthermore, she did not ascertain where concrete incentives might be desirable to the client, nor, if they were, what the incentives might be (Activities 3–5).

Incorporation of Skill Ratings on Recording Guides

As previously described, the connection between the descriptive information provided on the Case Recording Guides and the evaluation and feedback about skill performance is facilitated by incorporating the skill rating systems directly onto the Recording Guides. This is illustrated in Figure 13.1 from the Revised Profile and Figure 13.2 from the SAS.

As is apparent, the information sought is the same regardless of the rating system employed. The skills are numbered to facilitate locating skill definitions (for example, the 6, 5, 7 in Figure 13.2) and abbreviations of the skill definitions serve to prompt the student's and rater's memories. For example, the activities in skill 7, Figure 13.2, "develops a specification statement," are as follows: includes a stated frequency of occurrence (freq occ); includes a stated baseline period (baseline); is stated as a problem rather than as a goal (pr nt goal); and is one statement in a set that, taken together and altered, could logically be expected to change the state of the target problem from that described in the problem statement to that described in the goal statement (one in set).

Student Evaluation Form

The Student Evaluation Form is a summary which lists the skills that are being taught and a scale for evaluating them. To rate the student's skill in performance at the end of a marking period, the supervisor goes through the recording guides and tallies the ratings for each skill. The skills differ

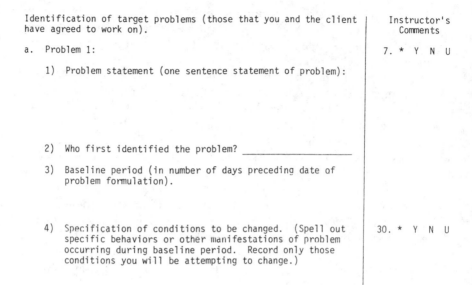

Identification of target problems (those that you and the client have agreed to work on).	Instructor's Comments
a. Problem 1:	7. * Y N U
1) Problem statement (one sentence statement of problem):	
2) Who first identified the problem? _____	
3) Baseline period (in number of days preceding date of problem formulation).	
4) Specification of conditions to be changed. (Spell out specific behaviors or other manifestations of problem occurring during baseline period. Record only those conditions you will be attempting to change.)	30. * Y N U

FIGURE 13.1 A page from the Initial Recording Guide incorporating the Revised Profile of Practice Skills

in the frequency with which they are rated. Initial phase skills such as targeting the problem and developing problem specifications are rated one to three times per case (once for each target problem). Middle-phase skills, such as generates tasks and task alternatives or reviews task progress in detail, are rated more frequently, depending on the number of interviews and tasks generated. Termination skills are normally rated once per case. The ratings are then transformed on a scale incorporated into the Student Evaluation form that takes into account the number of opportunities to perform the skill. Thus, the final evaluation contains no surprises for the student, who can relate her performance on each case directly to her final skill rating.

Advantages and Disadvantages

The Good News

The major advantages to the Skill Assessment Teaching Model are the increase in the number of skills that can be taught, the level at which they are taught, and the reduction in learning time. The Skill Assessment Scale includes 30 skills and 198 activities that might be performed in demon-

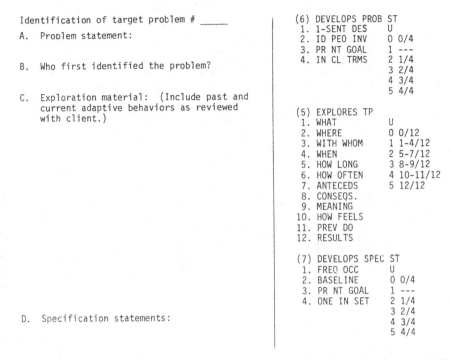

Identification of target problem # _____

A. Problem statement:

B. Who first identified the problem?

C. Exploration material: (Include past and
    current adaptive behaviors as reviewed
    with client.)

D. Specification statements:

(6) DEVELOPS PROB ST
 1. 1-SENT DES   U
 2. ID PEO INV   0 0/4
 3. PR NT GOAL   1 ---
 4. IN CL TRMS   2 1/4
                  3 2/4
                  4 3/4
                  5 4/4

(5) EXPLORES TP
 1. WHAT   U
 2. WHERE   0 0/12
 3. WITH WHOM   1 1-4/12
 4. WHEN   2 5-7/12
 5. HOW LONG   3 8-9/12
 6. HOW OFTEN   4 10-11/12
 7. ANTECEDS   5 12/12
 8. CONSEQS.
 9. MEANING
10. HOW FEELS
11. PREV DO
12. RESULTS

(7) DEVELOPS SPEC ST
 1. FREQ OCC   U
 2. BASELINE   0 0/4
 3. PR NT GOAL   1 ---
 4. ONE IN SET   2 1/4
                  3 2/4
                  4 3/4
                  5 4/4

FIGURE 13.2   A page from the Initial Recording Guide incorporating the Skill
                Assessment Scale

strating the skills. It is simply not possible for a supervisor to observe that
many dimensions of a student's work in such detail without a structured
instrument. Similarly, it is difficult to conceptualize and rate quality of
complex practice skills without the precise operational definitions offered
by the activity components of each skill.

Another advantage is that the skill rating instruments, especially the
Skill Assessment Scale, simplify the process of teaching skills and make it
more efficient. This is because most skills are defined by very simple
activities which require only that the students' attention is called to them
through the instruments. The battery of skills is encountered in the classroom during the normal process of teaching task-centered practice through
the usual means (role-play, modeling, and prepared case materials). There
are some exceptions, complex skills which require didactic presentations
and experiential exercises focused on the skills themselves. These include
the systematic provision of concrete rewards, an activity frequently performed when establishing rationale and incentives, and all the activities
necessary to produce the problem specification. Even with the special

attention to those skills, however, relatively little time is consumed by teaching the skills *per se*. In fact, since students must deal with these skills in every recording guide and after every interview, excessive attention in the classroom would probably be counterproductive.

Use of the Skill Assessment Teaching Model appears to reduce learning time by about one-half to one-third. The reduction occurred after the ratings were incorporated into the recording guides and hence students were receiving prompt, specific, and repetitive feedback about their skills. Prior to this, the average student had a good grasp of the skills by the end of the second quarter or beginning of the third. Now, comparable performance is demonstrated early in the second quarter. A useful approach to ensure rapid acquisition of the skills is for supervisors to rate skills more rather than less rigorously on early student cases. Students then take skill demonstration seriously and work hard to raise their performance so as to average out early ratings with which they are unsatisfied. Also, students react badly to the reverse—becoming more rigorous later— because they feel the rules are being changed.

Another advantage to this teaching model is the additional teaching and learning it enables. Once supervisors learn the method, they can provide feedback about skill performance expeditiously. As a result, they can spend more time and thought on the unique aspects of each case. They might, for example, discuss how the client's behavior demonstrates, or differs from, normal development, how the behavior might be explained by differing theories, or what creative tasks might be devised to alter it. Furthermore, this type of discussion is considerably more rewarding for supervisors than writing, for the umpteenth time, "Tasks are activities done by the client *outside* the session for the purpose of alleviating the target problems."

Similarly, supervisors who are facile with the method can handle more students at a time. We normally meet with students in group supervision once each week and supplement this with individual supervision when necessary. Group supervision is possible because of the amount of information and feedback about individual cases which is given through the recording guides. The group supervision time can then be used to discuss common issues or to delve more deeply into particularly challenging clients and problems or particularly intriguing and successful interventions. A secondary gain from group supervision appears to be the amount of vicarious learning that occurs. Students have the opportunity, in the group, to learn about clients and problems encountered in different settings as well as to observe and support one another's intellectual and emotional struggles.

The students' response to the Skill Assessment Teaching Model is mixed. On the positive side, the overwhelming majority recognize the "fairness" of the approach and like the clear expectations. A small percentage of intelligent but unsure students seem overly exuberant about it and it is hard to get them to do anything else.

Finally, the approach has two important advantages which have yet to be exploited. These are its usefulness for research and its "expandability." It can be used for research in a number of areas such as examining case outcome in relation to practitioner skill or measuring the efficacy of various teaching approaches. Its expandability permits adding new skills as appropriate, and the basic approach can be used with an entirely different set of skills derived from different models of practice.

The Bad News

The Skill Assessment Teaching Model does only what it is intended to do: teach task-centered and a few related practice skills. It does not teach interviewing skills nor does it teach students to make theoretically derived assessments. Thus, it must be supported by other content as well as other forms of teaching, for example, listening to tape recordings of student interviews to assess interviewing skills.

As a corollary to this, as noted above, it does do what it is intended to do effectively: focus attention on skills. A few students have difficulty focusing on more than one issue at a time and, as a result, this emphasis on skills is sometimes to the detriment of a more important concern, client problem alleviation. This difficulty is a serious one for competency-based methods of field instruction because the overall purpose of seeing clients can get lost in the effort to develop individual skills. For example, one videotape of a task-centered case with a successful outcome includes some scenes with less-than-perfect interviewing techniques. Students trained in microcounseling skills (Ivey and Authier, 1978) tend to be very critical because the practitioner does not make frequent eye contact, sits on a chair which is higher than that of the client, and so on. It is difficult to get such students to notice that the client has given up alcohol, secured adequate housing, learned to negotiate the social service system, regained custody of her children, and in other ways exceeded expectations for such a complex case.

The tendency for students to be overly concerned with skills and not enough with problem alleviation is quickly revealed and usually easily rectified because of the emphasis on continual task review, problem review, and outcome in the task-centered model. In addition, the design of the Recording Guides and Skill Assessment Scale is intended to minimize overemphasis on skill: the student must give information on *each* target problem and each task, rather than selectively reporting only the skillful aspects of intervention.

As previously observed, student response to the Skill Assessment Teaching Model has been mixed. One complaint is that the teaching model is too confining; that is, it holds them responsible for doing task-centered practice. This can be viewed as an advantage or disadvantage depending on the purpose of the course. If the purpose is to teach task-centered practice, then the expectation that they will implement the model is appropriate. If, however, the course is more eclectic, then the use of the Skill Assessment Teaching Model may overemphasize task-centered practice.

Another complaint from some students is that the Skill Assessment Teaching Model measures what they write and teaches them what to write rather than measuring what they actually do in practice. To a certain extent this is true, but it is equally true of all forms of supervision: students may distort what happened in line with what supervisors wish to hear (Muslin et al., 1967; Rosenblatt and Meyer, 1975). When students suggest that they are being evaluated on their writing rather than their performance, we point out that (1) we listen to tape recordings and this source of data is not ignored, and (2) understanding in thinking and writing is, for most students, a necessary precursor to performing. This response appears to make sense to most students.

Occasionally, a student will question the need for any kind of written report about interviews, especially with the ready availability of cassette recorders. Tape recordings are necessary for evaluating and teaching interviewing skills, but they do nothing to increase the student's ability to observe or to think. In fact, the burden of conceptualizing the interview falls on the listener, the supervisor, who already possesses the skills that are to be imparted. Thus, for almost all practice-education situations, a combination of tape recordings and conceptually oriented written recordings are necessary.

A very small percentage of students, about equal to those who "love" this method of instruction, find it unfair and extremely difficult. These are usually students who are not able to conceptualize practice easily, and the problem is normally revealed early when the student's first Case Recording Guide is a narrative or process report. Such students feel, often correctly, that they are practicing skillfully or, at least, doing some "good things" in practice, and that it is unfair to grade them on conceptual ability. However, there is tentative evidence that cognitive ability is related to better exploration and diagnostic skill (Duehn and Mayadas, 1979; Holloway and Wolleat, 1980). Furthermore, conceptualizing practice is essential to performing well in future roles such as supervisor.

Finally, most students complain that completing the recording guides is too time consuming. Some students have spent as long as four hours on the Initial Recording Guides with their first clients. However, the amount of time diminishes with experience, and once familiar with the model and the skills, the average student spends less than an hour on a recording guide.

The students' concerns about the teaching model are, to some extent, an intrinsic part of the reaction of first-year graduate students to field work. This does not mean that the criticisms should be discounted, however. For example, as a result of inviting students to critique the approach, we learned that the approach can be overused. Once the skills are mastered, continued focus on them leads to oversatiation and unnecessary redundancy.

Students' concerns also provoked another question: Is the Revised Profile superior to the Skill Assessment Scale for educational purposes? The amount of student frustration encountered while using the Revised Profile appeared equivalent to the frustration expressed during any form of field education, whereas the dissatisfaction seemed to increase noticeably when the Skill Assessment Scale replaced the Revised Profile. Unfortunately, no students used both instruments, and so no one could provide comparative feedback; incorporation of the Skill Assessment Scale also coincided with the implementation of a major curriculum revision which was almost universally disliked by students. As a result, it is impossible to determine the extent to which the Skill Assessment Scale increased dissatisfaction, and the relative usefulness of the two instruments for educational purposes is yet to be examined. It may be that the Skill Assessment Scale, with its greater detail, is appropriate for initial learning and that the Profile of Practice Skills should be substituted once students are well on their way to mastery. On the other hand, the SAS may be too detailed, leading to unnecessary student frustration, and should be reserved for research use only. The intention at this point is to engage future students in examining whether the SAS or the Profile is preferable for educational purposes.

The advantages in the amount and quality of feedback supervisors are able to offer students by using the Skill Assessment Teaching Model have been described. However, the start-up time poses difficulties for supervisors. First, supervisors must learn not only the process but, in some cases, the skills themselves. Second, supervisors' efforts to use the approach are at first quite time consuming. While initially the need to refer to the definitions takes time, with practice the skills become committed to memory and reference to the Profile or the SAS is infrequently needed. Consequently, supervisors often prefer to begin with only one or two students. In fact, however, supervisors learn the method much more quickly and thoroughly if they use it with a number of students because of the repetition and because different students and clients present them with more challenges in assessing the skills.

A disadvantage consistently anticipated but not yet experienced is resistance on the part of supervisors to learning and using the method. The initial reaction to what at first glance appears to be a very complicated model is doubt and fear: "Will I ever be able to learn this? The students will know more than I do." Thus far, however, all supervisors have plunged in and learned the model rapidly. Usually three sessions, one for each of the phases of treatment, are sufficient to teach the approach. Once supervisors realize that they will be taken through the method gradually, their fears are allayed and they become most supportive.

One final observation about the use of the method by supervisors merits attention: the accuracy of rating skills varies among supervisors. For teaching purposes, this is not particularly problematic if supervisors develop a level of consistency which enables students to identify the supervisor's expectations. Needless to say, this variation is intolerable if the method is used for research.

Conclusions

The Skill Assessment Teaching Model appears to be a very powerful approach to teaching effective task-centered practice. Deriving skills and skill definitions from the teaching model has enhanced our ability to teach task-centered practice efficiently. The examination of the effect of skills on clients has, in turn, played a role in developing task-centered practice. The Skill Assessment Scale, as it currently exists, is an outline for task-centered practice that should be equally useful in teaching or research and, because of its dual purpose, for both simultaneously. On hindsight, it is not surprising that a treatment model which was developed with the intention of being researchable should produce an equally researchable teaching method.

Epilogue

Anne E. Fortune

The task-centered model has shared with social work several professional trends: increasing consciousness of issues in accountability; increasing reliance on empirical evidence; interest in alternatives to traditional long-term or open-ended treatment; and a willingness to accept more limited treatment goals. The model has developed within that social climate since the publication of *Task-Centered Casework* (Reid and Epstein) in 1972. At that time, the task-centered approach was seen as limited to adults and older children who had difficulties which fell into a restricted range of target problems and whose problems met the criteria mentioned in my introductory chapter (client acknowledgement, resources available to alleviate problem, and specificity). Reid and Epstein (1972) suggested several areas for development of the model, all of which have been subsequently explored: in long-term care, with children, with families, in situational crises, and in authoritative casework situations. This volume and preceding work include field tests or controlled experiments in each of those areas, as well as in others. This chapter reviews some of the trends in task-centered practice since 1972 and previews some of the potential future developments.

Developments in the Task-Centered Model

Expanded Applicability of the Model

Since 1972, the task-centered model has been used with expanded age ranges of clients, target problems, modalities, and service systems. It is now appropriate for children as young as six years (Epstein, 1977; Reid et al., 1980; R. Rossi, 1977). Adaptations for work with young children include more concrete, behavioral problem specification, more tasks of an incremental nature, and more concrete aids such as drawings, task lists, and games (Epstein, 1977; Fortune, 1979a; Tolson, Chapter 13, this volume). At the other end of the life cycle, the approach has been used with well and frail elderly in the community (Cormican, 1977; Dierking, Brown, and Fortune, 1980; Rathbone-McCuan, Chapter 8, this volume; Toseland and Coppola, Chapter 5). Adaptations for the elderly include greater practitioner activity in carrying out tasks; more physical aids to memory such as notes; and more actively pursuing family involvement (Fortune and Rathbone-McCuan, 1981; Toseland and Coppola, Chapter 5).

A second trend is expansion of target problems for which the task-centered model is appropriate. In Reid's (1978) *The Task-Centered System*, the scope of target problems was expanded and the original requirement that a problem in living fall into a category in the typology of target problems was dropped. However, the focus of the model—problems in living—has not changed. Thus, the model has now been applied to alleviate hallucinations, suicidal impulses, and problems with parents among disturbed individuals, but the model does not deal with the personality characteristics or intrapsychic processes of the disturbed individual (Brown, 1977; Gibbons et al., 1978; Newcome, Chapter 3, this volume).

The third trend, expansion into group and family treatment, is the subject of this volume and will not be elaborated further. However, the task-centered model has not yet tested when group or family treatment would be preferable to individual treatment.

The fourth trend is extension of the model to a variety of service systems, including authoritative or protective settings and other long-term care settings. The model's requirement that the client acknowledge problems makes its use in authoritative settings problematic because of the difficulty of separating the coercive aura of service sponsorship from the service offered by a task-centered practitioner. Yet the model has been successful in such settings as probation (Bass, 1977; Hofstad, 1977), foster care (Rooney, 1975; Rzepnicki, Chapter 10, this volume; Salmon, 1977), and protective service (Rooney and Wanless, Chapter 11, this volume). The success may be due to the emphasis on client-stated problems, which can engage a client when imposed problems may not. In public services, this client orientation was retained by practitioners trained in task-centered practice when other elements of the model were not (Rooney, 1983). However, it is this emphasis which makes the model so difficult to implement in such settings, and implementation has been erratic and incomplete (Reid and Beard, 1980; Rooney, 1983). The task-centered model cannot solve all problems in delivery of social services and must be implemented carefully in authoritative settings.

A related development is the model's use in long-term care settings, including authoritative agencies but also geriatric life care and voluntary psychiatric care (Dierking, Brown, and Fortune, 1980; Newcome, Chapter 3, this volume). Integration of short-term treatment into long-term care is discussed in detail in the introductory chapter to this book. Still a difficulty in such integration is determining when task-centered service should be offered and when terminated, especially since monitoring is generally not effective in detecting incipient problems (Epstein, 1980). However, in Chapter 11, Rooney and Wanless offer a case management approach which appears to make long-term service more efficient and rational, if not more effective.

Greater Specificity of Treatment Procedures

The task-centered model, as mentioned, has developed through testing of treatment procedures and incorporation of successful techniques. An example is the development of the problem-solving steps, the task-planning and implementation sequence (Hepworth, 1979; Reid, 1975, 1978; Reid et al., 1980; Tolson, 1976). The strategies for attacking target problems offered in the introductory chapter is another attempt to be more specific about treatment approach. Yet the task-centered model —like social work—is a long way from being highly specific and prescriptive. This is appropriate, since each client is an individual, but the search to find demonstrably effective means of resolving problems continues.

Supervision and Teaching

Task-centered practice teachers and supervisors have become increasingly concerned with how to teach treatment techniques once they are specified. Tolson's Skill Assessment Teaching Model (Chapter 13), for example, was developed to improve teaching the model's clinical problem-solving skills to social work students. Larsen has developed another approach, incorporating empathic and listening skills (Larsen and Hepworth, 1982). Both efforts reflect a field-wide movement to formulate practice skills, to teach specific skills, and to measure acquisition of those skills, and are accompanied by a shift in student supervision from a case-focused approach to a skill-focused approach. This development is still in its infancy, but the next step is to compare different teaching approaches to imparting those skills.

Future Developments

As the previous section implies, there are a number of areas in which the task-centered model must continue to develop. These directions are not exclusive to the task-centered approach, but are shared by the field of social work. They include (1) increasing knowledge and sophistication about effective treatment strategies; (2) increasing ability to select a treatment modality, to determine for whom and for what problems individual or group or family treatment is most effective; (3) determining which practitioner skills are most essential to outcome, and how to teach the skills most effectively; and (4) determining how to manage service so that intervention is offered and used more effectively and efficiently. The teaching of task-centered skills to students is the subject of Chapter 13 in this volume, and service management in Chapters 11 and 12.

Tolson's material on specifying and teaching task-centered problem-solving skills (Chapter 13) should be an assist to the educational process, but further work is needed on translating and supplementing her model for practice with families and groups. In addition, the task-centered model must examine other relevant practitioner skills. For example, Can the concept of responsive versus systematic communication (Reid and Epstein, 1972; Fortune, introductory chapter, this volume) be operationally defined and the appropriate balance determined and taught? What level of empathy is minimal for effective task-centered practice?

As with the expansion of task-centered practice to families and groups, there is a trend to broaden the use of the model to inform administration and case management. Rooney and Wanless (Chapter 11) offer an approach to case management based on the task-centered model, while Parihar (Chapter 12) applies the model to problems in agency administration. As Parihar notes, basing a management approach on a practice model has the advantage that practitioners—who are the majority of agency administrative staff—can translate their practice skills rapidly to administrative skills. These developments hold promise for the future, as they appear to increase service delivery efficiency, but they have not yet been tested for effectiveness or flexibility in different service delivery systems, and more research is needed.

References

Abramson, Marcia. 1981. "Ethical Dilemmas for Social Workers in Discharge Planning." *Social Work in Health Care* 6 (Summer): 33-42.

Anderson, Barbara J., and Auslander, Wendy F. 1980. "Research on Diabetes Management and the Family: A Critique." *Diabetes Care* 3 (November-December): 696-702.

Anderson, Lowell; Fodor, Iris; and Alpert, Murray. 1976. "A Comparison of Methods for Training Self-Control." *Behavior Therapy* 7 (October): 649-658.

Anderson, Ralph E., and Carter, Irl. 1978. *Human Behavior in the Social Environment: A Social Systems Approach*, 2nd ed. New York: Aldine.

Angell, Donald L., and DeSau, George T. 1974. "Rare Discordant Verbal Roles and the Development of Group Problem-Solving Conditions." *Small Group Behavior* 5 (February): 45-55.

Aponte, Harry J., and Van Deusen, John M. 1981. "Structural Family Therapy." In *Handbook of Family Therapy*. Edited by Alan S. Gurman and David P. Kniskern. New York: Brunner/Mazel.

Atchley, Robert C. 1975. "Dimensions of Widowhood in Later Life." *Gerontologist* 15 (April): 176-178.

Azrin, Nathan H.; Naster, Barry J.; and Jones, Robert, 1973. "Reciprocity Counseling: A Rapid Learning-Based Procedure for Marital Counseling." *Behavior, Research, and Therapy* 11 (November): 365-382.

Babad, Elisha Y., and Amir, Liora. 1978. "Bennis and Shepard's Theory of Group Development: An Empirical Examination." *Small Group Behavior* 9 (November): 477-492.

Bach, George R., and Wyden, Peter. 1981. *Intimate Enemy: How to Fight Fair in Love and Marriage*. New York: Avon.

Bachman, Jerald G.; O'Malley, Patrick M.; and Johnston, Jerome. 1978. *Adolescence to Adulthood: Change and Stability in the Lives of Young Men*. Youth in Transition, Vol. 6. Ann Arbor, MI: Institute for Social Research, University of Michigan.

Baekeland, Frederick, and Lundwall, Lawrence. 1975. "Dropping Out of Treatment: A Critical Review." *Psychological Bulletin* 82 (September): 738-783.

Balch, Philip; McWilliams, Spencer; Lewis, Susan; and Ireland, John. 1978. "Clients' Treatment Expectations at a Community Mental Health Clinic." *American Journal of Community Psychology* 6: 105-113.

Bandura, Albert. 1969. *Principles of Behavior Modification.* New York: Holt, Rinehart and Winston.

Bank, Stephen P., and Kahn, Michael D. 1982. *The Sibling Bond.* New York: Basic.

———. 1975. "Sisterhood-Brotherhood Is Powerful: Sibling Subsystems and Family Therapy." *Family Process* 14 (September): 311-337.

Barnhill, Laurence; Rubenstein, Gerald; and Rocklin, Neil. 1979. "From Generation to Generation: Fathers-to-Be in Transition." *Family Coordinator* 28 (April): 229-239.

Bass, Michael. 1977. "Toward a Model of Treatment for Runaway Girls in Detention." In *Task-Centered Practice.* Edited by William J. Reid and Laura Epstein. New York: Columbia University Press.

Baucom, Donald H. 1982. "A Comparison of Behavioral Contracting and Problem-Solving/Communications Training in Behavioral Marital Therapy." *Behavior Therapy* 13 (March): 162-174.

Beck, Aaron T. 1976. *Cognitive Therapy and the Emotional Disorders.* New York: International Universities Press.

Beck, Dorothy Fahs. 1975. "Research Findings on the Outcomes of Marital Counseling." *Social Casework* 56 (March): 153-181.

Beck, Dorothy Fahs, and Jones, Mary Ann. 1973. *Progress on Family Problems: A Nationwide Study of Clients' and Counselors' Views on Family Agency Services.* New York: Family Service Association of America.

Bednar, Richard L., and Kaul, Theodore J. 1978. "Experiential Group Research: Current Perspectives." In *Handbook of Psychotherapy and Behavior Change: An Empirical Analysis,* 2nd ed. Edited by Sol L. Garfield and Allen E. Bergin. New York: Wiley.

Bell, C., and Mlyniec, W. J. 1974. "Preparing for a Neglect Proceeding: A Guide for the Social Worker." *Public Welfare* 32: 26-37.

Bennis, Warren G. 1966. *Changing Organizations.* New York: McGraw-Hill.

Bequaert, Lucia. 1976. *Single Women Alone and Together.* Boston: Beacon.

Berlin, Sharon B. 1983. "Single-Case Evaluation: Another Version." *Social Work Research and Abstracts* 19 (Spring): 3-11.

———. 1980. "Cognitive-Behavioral Intervention for Problems of Self-Criticism among Women." *Social Work Research and Abstracts* 16 (Winter): 19-28.

Bernal, Guillermo, and Baker, Jeffrey. 1979. "Toward a Metacommunicational Framework of Couple Interaction." *Family Process* 18 (September): 293-302.

Bertcher, Harvey J., and Maple, Frank F. 1977. *Creating Groups.* Sage Human Services Guide, Vol. 2. Beverly Hills, CA: Sage.

Blazer, Dan. 1980. "The Epidemiology of Mental Illness in Late Life." In *Handbook of Geriatric Psychiatry.* Edited by Ewald W. Busse and Dan G. Blazer. New York: Van Nostrand Reinhold.

Blenkner, Margaret. 1965. "Social Work and Family Relationships in Later Life with Some Thoughts on Filial Maturity." In *Social Structure and the Family: Generational Relations.* Edited by Ethyl Shanas and Gordon Streib. Englewood Cliffs, NJ: Prentice-Hall.

Blenkner, Margaret; Bloom, Martin; and Neilson, Margaret. 1971. "A Research and Demonstration Project of Protective Services." *Social Casework* 52 (October): 483–499.

Blizinsky, Marlin, and Reid, William J. 1980. "Problem Focus and Outcome in Brief Treatment." *Social Work* 25 (March): 89–98.

Bloom, Martin, and Monro, Alexander. 1972. "Social Work and the Aging Family." *Family Coordinator* 21 (January): 103–115.

Boettcher, Richard E., and Schie, Roger Vander. 1975. "Milieu Therapy with Chronic Mental Patients." *Social Work* 20 (March): 130–134.

Boszormenyi-Nagy, Ivan, and Spark, Geraldine M. 1973. *Invisible Loyalties: Reciprocity in Intergenerational Family Therapy.* Hagerstown, MD: Harper and Row.

Botwinick, Jack. 1977. "Intellectual Abilities." In *Handbook of the Psychology of Aging.* Edited by James E. Birren and K. Warren Schaie. New York: Van Nostrand Reinhold.

Bowen, Murray. 1977. "Aging: A Symposium." *Georgetown Medical Bulletin* 30 (Spring): 6–14.

Bradshaw, William H. 1982. "PASST (Primary Attending and Socialization Skills Training): Filling the Gap between Hospital and Community for Chronic Schizophrenics." *International Journal of Partial Hospitalization* 1 (January): 59–66.

Brandwein, Ruth A.; Brown, Carol A.; and Fox, Elizabeth Maury. 1974. "Women and Children Last: The Social Situation of Divorced Mothers and Their Families." *Journal of Marriage and the Family* 36 (August): 498–514.

Brodland, Gene A., and Andreasen, N. J. C. 1977. "Adjustment Problems of the Family of the Burn Patient." In *Coping with Physical Illness.* Edited by Rudolf H. Moos. New York: Plenum.

Brody, Elaine. 1981. "Women in the Middle and Family Help to Older People." *Gerontologist* 21 (October): 471–480.

———. 1977. *Long Term Care for Older People.* New York: Human Science Press.

———. 1966. "The Aging Family." *Gerontologist* 6: 201–206.

Brown, Lester B. 1980. "Client Problem Solving Learning in Task Centered Social Treatment." Ph.D. dissertation, University of Chicago.

———. 1977. "Treating Problems of Psychiatric Patients." In *Task-Centered Practice.* Edited by William J. Reid and Laura Epstein. New York: Columbia University Press.

Budman, Simon H. 1981. "Looking toward the Future." In *Forms of Brief Therapy.* Edited by Simon H. Budman. New York: Guilford.

Burgess, A. W., and Holmstrom, L. L. 1974. "Rape Trauma Syndrome." *American Journal of Psychiatry* 131: 981–986.

Burnside, Irene. 1978. *Working with the Elderly: Group Processes and Techniques.* Belmont, CA: Duxbury.

Butcher, James N., and Koss, Mary P. 1978. "Research on Brief and Crisis-Oriented Psychotherapies." In *Handbook of Psychotherapy and Behavior Change: An Empirical Analysis*, 2nd ed. Edited by Sol L. Garfield and Allen E. Bergin. New York: Wiley.

Butler, Janet; Bow, Irene; and Gibbons, Jane. 1978. "Task-Centered Casework with Marital Problems." *British Journal of Social Work* 8 (Summer): 393-409.

Butler, Robert. 1975. "Psychiatry and the Elderly: An Overview." *American Journal of Psychiatry* 132 (September): 893-900.

Butler, Timothy, and Fuhriman, Addie. 1980. "Patient Perspective on the Curative Process: A Comparison of Day Treatment and Outpatient Psychotherapy Groups." *Small Group Behavior* 11 (May): 371-388.

Campbell, Angus. 1981. *The Sense of Well-Being in America*. New York: McGraw-Hill.

Cantor, Nancy L., and Gelfand, Donna M. 1977. "Effects of Responsiveness and Sex of Children on Adults' Behavior." *Child Development* 48 (March): 232-238.

Caple, Richard B. 1978. "The Sequential Stages of Group Development." *Small Group Behavior* 9 (November): 470-476.

Cargan, Leonard, and Melko, Matthew. 1982. *Singles: Myths and Realities*. Beverly Hills, CA: Sage.

Carter, Elizabeth A., and McGoldrick, Monica. 1980. "The Family Life Cycle and Family Therapy: An Overview." In *The Family Life Cycle: A Framework for Family Therapy*. Edited by Elizabeth A. Carter and Monica McGoldrick. New York: Gardner.

Cartwright, Dorwin, and Zander, Alvin. 1968a. "Leadership and Performance of Group Functions: Introduction." In *Group Dynamics: Research and Theory*, 3rd ed. Edited by Dorwin Cartwright and Alvin Zander. New York: Harper-Row.

———. 1968b. "Pressures to Uniformity in Groups: Introduction." In *Group Dynamics: Research and Theory*, 3rd ed. Edited by Dorwin Cartwright and Alvin Zander. New York: Harper-Row.

Churchill, Sallie R., and Glasser, Paul H. 1974. "Small Groups in the Mental Hospital." In *Individual Change through Small Groups*. Edited by Paul Glasser, Rosemary Sarri, and Robert Vinter. New York: Free Press.

Colapinto, Jorge. 1979. "The Relative Value of Empirical Evidence." *Family Process* 18 (December): 427-491.

Compton, Beulah Roberts, and Galaway, Burt, Eds. 1979. *Social Work Processes*, rev. ed. Homewood, IL: Dorsey.

Conway, John B., and Bucher, Bradley D. 1976. "Transfer and Maintenance of Behavior Change in Children: A Review and Suggestions." In *Behavior Modification and Families*. Edited by Eric J. Mash, Leo A. Hamerlynck, and Lee C. Handy. New York: Brunner/Mazel.

Conyard, Shirley; Krishnamurthy, Muthuswamy; and Dosik, Harvey. 1980. "Psychosocial Aspects of Sickle Cell Anemia in Adolescents." *Health and Social Work Journal* 5 (February): 20-26.

Copeland, Harriet. 1980. "The Beginning Group." *International Journal of Group Psychotherapy* 30 (April): 201-212.

Corden, John. 1980. "Contracts in Social Work Practice." *British Journal of Social Work* 10 (Summer): 143-161.

Cormican, Elin. 1977. "Task-Centered Model for Work with the Aged." *Social Casework* 58 (October): 490-494.

Corsini, Raymond J., and Rosenberg, Bina. 1955. "Mechanisms of Group Psychotherapy: Process and Dynamics." *Journal of Abnormal and Social Psychology* 51 (November): 406-411.

Corson, John A. 1976. "Families as Mutual Control Systems: Optimization by Systematization of Reinforcement." In *Behavior Modification and Families*. Edited by Eric J. Mash, Leo A. Hamerlynck, and Lee C. Handy. New York: Brunner/Mazel.

Crandall, Rick. 1978. "The Assimilation of Newcomers into Groups." *Small Group Behavior* 9 (August): 331-336.

Crews, Catherine Y., and Melnick, Joseph. 1976. "Use of Initial and Delayed Structure in Facilitating Group Development." *Journal of Counseling Psychology* 23 (March): 92-98.

Crousby, Barbara J. 1979. "Task-Centered Practice with Groups of Community-based Elderly." Unpublished.

Daley, Michael R. 1979. "Burnout: Smoldering Problem in Protective Services." *Social Work* 24 (September): 375-379.

David, Henry P., and Baldwin, Wendy P. 1979. "Childbearing and Child Development: Demographic and Psychosocial Trends." *American Psychologist* 34 (October): 866-871.

Davis, Frederick B., and Lohr, Naomi E. 1971. "Special Problems with the Use of Cotherapists in Group Psychotherapy." *International Journal of Group Psychotherapy* 21 (April): 143-158.

Davison, Gerald C., and Valins, Stuart. 1969. "Maintenance of Self-attributed and Drug-attributed Behavior Change." *Journal of Personality and Social Psychology* 11 (January): 25-33.

DeWitt, Kathryn Nash. 1978. "The Effectiveness of Family Therapy: A Review of Outcome Research." *Archives of General Psychiatry* 35 (May): 549-560.

Dierking, Barbara; Brown, Margot; and Fortune, Anne E. 1980. "Task-Centered Treatment in a Residential Facility for the Elderly: A Clinical Trial." *Journal of Gerontological Social Work* 2 (Spring): 225-240.

Dies, Robert R. 1979. "Group Psychotherapy: Reflections on Three Decades of Research." *Journal of Applied Behavioral Science* 15: 361-373.

Douglas, Tom. 1979. *Group Processes in Social Work: A Theoretical Synthesis*. Chichester: Wiley.

Dowd, James J. 1981. "Conversation and Social Exchange: Managing Identities in Old Age." *Human Relations* 34 (July): 541-553.

Duehn, Wayne D., and Mayadas, Nazneed Sada. 1979. "Starting Where the Client Is: An Empirical Investigation." *Social Casework* 60 (February): 67-74.

Duehn, Wayne D., and Proctor, Enola K. 1977. "Initial Clinical Interaction and Premature Discontinuance in Treatment." *American Journal of Orthopsychiatry* 47 (April): 284-290.

Duvall, Evelyn Millis. 1977. *Marriage and Family Development*, 5th ed. New York: Harper and Row.

D'Zurilla, Thomas J., and Goldfried, Marvin R. 1971. "Problem-Solving and Behavior Modification." *Journal of Abnormal Psychology* 78 (August): 107–126.

D'Zurilla, Thomas J., and Nezu, Arthur. 1980. "A Study of the Generation-of-Alternatives Process in Social Problem Solving." *Cognitive Therapy and Research* 4 (March): 67–72.

Ellis, Albert. 1978. *Rational Emotive Cognitive Therapy in the Treatment of Schizophrenia*. New York: BMA Audio Cassettes, Guilford.

Ellis, Albert, and Grieger, Russell. 1977. *Handbook of Rational-Emotive Therapy*. New York: Springer.

Emlen, Arthur; Lahti, Janet; Downs, Glenn; McKay, Alec; and Downs, Susan. 1978. *Overcoming Barriers to Planning for Children in Foster Care*. Prepared for U.S. Children's Bureau, Administration for Children, Youth, and Families, U.S. Department of Health, Education, and Welfare. DHEW Publication No. (OHDS) 78-30138. Washington, D.C.: United States Government Printing Office.

Emshoff, James G.; Redd, William H.; and Davidson, William S. 1976. "Generalization Training and the Transfer of Prosocial Behavior in Delinquent Adolescents." *Journal of Behavior Therapy and Experimental Psychiatry* 7 (June): 141–144.

Entwisle, Doris R., and Doering, Susan G. 1981. *The First Birth: A Family Turning Point*. Baltimore: Johns Hopkins University Press.

Epstein, Laura. 1980. *Helping People: The Task-Centered Approach*. St. Louis: Mosby.

———. 1977. "A Project in School Social Work." In *Task-Centered Practice*. Edited by William J. Reid and Laura Epstein. New York: Columbia University Press.

Epstein, Laura; Tolson, Eleanor R.; and Reid, William J. 1978. "Dissemination." In *The Task-Centered System*. Edited by William J. Reid. New York: Columbia University Press.

Ericksen, Julia A.; Yancey, William L.; and Ericksen, Eugene P. 1979. "The Division of Family Roles." *Journal of Marriage and the Family* 41 (May): 301–313.

Evans, Ron L., and Jaureguy, Beth M. 1982. "Phone Therapy Outreach for Blind Elderly." *Gerontologist* 22 (February): 32–35.

———. 1981. "Group Therapy by Phone: A Cognitive Behavioral Program for Visually Impaired Elderly." *Social Work in Health Care* 7 (Winter): 79–80.

Ewalt, Patricia L. 1977. "A Psychoanalytically Oriented Child Guidance Setting." In *Task-Centered Practice*. Edited by William J. Reid and Laura Epstein. New York: Columbia University Press.

———. 1976. "The Case for Immediate Brief Intervention." *Social Work* 21 (January): 63–65.

Ewing, Charles P. 1978. *Crisis Intervention as Psychotherapy*. New York: Oxford University Press.

Fairweather, George W.; Sanders, David H.; Maynard, Hugo; and Cressler, David L. 1969. *Community Life for the Mentally Ill: An Alternative to Institutional Care*. Chicago: Aldine.

Fanshel, David, and Shinn, Eugene B. 1978. *Children in Foster Care: A Longitudinal Investigation.* New York: Columbia University Press.

Fayol, Henry. 1949. *General and Industrial Management.* Translated by Constance Storrs. London: Pitman.

Feldman, Ronald A., and Wodarski, John S. 1975. *Contemporary Approaches to Group Treatment.* San Francisco: Jossey-Bass.

Festinger, Trudy Bradley. 1975. "The New York Court Review of Children in Foster Care." *Child Welfare* 54 (April): 211–245.

Firestein, Stephen K. 1978. *Termination in Psychoanalysis.* New York: International Universities Press.

Fisch, Richard; Weakland, John H.; and Segal, Lynn. 1982. *The Tactics of Change: Doing Therapy Briefly.* San Francisco: Jossey-Bass.

Fischer, Joel. 1978. *Effective Casework Practice: An Eclectic Approach.* New York: McGraw-Hill.

———. 1971. "A Framework for the Analysis and Comparison of Clinical Theories of Induced Change." *Social Service Review* 45 (December): 440–454.

Fischer, Lucy Rose. 1983. "Mothers and Mothers in-law." *Journal of Marriage and the Family* 45 (February): 187–192.

Fisher, Stuart G. 1980. "The Use of Time Limits in Brief Psychotherapy: A Comparison of Six-Session, Twelve-Session, and Unlimited Treatment with Families." *Family Process* 19 (December): 377–392.

Fishman, Steven T., and Lubetkin, Barry S. 1980. "Maintenance and Generalization of Individual Behavior Therapy Programs: Clinical Observations." In *Improving the Long-Term Effects of Psychotherapy: Models of Durable Outcome.* Edited by Paul Karoly and John J. Steffen. New York: Gardner.

Ford, Donald H., and Urban, Hugh B. 1963. *Systems of Psychotherapy: A Comparative Study.* New York: Wiley.

Fortune, Anne E. 1981. "Termination in Task-Centered Treatment." Chicago: University of Chicago. Mimeo.

———. 1979a. "Communication in Task-Centered Treatment." *Social Work* 24 (September): 390–396.

———. 1979b. "Problem-Solving Processes in Task-Centered Treatment with Adults and Children." *Journal of Social Service Research* 2 (Summer): 357–371.

———. 1978. "Verbal Communication in Task-Centered Treatment." Ph.D. dissertation, University of Chicago.

———. 1976. *Task-Centered Tasks in Relation to Client Problems.* Chicago: School of Social Service Administration, University of Chicago. Offset.

Fortune, Anne E., and Rathbone-McCuan, Eloise. 1981. "Education in Gerontological Social Work: Application of the Task-Centered Model." *Journal of Education for Social Work* 17 (Fall): 98–105.

Frank, Arlene; Eisenthal, Sherman; and Lazare, Aaron. 1978. "Are There Social Class Differences in Patients' Treatment Conceptions? Myths and Facts." *Archives of General Psychiatry* 35 (January): 61–69.

Fuchs, Carilyn Z., and Rehm, Lynn P. 1977. "A Self-control Behavior Therapy Program for Depression." *Journal of Consulting and Clinical Psychology* 45 (April): 206–215.

Gambrill, Eileen. 1977. *Behavior Modification: Handbook of Assessment, Intervention, and Evaluation*. San Francisco: Jossey-Bass.

Gambrill, Eileen D., and Wiltse, Kermit T. 1974. "Foster Care: Plans and Activities." *Public Welfare* 32 (Spring): 12-21.

Garcia, Eugene. 1974. "The Training and Generalization of a Conversational Speech Form in Nonverbal Retardates." *Journal of Applied Behavior Analysis* 7 (Spring): 137-149.

Garfield, Sol L. 1978. "Research on Client Variables in Psychotherapy." In *Handbook of Psychotherapy and Behavior Change: An Empirical Analysis*, 2nd ed. Edited by Sol L. Garfield and Allen E. Bergin. New York: Wiley.

Garland, James A.; Jones, Hubert E.; and Kolodny, Ralph L. 1973. "A Model for Stages of Development in Social Work Groups." In *Explorations in Group Work: Essays in Theory and Practice*. Edited by Saul Bernstein. Boston: Milford House.

Garvin, Charles. 1981. *Contemporary Group Work*. Englewood Cliffs, NJ: Prentice-Hall.

———. 1977. "Strategies for Group Work with Adolescents." In *Task-Centered Practice*. Edited by William J. Reid and Laura Epstein. New York: Columbia University Press.

———. 1974. "Task-Centered Group Work." *Social Service Review* 48 (December): 494-507.

Garvin, Charles D.; Reid, William; and Epstein, Laura. 1976. "A Task-Centered Approach." In *Theories of Social Work with Groups*. Edited by Robert W. Roberts and Helen Northen. New York: Columbia University Press.

Gelles, Richard J. 1980. "Violence in the Family: A Review of Research in the Seventies." *Journal of Marriage and the Family* 42 (November): 873-884.

Germain, Carel B. 1976. "Time: An Ecological Variable in Social Work Practice." *Social Casework* 57 (July): 419-462.

Gibbons, J. S.; Butler, J.; Urwin, P.; and Gibbons, J. L. 1978. "Evaluation of a Social Work Service for Self-Poisoning Patients." *British Journal of Psychiatry* 133: 111-118.

Gibson, James; Ivancevich, John; and Donnelly, James Jr. 1976. *Organizations*. Dallas, TX: Business Publications.

Giele, Janet Zollinger. 1982. "Women in Adulthood: Unanswered Questions." In *Women in the Middle Years: Current Knowledge and Directions for Research and Policy*. Edited by Janet Zollinger Giele. New York: Wiley.

Giovannoni, Jeanne M., and Billingsley, Andrew. 1970. "Child Neglect among the Poor: A Study of Parental Adequacy in Families of Three Ethnic Groups." *Child Welfare* 49 (April): 196-204.

Glaser, Barney C., and Strauss, Anselon L. 1967. *The Discovery of Grounded Theory: Strategies for Qualitative Research*. Chicago: Aldine.

Glick, Paul C. 1977. "Updating the Life Cycle of the Family." *Journal of Marriage and the Family* 39 (February): 5-13.

Glogower, Fred, and Sloop, E. Wayne. 1976. "Two Strategies of Group Training of Parents as Effective Behavior Modifiers." *Behavior Therapy* 7: 177-184.

Golan, Naomi. 1981. *Passing Through Transitions: A Guide for Practitioners*. New York: Free Press.

———. 1979. "Crisis Theory." In *Social Work Treatment*, 2nd ed. Edited by Francis J. Turner. New York: Free Press.

———. 1978. *Treatment in Crisis Situations*. New York: Free Press.

———. 1969. "When Is a Client in Crisis?" *Social Casework* 50 (July): 389-394.

Goldfried, Marvin R., and D'Zurilla, Thomas J. 1969. "A Behavior Analytic Model for Assessing Competence." In *Current Topics in Clinical and Community Psychology*, Vol. 1. Edited by C. D. Spielberger. New York: Academic.

Goldsmith, Jean B., and McFall, Richard M. 1975. "Development and Evaluation of an Interpersonal Skill-Training Program for Psychiatric Inpatients." *Journal of Abnormal Psychology* 84 (February): 51-58.

Goldstein, Arnold P.; Heller, Kenneth; and Sechrest, Lee B. 1966. *Psychotherapy and the Psychology of Behavior Change*. New York: Wiley.

Goldstein, Arnold P.; Lopez, Martita; and Greenleaf, David O. 1979. "Introduction." In *Maximizing Treatment Gains: Transfer Enhancement in Psychotherapy*. Edited by Arnold P. Goldstein and Frederick H. Kanfer. New York: Academic.

Goldstein, Arnold; Sprafkin, Robert P.; and Gershaw, N. Jane. 1976. *Skill Training for Community Living: Applying Structured Learning Therapy*. New York: Pergamon and Structured Learning Associates.

Goldstein, Howard. 1973. *Social Work Practice: A Unitary Approach*. Columbia, SC: University of South Carolina Press.

Goodyear, Rodney K. 1981. "Termination as a Loss Experience for the Counselor." *Personnel and Guidance Journal* 59 (February): 347-350.

Gordon, Thomas. 1955. *Group-Centered Leadership*. Cambridge, MA: Riverside.

Grandvold, Donald K., and Welch, Gary J. 1977. "Intervention for Postdivorce Adjustment Problems: The Treatment Seminar." *Journal of Divorce* 1 (Fall): 81-92.

Grinnell, Richard M., Jr. 1973. "Environmental Modification: Casework's Concern or Casework's Neglect?" *Social Service Review* 47 (June): 208-220.

Gruber, Ronald P. 1971. "Behavior Therapy: Problems in Generalization." *Behavior Therapy* 2 (July): 361-368.

Gurman, Alan S., and Kniskern, David P. 1981. "Family Therapy Outcome Research: Knowns and Unknowns." In *Handbook of Family Therapy*. Edited by Alan S. Gurman and David P. Kniskern. New York: Brunner/Mazel.

———. 1978. "Research on Marital and Family Therapy: Progress, Perspective, and Prospect." In *Handbook of Psychotherapy and Behavior Change: An Empirical Analysis*, 2nd ed. Edited by Sol L. Garfield and Allen E. Bergin. New York: Wiley.

Haley, Jay. 1980. *Leaving Home: The Therapy of Disturbed Young People*. New York: McGraw-Hill.

———. 1976. *Problem Solving Therapy*. San Francisco, CA: Jossey-Bass.

———. 1963. *Strategies of Psychotherapy*. New York: Grune and Stratton.

Hamilton, Adrianne K., and Noble, Dorinda N. 1983. "Assisting Families Through Genetic Counseling." *Social Casework* 64 (January): 18-25.

Harbert, Anita, and Ginsberg, Leon. 1979. *Human Services for Older Adults: Concepts and Skills*. Belmont, CA: Wadsworth.

Hare, A. Paul. 1976. *Handbook of Small Group Research*, 2nd ed. New York: Free Press.

Hare-Mustin, Rachel T.; Marecek, Jeanne; Kaplan, Alexandra G.; and Liss-Levinson, Nechama. 1979. "Rights of Clients, Responsibilities of Therapists." *American Psychologist* 34 (January): 3-16.

Hari, Veronica. 1977. "Instituting Short-Term Casework in a 'Long-Term' Agency." In *Task-Centered Practice*. Edited by William J. Reid and Laura Epstein. New York: Columbia University Press.

Harrison, W. David. 1980. "Role Strain and Burnout in Child-Protective Service Workers." *Social Service Review* 54 (March): 31-37.

Hart, Russell R. 1978. "Therapeutic Effectiveness of Setting and Monitoring Goals." *Journal of Consulting and Clinical Psychology* 46 (December): 1242-1245.

Hartford, Margaret E. 1972. *Groups in Social Work: Application of Small Group Theory and Research to Social Work Practice.* New York: Columbia University Press.

Hashimi, Joan K. 1981. "Environmental Modification: Teaching Social Coping Skills." *Social Work* 26 (July): 323-326.

Hepworth, Dean H. 1979. "Early Removal of Resistance in Task-Centered Case-Work." *Social Work* 24 (July): 317-322.

Herr, John, and Weakland, John. 1979. *Counseling Elders and Their Families: Practical Techniques for Applied Gerontology.* New York: Springer Publishing Co.

Hersen, Michel, and Bellack, Alan S. 1976. "Social Skills Training for Chronic Psychiatric Patients: Rationale, Research Findings and Future Directions." *Comprehensive Psychiatry* 17 (July/August): 557-580.

Hersey, Paul, and Blanchard, Kenneth. 1977. *Management of Organizational Behavior.* Englewood Cliffs, NJ: Prentice-Hall.

Herz, Marvin I.; Endicott, Jean; Spitzer, Robert L.; and Messnikoff, Alvin. 1971. "Day Versus Inpatient Hospitalization: A Controlled Study." *American Journal of Psychiatry* 127 (April): 107-118.

Hess, Beth B., and Waring, Joan M. 1978. "Changing Patterns of Aging and Family Bonds in Later Life." *Family Coordinator* 27 (October): 304-314.

Hetherington, E. Mavis. 1979. "Divorce: A Child's Perspective." *American Psychologist* 34 (October): 851-858.

Hetherington, E. Mavis; Cox, Martha; and Cox, Roger. 1976. "Divorced Fathers." *Family Coordinator* 25 (October): 417-428.

Hill, Barbara; Lippitt, Lawrence; and Serkownek, Kenneth. 1979. "The Emotional Dimensions of the Problem-Solving Process." *Group and Organization Studies* 4 (March): 93-102.

Hill, Reuben. 1949. *Families Under Stress.* New York: Harper and Row.

Hill, William Fawcett. 1975. "Further Considerations of Therapeutic Mechanisms in Group Therapy." *Small Group Behavior* 6 (November): 421-429.

Hill, William Fawcett, and Gruner, LeRoy. 1973. "A Study of Development in Open and Closed Groups." *Small Group Behavior* 4 (August): 355-381.

Hiltz, Starr Roxanne. 1978. "Widowhood: A Roleless Role." *Marriage and Family Review* 1 (November/December): 1-10.

Hinton, John. 1977. "Bearing Cancer." In *Coping with Physical Illness*. Edited by Rudolf H. Moos. New York: Plenum.

Hoffman, Lynn. 1981. *Foundations of Family Therapy*. New York: Basic.

Hofstad, Milton O. 1977. "Treatment in a Juvenile Court Setting." In *Task-Centered Practice*. Edited by William J. Reid and Laura Epstein. New York: Columbia University Press.

Hollis, Florence. 1967. "Explorations in the Development of a Typology of Casework Treatment." *Social Casework* 48 (June): 335-341.

———. 1964. *Casework: A Psychosocial Therapy*. New York: Random House.

Holloway, Elizabeth L., and Wolleat, Patricia L. 1980. "Relationship of Counselor Conceptual Level to Clinical Hypothesis Formation." *Journal of Counseling Psychology* 27 (November): 539-545.

Howard, Mary Ann, and Anderson, Richard J. 1978. "Early Identification of Potential School Dropouts: A Literature Review." *Child Welfare* 57 (April): 224-228.

Hudson, Walter W., and Glisson, Dianne H. 1976. "Assessment of Marital Discord in Social Work Practice." *Social Service Review* 50 (June): 311-326.

Ilfield, Frederic W., Jr. 1982. "Marital Stressors, Coping Styles, and Symptoms of Depression." In *Handbook of Stress. Theoretical and Clinical Aspects*. Edited by Leo Goldberger and Shlomo Breznitz. New York: Free Press.

Imber, Stanley D.; Lewis, Philip M.; and Loiselle, Robert H. 1979. "Uses and Abuses of the Brief Intervention Group." *International Journal of Group Psychotherapy* 19 (January): 39-49.

Institute for Judicial Administration, American Bar Association, Juvenile Justice Standards Project. 1977. *Standards Relating to Juvenile Records and Information Systems—Tentative Draft*. Cambridge, MA: Ballinger Publishing Co., 1977.

Israel, Allen C., and Saccone, Anthony J. 1979. "Follow-up of Effects of Choice of Mediator and Target of Reinforcement of Weight Loss." *Behavior Therapy* 10 (March): 260-265.

Ivey, Allen E., and Authier, Jerry. 1978. *Microcounseling*. Springfield, IL: Charles C. Thomas.

Jackson, Allene. 1979. "The Use of the Task-centered Approach in Helping the Family of an Elderly Person Decide on Appropriate Care." Unpublished.

Jacobson, Neil S. 1981. "Behavioral Marital Therapy." In *Handbook of Family Therapy*. Edited by Alan S. Gurman and David P. Kniskern. New York: Brunner/Mazel.

———. 1978. "A Review of the Research on the Effectiveness of Marital Therapy." In *Marriage and Marital Therapy: Psychoanalytic, Behavioral and Systems Theory Perspectives*. Edited by Thomas J. Paolino, Jr., and Barbara S. McCrady. New York: Brunner/Mazel.

Jacobson, Neil S., and Margolin, Gayla. 1979. *Marital Therapy: Strategies Based on Social Learning and Behavior Exchange Principles*. New York: Brunner/Mazel.

Jenkins, Shirley, and Norman, Elaine. 1975. *Beyond Placement: Mothers View Foster Care*. New York: Columbia University Press.

Johnson, Carole. 1974. "Planning for Termination of the Group." In *Individual*

Change through Small Groups. Edited by Paul Glasser, Rosemary Sarri, and Robert Vinter. New York: Free Press.

Johnson, Deborah Hazel, and Gelso, Charles J. 1980. "The Effectiveness of Time Limits in Counseling and Psychotherapy: A Critical Review." *Counseling Psychologist* 9: 70-83.

Johnson, Elizabeth S., and Bursk, Barbara J. 1977. "Relationships between the Elderly and Their Adult Children." *Gerontologist* 17: 90-96.

Johnson, Stephen M.; Bolstad, Orin D.; and Lobitz, Gretchen K. 1976. "Generalization and Contrast Phenomena in Behavior Modification with Children." In *Behavior Modification and Families.* Edited by Eric J. Mash, Leo A. Hamerlynck, and Lee C. Handy. New York: Brunner/Mazel.

June, Lee N., and Smith, Elsie J. 1983. "A Comparison of Client and Counselor Expectancies Regarding the Duration of Counseling." *Journal of Counseling Psychology* 30 (October): 596-599.

Kanfer, Frederick H. 1979. "Self-Management: Strategies and Tactics." In *Maximizing Treatment Gains: Transfer Enhancement in Psychotherapy.* Edited by Arnold P. Goldstein and Frederick H. Kanfer. New York: Academic.

Kanfer, Frederick H., and Grimm, Laurence G. 1978. "Freedom of Choice and Behavioral Change." *Journal of Consulting and Clinical Psychology* 46 (October): 873-878.

Karoly, Paul. 1980. "Person Variables in Therapeutic Change and Development." In *Improving the Long-term Effects of Psychotherapy: Models of Durable Outcome.* Edited by Paul Karoly and John J. Steffen. New York: Gardner.

Katz, S., and Mazur, M. A. 1979. *Understanding the Rape Victim: A Synthesis of Research Findings.* New York: Wiley.

Kazdin, Alan E., and Mascitelli, Sally. 1982. "Covert and Overt Rehearsal and Homework Practice in Developing Assertiveness." *Journal of Consulting and Clinical Psychology* 50 (April): 250-258.

Keeley, S. M.; Shemberg, K. M.; and Carbonell, Joyce. 1976. "Operant Clinical Intervention: Behavior Management or Beyond? Where Are the Data?" *Behavior Therapy* 7 (May): 292-305.

Keller, James, and Hughston, George. 1981. *Counseling the Elderly: A Systems Approach.* New York: Harper and Row.

Kennell, John; Voos, Diana; and Klaus, Marshall. 1976. "Parent-Infant Bonding." In *Child Abuse and Neglect: The Family and the Community.* Edited by Ray E. Helfer and C. Henry Dempe. New York: Ballinger.

Kent, Donald J., and Matson, Margaret B. 1972. "The Impact of Health on the Aged Family." *Family Coordinator* 21 (January): 29-36.

Kerr, Michael E. 1981. "Family Systems Theory and Therapy." In *Handbook of Family Therapy.* Edited by Alan S. Gurman and David P. Kniskern. New York: Brunner/Mazel.

Kimball, Chase Patterson. 1977. "Psychological Responses to the Experience of Open-Heart Surgery." In *Coping with Physical Illness.* Edited by Rudolf H. Moos. New York: Plenum.

Kiresuk, Thomas J., and Sherman, Robert E. 1968. "Goal Attainment Scaling: A General Method for Evaluating Comprehensive Community Mental Health Programs." *Community Mental Health* 4 (December): 443-453.

Kleinman, Judith; Rosenberg, Elinor; and Whiteside, Mary. 1979. "Common Developmental Tasks in Forming Reconstituted Families." *Journal of Marital and Family Therapy* 5 (April): 79–86.

Kniskern, David P., and Gurman, Alan S. 1980. "Clinical Implications of Recent Research in Family Therapy." In *Group and Family Therapy, 1980.* Edited by Lewis R. Wolberg and Marvin L. Aronson. New York: Brunner/Mazel.

Knitzer, Jane; Allen, Mary Lee; and McGowan, Brenda. 1978. *Children without Homes: An Examination of Public Responsibility to Children in Out-of-Home Care.* Washington, D.C.: Children's Defense Fund.

Knox, David. 1971. *Marriage Happiness: A Behavioral Approach.* Champaign, IL: Research Press.

Koegel, Robert L.; Egel, Andrew L.; and Williams, Julie A. 1980. "Behavioral Contrast and Generalization Across Settings in the Treatment of Autistic Children." *Journal of Experimental Child Psychology* 30 (December): 422–437.

Koran, Lorrin M., and Costell, Ronald M. 1973. "Early Termination from Group Psychotherapy." *International Journal of Group Psychotherapy* 23 (July): 346–359.

Koss, Mary P. 1979. "Length of Psychotherapy for Clients Seen in Private Practice." *Journal of Consulting and Clinical Psychology* 47 (February): 210–212.

Kuypers, Joseph A., and Trute, Barry. 1978. "The Older Family as the Locus of Crisis Intervention." *Family Coordinator* 27 (October): 405–411.

LaCommare, Patrick C. 1975. "The Day Treatment Center: A Community Alternative to State Hospitalization." *Psychiatric Annals* 5 (May): 178–183.

Lacoursiere, Roy B. 1980. *The Life Cycle of Groups: Group Developmental Stage Theory.* New York: Human Sciences Press.

LaFerriere, Lorraine, and Calsyn, Robert. 1978. "Goal Attainment Scaling: An Effective Treatment Technique in Short-Term Therapy." *American Journal of Community Psychology* 6 (June): 271–282.

Lamb, Richard. 1979a. "Roots of Neglect of the Long Term Client." *Psychiatry* 42 (August): 201–207.

———. 1979b. "Staff Burnout in Work with Long-Term Patients." *Hospital and Community Psychiatry* 30 (June): 396–398.

Lange, Arthur J., and Jakubowski, Patricia. 1976. *Responsible Assertive Behavior.* Champaign, IL: Research Press.

Langer, Ellen J., and Rodin, Judith. 1976. "The Effects of Choice and Enhanced Personal Responsibility for the Aged: A Field Experiment in an Institutional Setting." *Journal of Personality and Social Psychology* 34 (August): 191–198.

Larsen, JoAnn. 1980. "Accelerating Group Development and Productivity: An Effective Leader Approach." *Social Work with Groups* 3 (Summer): 25–39.

Larsen, JoAnn, and Hepworth, Dean H. 1982. "Enhancing the Effectiveness of Practicum Instruction: An Empirical Study." *Journal of Education for Social Work* 18 (Spring): 50–59.

Larsen, JoAnn, and Mitchell, Craig T. 1980. "Task-Centered, Strength-Oriented Group Work with Delinquents." *Social Casework* 61 (March): 154–163.

Leak, Gary K. 1980. "Effects of Highly Structured Versus Nondirective Group Counseling Approaches on Personality and Behavioral Measures of Adjustment in Incarcerated Felons." *Journal of Counseling Psychology* 27 (September): 520-523.

Lee, Gary R. 1980. "Kinship in the Seventies: A Decade Review of Research and Therapy." *Journal of Marriage and the Family* 42 (November): 923-934.

Lemon, Elizabeth C., and Goldstein, Shirley. 1978. "The Use of Time Limits in Planned Brief Casework." *Social Casework* 59 (December): 588-596.

Levinson, Daniel J.; with Darrow, Charlotte N.; Klein, Edward B.; Levinson, Maria H.; and McKee, Braxton. 1978. *The Seasons of a Man's Life.* New York: Alfred A. Knopf.

Levinson, Hilliard L. 1977. "Termination of Psychotherapy: Some Salient Issues." *Social Casework* 58 (October): 480-489.

Lewis, Benjamin F. 1978. "An Examination of the Final Phase of a Group Development Theory. *Small Group Behavior* 9 (November): 507-517.

Lieberman, Morton A., and Tobin, Sheldon S. 1983. *The Experience of Old Age.* New York: Basic.

Lieberman, Morton A.; Yalom, Irvin D.; and Miles, Matthew B. 1973. *Encounter Groups: First Facts.* New York: Basic.

Likert, Rensis. 1961. *New Patterns of Management.* New York: McGraw-Hill.

Lishman, Joyce. 1978. "A Clash in Perspective? A Study of Worker and Client Perceptions of Social Work." *British Journal of Social Work* 8 (Autumn): 301-311.

Long, Larry D., and Cope, Corrine S. 1980. "Curative Factors in a Male Felony Offender Group." *Small Group Behavior* 11 (November): 389-398.

Lowenthal, Marjorie Fiske; Thurnher, Majda; Chiriboga, David; and Associates. 1975. *Four Stages of Life: A Comparative Study of Women and Men Facing Transitions.* San Francisco: Jossey-Bass.

Lowy, Louis. 1979. *Social Work With the Aging.* New York: Harper and Row.

Lueck, Marjorie; Orr, Ann C.; and O'Connell, Martin. 1982. *Trends in Child Care Arrangements of Working Mothers.* U.S. Census, Current Population Reports, Special Studies, P-23, No. 117, June.

Lukton, Rosemary Creed. 1982. "Myths and Realities of Crisis Intervention." *Social Casework* 63 (May): 276-285.

Maas, Henry, and Engler, Richard. 1959. *Children in Need of Parents.* New York: Columbia University Press.

Macklin, Eleanor D. 1980. "Nontraditional Family Forms: A Decade of Research." *Journal of Marriage and the Family* 42 (November): 905-922.

Madanes, Cloe. 1981. *Strategic Family Therapy.* California: Jossey-Bass.

Maluccio, Anthony N. 1979. "Perspectives of Social Workers and Clients on Treatment Outcome." *Social Casework* 60 (July) 394-401.

Maluccio, Anthony N., and Marlow, Wilma D. 1974. "The Case for the Contract." *Social Work* 19 (January): 28-36.

Marholin, David, and Touchette, Paul E. 1979. "The Role of Stimulus Control and Response Consequences." In *Maximizing Treatment Gains: Transfer Enhancement in Psychotherapy.* Edited by Arnold P. Goldstein and Fredrick H. Kanfer. New York: Academic.

Maslow, Abraham H. 1954. *Motivation and Personality.* New York: Harper and Row.

Masten, Ann S. 1979. "Family Therapy as a Treatment for Children: A Critical Review of Outcome Research." *Family Process* 18 (September): 323-335.

Matarazzo, Ruth G. 1978. "Research on the Teaching and Learning of Psychotherapeutic Skills." In *Handbook of Psychotherapy and Behavior Change*, 2nd ed. Edited by Sol L. Garfield and Allen E. Bergin. New York: Wiley.

May, Katharyn A. 1982. "Factors Contributing to First-Time Fathers' Readiness for Fatherhood: An Exploratory Study." *Family Relations* 31 (July): 353-361.

McCubbin, Hamilton I.; Joy, Constance B.; Cauble, A. Elizabeth; Comrau, Joan K.; Patterson, Joan M.; and Needle, Richard. 1980. "Family Stress and Coping: A Decade Review." *Journal of Marriage and the Family* 42 (November): 855-871.

McGoldrick, Monica. 1980. "The Joining of Families through Marriage: The New Couple." In *The Family Life Cycle: A Framework for Family Therapy.* Edited by Elizabeth A. Carter and Monica McGoldrick. New York: Gardner.

McGoldrick, Monica, and Carter, Elizabeth A. 1982. "The Family Life Cycle." In *Normal Family Processes.* Edited by Froma Walsh. New York: Guilford.

McGregor, Douglas. 1960. *The Human Side of Enterprise.* New York: McGraw-Hill.

Meadow, Diane. 1981. "Connecting Theory and Practice: The Effect of Pre-Group Preparation on Individual and Group Behavior." Paper presented at the Fourth Annual Symposium on Social Work with Groups, Toronto, Canada, October.

Mendes, Helen A. 1979. "Single-Parent Families: A Typology of Life-Styles." *Social Work* 24 (May): 193-200.

Miller, Dorothy A. 1981. "The 'Sandwich' Generation: Adult Children of the Aging." *Social Work* 26 (September): 419-423.

Minahan, Ann. 1980. "Burnout and Organizational Change." *Social Work* 25 (March): 87.

Minuchin, Salvador. 1974. *Families and Family Therapy.* Cambridge, MA: Harvard University Press.

Minuchin, Salvador, and Fishman, Charles. 1981. *Family Therapy Techniques.* Cambridge, MA: Harvard University Press.

Mooney, James D. 1947. *The Principles of Organization.* New York: Harper.

Moss, Sidney A., and Moss, Miriam S. 1967. "When a Caseworker Leaves an Agency: The Impact on Worker and Client." *Social Casework* 48 (July): 433-437.

Mullen, Edward J., and Dumpson, James (Eds.). 1972. *Evaluation of Social Intervention.* San Francisco: Jossey-Bass.

Muslin, Hyman L.; Burstein, Alvin G.; Gedo, John E.; and Sadow, Leo. 1967. "Research on the Supervisory Process: I. Supervisor's Appraisal of the Interview Data." *Archives of General Psychiatry* 16 (April): 427-431.

Nathanson, Constance A., and Lorenz, Gerda. 1982. "Women and Health: The Social Dimensions of Biomedical Data." In *Women in the Middle Years: Current Knowledge and Directions for Research and Policy.* Edited by Janet Zollinger Giele. New York: Wiley.

National Council of Juvenile and Family Court Judges. 1981. *Judicial Review of*

Children in Placement Deskbook. Reno, Nevada: National Council of Juvenile and Family Court Judges.

Nelsen, Judith C. 1980. "Support: A Necessary Condition for Change." *Social Work* 25 (September): 388–393.

Neugarten, Bernice. 1977. "Personality and Aging." In *Handbook of the Psychology of Aging.* Edited by James E. Birren and K. Warren Schaie. New York: Van Nostrand Reinhold.

Newcome, Kent. 1979. "Task-Centered Case Management: Coordinating the Long-Term Mentally Ill in the Community." Mimeo.

———. 1978. "An Organizational Analysis of a Day Treatment Program." Mimeo.

Nezu, Arthur, and D'Zurilla, Thomas J. 1981. "Effects of Problem Definition and Formulation on the Generation of Alternatives in the Social Problem-Solving Process." *Cognitive Therapy and Research* 5 (September): 265–271.

———. 1979. "An Experimental Evaluation of the Decision-Making Process in Social Problem Solving." *Cognitive Therapy and Research* 3 (September): 269–277.

Nock, Steven L. 1979. "The Family Life Cycle: Empirical or Conceptual Tool?" *Journal of Marriage and the Family* 41 (February): 15–26.

Northen, Helen. 1982. *Clinical Social Work.* New York: Columbia University Press.

———. 1969. *Social Work with Groups.* New York: Columbia University Press.

Norton, Arthur J. 1983. "Family Life Cycle: 1980." *Journal of Marriage and the Family* 45 (May): 267–275.

Notman, Malkah T., and Nadelson, Carol. 1980. "Reproductive Crises." In *Women and Psychotherapy: An Assessment of Research and Practice.* Edited by Annette M. Brodsky and Rachel T. Hare-Mustin. New York: Guilford.

O'Leary, Susan G., and Dubey, Dennis B. 1979. "Applications of Self-Control Procedures by Children: A Review." *Journal of Applied Behavior Analysis* 12 (Fall): 449–465.

Olsen, Irene. 1970. "Some Effects of Increased Aid in Money and Social Services to Families Getting AFDC Grants." *Child Welfare* 49 (February): 94–100.

Olson, R. Paul, and Greenberry, David J. 1972. "Effects of Contingency Contracting and Decision-Making Groups with Chronic Mental Patients." *Journal of Consulting and Clinical Psychology* 38: 376–383.

Oxley, Genevieve B. 1977. "Involuntary Clients' Responses to a Treatment Experience." *Social Casework* 58 (December): 607–614.

Paquin, Michael J. R. 1981. "Self-Monitoring of Marital Communication in Family Therapy." *Social Casework* 62 (May): 267–272.

Parad, Libbie G., and Parad, Howard J. 1968. "A Study of Crisis-Oriented Planned Short-Term Treatment: Part II." *Social Casework* 49 (July): 418–426.

Parihar, Bageshwari. 1984. *Task-Centered Management in Human Services.* Springfield, IL: Charles C. Thomas.

———. 1982. "Management of Treatment Organizations: Problem-Oriented Approach." Ph.D. dissertation, University of Illinois-Chicago Circle.

Parkes, C. M. 1972. *Bereavement: Studies of Grief in Adult Life.* New York: International Universities Press.

Parloff, Morris B., and Dies, Robert T. 1977. "Group Psychotherapy Outcome

Research 1966-1975." *International Journal of Group Psychotherapy* 27 (July): 281-319.

Parsons, Talcott. 1957. "The Mental Hospital as a Type of Organization." In *The Patient and the Mental Hospital.* Edited by Daniel J. Levinson and Richard H. Williams. Glencoe, IL: Free Press.

Patterson, G. R., and Fleischman, M. J. 1979. "Maintenance of Treatment Effects: Some Considerations Concerning Family Systems and Follow-up Data." *Behavior Therapy* 10 (March): 168-185.

Patti, Rino; Diedreck, Elenore; Olson, Dennis; and Crowell, Jill. 1979. "From Direct Service to Administration: A Study of Social Workers' Transition from Clinical to Management Roles, Part 1: Analysis." *Administration in Social Work* 3: 131-151.

Peck, Harris B. 1962. "The Role of the Psychiatric Day Hospital in a Community Mental Program: A Group Process Approach." *American Journal of Orthopsychiatry* 32 (March): 229-230.

Pendleton, Linda R.; Shelton, John L.; and Wilson, Susan E. 1976. "Social Inter action Training Using Systematic Homework." *Personnel and Guidance Journal* 54 (May): 484 401.

Perlman, Helen Harris. 1970. "The Problem-Solving Model in Social Casework." In *Theories of Social Casework.* Edited by Robert W. Roberts and Robert H. Nee. Chicago: University of Chicago Press.

———. 1957. *Social Casework: A Problem-Solving Process.* Chicago: University of Chicago Press.

Pines, Ayala, and Kafry, Ditsa. 1978. "Occupational Tedium in the Social Services." *Social Work* 23 (November): 499-507.

Platt, Jerome J., and Siegel, Jerome M. 1976. "MMPI Characteristics of Good and Poor Social Problem-Solvers among Psychiatric Patients. *Journal of Psychology* 94 (September): 245-251.

Platt, Jerome J.; Siegel, Jerome M.; and Spivack, George. 1975. "Do Psychiatric Patients and Normals See the Same Solution as Effective in Solving Inter-personal Problems?" *Journal of Consulting and Clinical Psychology* 43 (April): 279.

Platt, Jerome J., and Spivack, George. 1974. "Means of Solving Real Life Problems: I. Psychiatric Patients Versus Controls and Cross-Cultural Comparisons of Normal Females." *Journal of Community Psychology* 2: 45-48.

———. 1972. "Problem-Solving Thinking of Psychiatric Patients." *Journal of Consulting and Clinical Psychology* 39 (August): 148-151.

Practice Digest. 1982. "Special Section on Case Management." 4 (March).

Price, Richard J. 1979. "The Social Ecology of Treatment Gain." In *Maximizing Treatment Gains: Transfer Enhancement in Psychotherapy.* Edited by Arnold P. Goldstein and Frederick H. Kanfer. New York: Academic.

Price-Bonham, Sharon, and Balswick, Jack O. 1980. "The Noninstitutions: Divorce, Desertion, and Remarriage." *Journal of Marriage and the Family* 42 (November): 959-972.

Rappaport, Alan F., and Harrell, Jay. 1972. "A Behavioral-Exchange Model for Marital Counseling." *Family Coordinator* 21 (April): 203-212.

Rapoport, Lydia. 1970. "Crisis Intervention as a Mode of Brief Treatment." In

Theories of Social Casework. Edited by Robert W. Roberts and Robert H. Nee. Chicago: University of Chicago Press.

Raschke, Helen J. 1977. "The Role of Social Participation in Postseparation and Postdivorce Adjustment." *Journal of Divorce* 1 (Winter): 129-140.

Raskind, Murray A., and Storrie, Michael C. 1980. "The Organic Mental Disorders." In *Handbook of Geriatric Psychiatry.* Edited by Ewald W. Busse and Dan G. Blazer. New York: Van Nostrand Reinhold.

Rathbone-McCuan, Eloise. 1982. "Mental Health of Older Woman Training Project." St. Louis: George Warren Brown School of Social Work, Washington University.

Rathbone-McCuan, Eloise, and Hashimi, Joan. 1982. *Isolated Elders: Health and Social Interventions.* Rockville: Aspen Systems Corporation.

Rathbone-McCuan, Eloise; Travis, Ann; and Voyles, Barbara. 1983. "Family Interventions: Applying the Task-Centered Approach." In *The Abuse and Maltreatment of the Elderly.* Edited by Jordan I. Koesberg. Littleton, MA: PSG.

Reder, Peter, and Tyson, Robert L. 1980. "Patient Dropout from Individual Psychotherapy: A Review and Discussion." *Bulletin of the Menninger Clinic* 44: 229-252.

Reid, William J. In press. *Family Problem Solving.* New York: Columbia University Press.

———. 1981. "Family Treatment Within a Task-Centered Framework." In *Models of Family Treatment.* Edited by Eleanor Reardon Tolson and William J. Reid. New York: Columbia University Press.

———. 1979. "The Model Development Dissertation." *Journal of Social Service Research* 3 (Winter): 215-225.

———. 1978. *The Task-Centered System.* New York: Columbia University Press.

———. 1977a. "Process and Outcome in the Treatment of Family Problems." In *Task Centered Practice.* Edited by William J. Reid and Laura Epstein. New York: Columbia University Press.

———. 1977b. "Task-Centered Treatment and Trends in Clinical Social Work." In *Task-Centered Practice.* Edited by William J. Reid and Laura Epstein. New York: Columbia University Press.

———. 1975. "A Test of a Task-Centered Approach." *Social Work* 20 (January): 3-9.

———. 1969/70. "Implications of Research for the Goals of Casework." *Smith College Studies in Social Work* 40:140-154.

Reid, William J., and Beard, Christine. 1980. "An Evaluation of In-Service Training in a Public Welfare Setting." *Administration in Social Work* 4 (Spring): 71-85.

Reid, William J., and Epstein, Laura. 1972. *Task-Centered Casework.* New York: Columbia University Press.

Reid, William J., and Epstein, Laura (Eds.). 1977. *Task-Centered Practice.* New York: Columbia University Press.

Reid, William J.; Epstein, Laura; Brown, Lester; Tolson, Eleanor; and Rooney, Ronald H. 1980. "Task-Centered School Social Work." *Social Work in Education* 2 (January): 7-24.

Reid, William J., and Hanrahan, Patricia. 1982. "Recent Evaluations of Social Work: Grounds for Optimism." *Social Work* 27 (June): 328-340.

Reid, William J., and Shyne, Ann W. 1969. *Brief and Extended Casework.* New York: Columbia University Press.

Rhodes, Sonya L. 1977a. "Contract Negotiation in the Initial Stage of Casework Service." *Social Service Review* 51 (March): 123-140.

———. 1977b. "A Developmental Approach to the Life Cycle of the Family." *Social Casework* 58 (May): 301-311.

Richards, C. Steven, and Perri, Michael G. 1978. "Do Self-Control Treatments Last? An Evaluation of Behavioral Problem Solving and Faded Counselor Contact as Treatment Maintenance Strategies." *Journal of Counseling Psychology* 25: 376-383.

Riley, Matilda W., and Foner, Anne. 1968. *Aging and Society, Vol. 1: An Inventory of Research Findings.* New York: Russell Sage Foundation.

Robin, Arthur L. 1979. "Problem-Solving Communication Training: A Behavioral Approach to the Treatment of Parent-Adolescent Conflict." *American Journal of Family Therapy* 7 (Summer): 69-82.

Rodin, Judith, and Langer, Ellen J. 1977. "Long-term Effects of a Control-Relevant Intervention with the Institutionalized Aged." *Journal of Personality and Social Psychology* 35 (December): 897-902.

Rohrbaugh, Michael, and Bartel, Bryan D. 1975. "Participants' Perception of 'Curative Factors' in Therapy and Growth Groups." *Small Group Behavior* 6 (November): 430-456.

Rohrlich, John A.; Ranier, Ruth; Berg-Cross, Linda; and Berg-Cross, Gary. 1977. "The Effects of Divorce: A Research Review with a Developmental Perspective." *Journal of Clinical Child Psychology* 6 (Summer): 15-20.

Rooney, Ronald H. 1983. "Can Public Agency Social Workers Learn and Practice the Task-Centered Approach? Results of a Pilot Study of Task-Centered Dissemination." Paper presented at the Council on Social Work Education Annual Program Meeting, Fort Worth, Texas, March 14.

———. 1981. "A Task-Centered Reunification Model for Foster Care." In *The Challenge of Partnership: Working with Parents of Children in Foster Care.* Edited by Anthony N. Maluccio and Paula A. Sinanoglu. New York: Child Welfare League of America.

———. 1978. "Separation through Foster Care: Toward a Problem-Oriented Practice Model Based on Task-Centered Casework." Ph.D. dissertation, University of Chicago.

———. 1977. "Adolescent Groups in Public Schools." In *Task-Centered Practice.* Edited by William J. Reid and Laura Epstein. New York: Columbia University Press.

———. 1975. "A Guide to Operating Task-Centered Groups." Chicago: University of Chicago. Offset.

Rose, Sheldon D. 1977. *Group Therapy: A Behavioral Approach.* Englewood Cliffs, NJ: Prentice-Hall.

———. 1972. Treating Children in Groups. San Francisco: Jossey-Bass.

Rosenberg, Blanca N., and Klein, Joan M. 1980. "A Family Integrates Planned Short-Term Treatment." *Social Casework* 61 (December): 619-628.

Rosenblatt, Aaron, and Meyer, John E. 1975. "Objectionable Supervisory Styles: Students' Views." *Social Work* 20 (May): 184-189.

Rossi, Alice S. 1968. "Transition to Parenthood." *Journal of Marriage and the Family* 30 (February): 26–39.

Rossi, Robert B. 1977. "Helping a Mute Child." In *Task-Centered Practice*. Edited by William J. Reid and Laura Epstein. New York: Columbia University Press.

Rothman, Jack. 1980. *Social R & D: Research and Development in the Human Services*. Englewood Cliffs, NJ: Prentice Hall.

Rubenstein, Hiasaura, and Bloch, Mary H. 1978. "Helping Clients Who Are Poor: Worker and Client Perceptions of Problems, Activities, and Outcomes." *Social Service Review* 52 (March): 69–84.

Russo, Nancy Felipe. 1979. "Overview: Sex Roles, Fertility and the Motherhood Mandate." *Psychology of Women Quarterly* 4 (Fall): 7–15.

Rzepnicki, Tina L. 1982. "Task-Centered Intervention: An Adaptation and Test of Effectiveness in Foster Care Services." Ph.D. dissertation, University of Chicago.

Sager, Clifford J.; Brown, Hollis Steer; Crohn, Helen; Engel, Tamara; Rodstein, Evelyn; and Walker, Libby. 1983. *Treating the Remarried Family*. New York: Brunner/Mazel.

Salmon, Wilma. 1977. "A Service Program in a State Public Welfare Agency." In *Task-Centered Practice*. Edited by William J. Reid and Laura Epstein. New York: Columbia University Press.

Sanders, L. Thomas, and Seelbach, Wayne C. 1981. "Variations in Preferred Care Alternatives for the Elderly: Family Versus Nonfamily Sources." *Family Relations* 30 (July): 447–451.

Sarri, Rosemary C., and Galinsky, Maeda J. 1974. "A Conceptual Framework for Group Development." In *Individual Change through Small Groups*. Edited by Paul Glasser, Rosemary Sarri, and Robert Vinter. New York: Free Press.

Scanzoni, John, and Szinovacz, Maximiliane. 1980. *Family Decision-Making: A Developmental Sex Role Model*. Sage Library of Social Research, Vol. III. Beverly Hills, CA: Sage.

Schein, Edgar H. 1965. *Organizational Psychology*. Englewood Cliffs, NJ: Prentice-Hall.

Scherz, Frances H. 1971. "Maturational Crises and Parent–Child Interaction." *Social Casework* 52 (June): 362–369.

Schiff, Sheldon. 1962. "Termination of Therapy: Problems in a Community Psychiatric Outpatient Clinic." *Archives of General Psychiatry* 6 (January): 77–82.

Schinke, Steven. 1981. *Behavioral Methods in Social Welfare*. New York: Aldine.

Schlenoff, Marjorie Litwin, and Busa, Sandra Hricko. 1981. "Student and Field Instructor as Group Co-therapists: Equalizing an Unequal Relationship." *Journal of Education for Social Work* 17 (Winter): 29–35.

Schlesinger, Benjamin. 1978. *The One-Parent Family: Perspectives and Annotated Bibliography*. Toronto: University of Toronto Press.

Schvaneveldt, Jay D., and Ihinger, Marilyn. 1979. "Sibling Relationships in the Family." In *Contemporary Theories about the Family: Research-Based Theories*, Vol. I. Edited by Wesley R. Burr, Reuben Hill, F. Ivan Nye, and Ira L. Reiss. New York: Free Press.

Schwartz, Arthur, and Goldiamond, Israel. 1975. *Social Casework: A Behavioral Approach*. New York: Columbia University Press.

Schwartz, Edward E., and Sample, William C. 1972. *The Midway Office*. New York: National Association of Social Workers.

Seabury, Brett A. 1976. "The Contract: Uses, Abuses, and Limitations." *Social Work* (January): 16-21.

Seymour, Frederick W., and Stokes, Trevor F. 1976. "Self-Recording in Training Girls to Increase Work and Evoke Staff Praise in an Institution for Offenders." *Journal of Applied Behavior Analysis* 9 (Spring): 41-54.

Shanas, Ethel. 1980. "Older People and Their Families: The New Pioneers." *Journal of Marriage and the Family* 42 (February): 9-15.

———. 1979. "Social Myth as Hypothesis: The Case of Family Relations of Old People." *Gerontologist* 19 (February): 3-9.

Shapiro, Constance Hoenk. 1982. "The Impact of Infertility on the Marital Relationship." *Social Casework* 63 (September): 387-393.

———. 1980. "Termination: A Neglected Concept in the Social Work Curriculum." *Journal of Education for Social Work* 16 (Spring): 13-19.

Shapiro, Deborah. 1976. *Agencies and Foster Children*. New York: Columbia University Press.

Shepherd, Geoff. 1978. "Social Skills Training: The Generalization Problem— Some Further Data." *Behavioral Research and Therapy* 16: 287-288.

———. 1977. "Social Skills Training: The Generalization Problem." *Behavior Therapy* 8 (November): 1008-1119.

Sherman, Edmund. 1981. *Counseling the Aging: An Integrative Approach*. New York: Free Press.

Sherry, Patrick, and Hurley, John R. 1976. "Curative Factors in Psychotherapeutic and Growth Groups." *Journal of Clinical Psychology* 32 (October): 835-837.

Shulman, Lawrence. 1979. *The Skills of Helping Individuals and Groups*. Itasca, IL: F. E. Peacock.

Siegel, Jerome M., and Spivack, George. 1973. *Problem-Solving Therapy: A New Program for Chronic Schizophrenic Patients*. Research and Evaluation Report No. 23. Philadelphia: Hahemann Medical College and Hospital.

Sifneos, Peter E. 1981. "Short-Term Anxiety-Provoking Psychotherapy: Its History, Technique, Outcome, and Instruction." In *Forms of Brief Therapy*. Edited by Simon H. Budman. New York: Guilford.

———. 1979. *Short-Term Dynamic Psychotherapy: Evaluation and Technique*. New York: Plenum.

Silverman, Phyllis Rolfe. 1970. "A Reexamination of the Intake Procedure." *Social Casework* 51 (December): 625-632.

Simon, Herbert A. 1961. *Administrative Behavior*. New York: Macmillan.

Sirles, Elizabeth A. 1982. "Client-Counselor Agreement on Problem and Change." *Social Casework* 63 (June): 348-353.

Sluzki, Carlos E. 1978. "Marital Therapy from a Systems Theory Perspective." In *Marriage and Marital Therapy: Psychoanalytic, Behavioral and Systems Theory Perspectives*. Edited by Thomas J. Paolino, Jr., and Barbara S. McCrady. New York: Brunner/Mazel.

Solomon, Robert W., and Wahler, Robert F. 1973. "Peer Reinforcement Control of Classroom Problem Behavior." *Journal of Applied Behavior Analysis* 6 (Spring): 49-56.

Sonne, Janet L., and Janoff, Dean. 1979. "The Effect of Treatment Attributions on the Maintenance of Weight Reduction: A Replication and Extension." *Cognitive Therapy and Research* 3 (December): 389-397.

Spanier, Graham B. 1976. "Measuring Dyadic Adjustment: New Scales for Assessing the Quality of Marriage and Similar Dyads." *Journal of Marriage and the Family* 38 (February): 15-28.

Spanier, Graham B., and Glick, Paul C. 1981. "Marital Instability in the United States: Some Correlates and Recent Changes." *Family Relations* 31 (July): 329-338.

Spanier, Graham B., and Lewis, Robert A. 1980. "Marital Quality: A Review of the Seventies." *Journal of Marriage and the Family* 42 (November): 825-839.

Spanier, Graham B.; Sauer, William; and Larzelere, R. 1979. "An Empirical Evaluation of the Family Life Cycle." *Journal of Marriage and the Family* 41 (February): 27-38.

Spivack, George; Platt, Jerome J.; and Shure, Myrna B. 1976. *The Problem-Solving Approach to Adjustment.* San Francisco: Jossey-Bass.

Stabler, Nora. 1981. "The Use of Groups in Day Centers for Older Adults." *Social Work with Groups* 4 (Fall/Winter): 49-58.

Stafford, Juliene L., and Bringle, Robert G. 1980. "The Influence of Task Success on Elderly Women's Interest in New Activities." *Gerontologist* 20 (December): 642-648.

Stanton, M. Duncan. 1981. "Strategic Approaches to Family Therapy." In *Handbook of Family Therapy.* Edited by Alan S. Gurman and David P. Kniskern. New York: Brunner/Mazel.

Starfield, Barbara; Wray, Christine; Hess, Kelliann; Gross, Richard; Birk, Peter S.; and D'Lugoff, Burton C. 1981. "The Influence of Patient-Practitioner Agreement on Outcome of Care." *American Journal of Public Health* 71 (February): 127-131.

Steiman, Leo A., and Hunt, Robert C. 1961. "A Day Care Center in a State Hospital." *American Journal of Psychiatry* 117 (June): 1109-1112.

Stein, Theodore J.; Gambrill, Eileen D.; and Wiltse, Kermit T. 1978. *Children in Foster Homes: Achieving Continuity of Care.* New York: Praeger.

Stokes, Trevor F.; Fowler, Susan A.; and Baer, Donald M. 1978. "Training Preschool Children to Recruit Natural Communities of Reinforcement." *Journal of Applied Behavioral Analysis* 11 (Summer): 285-303.

Stoller, Eleanor Palo, and Earl, Lorna L. 1983. "Help with Activities of Everyday Life: Sources of Support for the Noninstitutionalized Elderly." *Gerontologist* 23 (February): 64-70.

Stone, L. Joseph, and Church, Joseph. 1973. *Childhood and Adolescence: A Psychology of the Growing Person,* 3rd ed. New York: Random House.

Stone, Margaret E., and Nelson, Gary L. 1979. "Coordinated Treatment for Long-Term Psychiatric Inpatients." *Social Work* 24 (September): 406-410.

Streib, Gordon F., and Beck, Rubye Wilkerson. 1980. "Older Families: A Decade Review." *Journal of Marriage and the Family* 42 (November): 937-956.

Stuart, Richard B. 1980. *Helping Couples Change: A Social Learning Approach to Marital Therapy.* New York: Guilford.

———. 1971. "Behavioral Contracting Within the Families of Delinquents." *Journal of Behavior Therapy and Experimental Psychiatry* 2: 1-11.

———. 1968. "Token Reinforcement in Marital Treatment." In *Advances in Behavior Therapy*, Vol. 6. Edited by Richard D. Rubin and Cyril M. Franks. New York: Academic.

Stuart, Richard B., and Stuart, Freida. 1973. *Marital Pre-Counseling Inventory.* Champaign, IL: Research Press.

Studt, Eliot. 1968. "Social Work Theory and Implications for the Practice of Methods." *Social Work Education Reporter* 16: 22-46.

Sucato, Vincent. 1978. "The Problem-solving Process in Short-Term and Long-Term Service." *Social Service Review* 52 (June): 244-264.

Sue, Derald W. 1981. *Counseling the Culturally Different: Theory and Practice.* New York: Wiley.

Taylor, Carvel. 1977. "Counseling in a Service Industry." In *Task-Centered Practice.* Edited by William J. Reid and Laura Epstein. New York: Columbia University Press.

Taylor, Frederick W. 1911. *Principles of Scientific Management.* New York: Harper & Brothers.

Taylor, John W. 1980. "Using Short-Term Structured Groups with Divorced Clients." *Social Work* 61 (September): 433-437.

Teitelbaum, Lee E., and Gough, Aidan R., Eds. 1977. *Beyond Control: Status Offenders in the Juvenile Court.* Cambridge, MA: Ballinger.

Terkelsen, Kenneth G. 1980. "Toward a Theory of the Family Life Cycle." In *The Family Life Cycle: A Framework for Family Therapy.* Edited by Elizabeth A. Carter and Monica McGoldrick. New York: Gardner.

Thomas, Edwin J. 1978a. "Mousetraps, Developmental Research and Social Work." *Social Service Review* 52 (September): 468-483.

———. 1978b. "Generating Innovation in Social Work: The Paradigm of Developmental Research." *Journal of Social Service Research* 1 (Fall): 95-116.

———. 1977. *Marital Communication and Decision Making: Analysis, Assessment, and Change.* New York: Free Press.

Tobin, Sheldon S. 1982. "Psychodynamic Treatment of the Family and the Institutionalized Individual." Paper presented at the NIMH Conference on Psychodynamic Research Perspectives on Development, Psychopathology and Treatment in Later Life, Rockville, Maryland, November 6-8.

Tolson, Eleanor Reardon. 1977. "Alleviating Marital Communication Problems." In *Task-Centered Practice.* Edited by William J. Reid and Laura Epstein. New York: Columbia University Press.

———. 1976. "A Single Organism Design for Evaluating the Effectiveness of the Task Implementation Sequence in Modifying Marital Communication Problems." Ph.D. dissertation, University of Chicago.

———. Personal communication, 1982.

Torczyner, J., and Pare, Arleen. 1979. "The Influence of Environmental Factors on Foster Care." *Social Service Review* 53 (September): 358-377.

Toseland, Ron. 1980. "Group Problem Solving with the Elderly." In *A Casebook in Group Therapy.* Edited by Sheldon D. Rose. Englewood Cliffs, NJ: Prentice-Hall.

———. 1977. "A Problem-Solving Group Workshop for Older Persons." *Social Work* 22 (July): 325–326.

Toseland, Ron, and Rivas, Robert. 1984. *An Introduction to Group Work Practice.* New York: Macmillan.

Toseland, Ron, and Rose, Sheldon D. 1978. "Evaluating Social Skills Training for Older Adults in Groups." *Social Work Research and Abstracts* 14 (Spring): 25–33.

Toseland, Ron; Sherman, Edmund; and Bliven, Stephen. 1981. "The Comparative Effectiveness of Two Group Work Approaches for the Development of Mutual Support Groups Among the Elderly." *Social Work with Groups* 4 (Spring/Summer): 137–153.

Treas, Judith. 1977. "Family Support Systems for the Aged: Some Social and Demographic Considerations." *Gerontologist* 17 (December): 486–491.

Troll, Lillian E. 1971. "The Family of Later Life: A Decade Review." *Journal of Marriage and the Family* 33 (May): 263–290.

Tsukada, Grace K. 1979. "Sibling Interaction: A Review of the Literature." *Smith College Studies in Social Work* 49 (June): 229–247.

Tuckman, Bruce W., and Jensen, Mary Ann C. 1977. "Stages of Small Group Development Revisited." *Group and Organization Studies* 2 (December): 419–427.

Uhlenberg, Peter. 1974. "Cohort Variations in Family Life Cycle Experiences of U.S. Females." *Journal of Marriage and the Family* 36 (May): 284–292.

U.S. Census. 1982. *Marital Status and Living Arrangements: March 1981.* Current Population Reports, Population Characteristics, Series P-20, No. 372. June.

U.S. Census. 1977. *Marriage, Divorce, Widowhood, and Remarriage by Family Characteristics: June 1975.* Current Population Reports, Population Characteristics, Series P-20, No. 312. August.

U.S. Census. 1976. *Number, Timing, and Duration of Marriages and Divorces in the United States: June 1975.* Current Population Reports, Population Characteristics, Series P-20, No. 297. October.

Urbain, Eugene S., and Kendall, Philip C. 1980. "Review of Social-Cognitive Problem-Solving Interventions with Children." *Psychological Bulletin* 88 (July): 109–143.

VanDyck, Barry J. 1980. "An Analysis of Selection Criteria for Short-Term Group Counseling Clients." *Personnel and Guidance Journal* 29 (December): 226–230.

Vasaly, S. M. 1976. *Foster Care in Five States: A Synthesis and Analysis of Studies from Arizona, California, Iowa, Massachusetts, and Vermont.* Washington, DC: Social Work Research Group, George Washington University, June.

Verbrugge, Lois M. 1979. "Marital Status and Health." *Journal of Marriage and the Family* 41 (May): 267–285.

Veroff, Joseph; Douvan, Elizabeth; and Kulka, Richard A. 1981. *The Inner American: A Self-Portrait from 1957 to 1976.* New York: Basic.

Veroff, Joseph; Kulka, Richard A.; and Douvan, Elizabeth. 1981. *Mental Health in America: Patterns of Help-seeking from 1957 to 1976.* New York: Basic.

Vincent, John P.; Weiss, Robert L.; and Birchler, Gary R. 1975. "A Behavioral

Analysis of Problem Solving in Distressed and Nondistressed Married and Stranger Dyads." *Behavior Therapy* 6: 475-487.

Vinter, Robert D. 1963. "Analysis of Treatment Organizations." *Social Work* 8 (July): 3-15.

Wallace, Charles J.; Nelson, Connie J.; Liberman, Robert Paul; Aitchison, Robert A.; Lukoff, David; Elder, John P.; and Ferris, Chris. 1980. "A Review and Critique of Social Skill Training with Schizophrenic Patients." *Schizophrenia Bulletin* 6 (Winter): 42-63.

Wallace, David. 1967. "The Chemung County Evaluation of Casework Service to Dependent Multi-problem Families: Another Problem Outcome." *Social Service Review* 41 (December): 379-384.

Wallerstein, Judith S., and Kelly, Joan B. 1980. "Effects of Divorce on the Visiting Father-Child Relationship." *American Journal of Psychiatry* 137 (December): 1534-1539.

———. 1979. "Children and Divorce: A Review." *Social Work* 24 (November): 468-475.

Walters, James, and Walters, Lynda Henly. 1980. "Parent-Child Relationships: A Review, 1970-1979." *Journal of Marriage and the Family* 42 (November): 807-822.

Wattenberg, Esther, and Reinhardt, Hazel. 1979. "Female-Headed Families: Trends and Implications." *Social Work* 24 (November): 460-467.

Wattie, Brenda. 1973. "Evaluating Short-term Casework in a Family Agency." *Social Casework* 54 (December): 609-616.

Watzlawick, Paul; Beavin, Janet Helmick; and Jackson, Don D. 1967. *Pragmatics of Human Communication.* New York: Norton.

Waxer, Peter H. 1977. "Short-Term Group Psychotherapy: Some Principles and Techniques." *International Journal of Group Psychotherapy* 27 (January): 33-42.

Wayne, Julianne, and Avery, Nancy. 1979. "Activities as a Tool for Group Termination." *Social Work* 24 (January): 58-62.

Weber, Max. 1947. *The Theory of Social and Economic Organization.* Translated by A. M. Henderson and Talcott Parsons. New York: Oxford University Press.

Wechter, Sharon L. 1983. "Separation Difficulties Between Parents and Young Adults." *Social Casework* 64 (February): 97-104.

Weiner, Marcella; Brok, Albert; and Snadowsky, Alvin. 1978. *Working with the Aged.* Englewood Cliffs, NJ: Prentice-Hall.

Weiss, Robert L. 1975. "Contracts, Cognition and Change: A Behavioral Approach to Marriage Therapy." *Counseling Psychologist* 5: 15-26.

Weiss, Robert L.; Birchler, Gary R.; and Vincent, John. 1974. "Contractual Models for Negotiation Training in Marital Dyads." *Journal of Marriage and the Family* 36 (May): 321-330.

Weiss, Robert S. 1979a. *Going it Alone: The Family Life and Social Situation of the Single Parent.* New York: Basic.

———. 1979b. "Growing Up a Little Faster: The Experience of Growing Up in a Single-Parent Household." *Journal of Social Issues* 35 (Fall): 97-111.

Wells, Richard A. 1981. "The Empirical Base of Family Therapy: Practice Impli-

cations." In *Models of Family Treatment*. Edited by Eleanor Reardon Tolson
and William J. Reid. New York: Columbia University Press.

Wildman, Robert W. II, and Wildman, Robert W. 1980. "Maintenance and
Generalization of Institutional Behavior Modification Programs." In *Improving
the Long-Term Effects of Psychotherapy: Models of Durable Outcome*.
Edited by Paul Karoly and John J. Steffen. New York: Gardner.

Willer, Barry, and Miller, Gary H. 1976. "Client Improvement in Goal Setting and
Its Relationship to Therapeutic Outcome." *Journal of Clinical Psychology* 32
(July): 687–690.

Williams, Shirley, and Other Experts. 1981. *Youth Without Work: Three Countries
Approach the Problem*. Paris, France: Organization for Economic Cooperation and Development.

Wilson, G. Terence, and Brownell, Kelly D. 1980. "Behavior Therapy for Obesity:
An Evaluation of Treatment Outcome." *Advances in Behavior Research and
Therapy* 3: 49-86.

Winborn, Rebecca. 1983. "Adapting to Parenthood: Negotiating New Roles."
Social Casework 64 (December): 618-624.

Wise, Frances. 1977. "Conjoint Marital Treatment." In *Task-Centered Practice*.
Edited by William J. Reid and Laura Epstein. New York: Columbia University Press.

Wodarski, John S.; Saffir, Marcy; and Frazer, Malcolm. 1982. "Using Research to
Evaluate the Effectiveness of Task-Centered Casework." *Journal of Applied
Social Sciences* 7 (Spring): 70-82.

Wood, Katherine M. 1978. "Casework Effectiveness: A New Look at the Research
Evidence." *Social Work* 23 (November): 437-459.

Woods, Martha, and Melnick, Joseph. 1979. "A Review of Group Therapy Selection Criteria." *Small Group Behavior* 10 (May): 155-175.

Yalom, Irvin D. 1975. *The Theory and Practice of Group Psychotherapy*, 2nd ed.
New York: Basic.

Zimmerman, Shirley L. 1980. "The Family: Building Block or Anachronism."
Social Casework 61 (April): 195-204.

Index